# THE SILENT SERVICE'S FIRST HERO

*Dedicated to past, present and future qualified individuals of the United States Navy Submarine Force.*

## Henry Breault's Medal of Honor Citation

For heroism and devotion to duty while serving on board the U.S. submarine O-5 at the time of the sinking of that vessel. On the morning of 28 October 1923, the O-5 collided with the steamship Abangarez and sank in less than a minute. When the collision occurred, Breault was in the torpedo room. Upon reaching the hatch, he saw that the boat was rapidly sinking. Instead of jumping overboard to save his own life, he returned to the torpedo room to the rescue of a shipmate who he knew was trapped in the boat, closing the torpedo room hatch on himself. Breault and Brown remained trapped in this compartment until rescued by the salvage party 31 hours later.

Cover picture from Library of Congress

# THE SILENT SERVICE'S FIRST HERO

## THE FIRST SUBMARINER TO RECEIVE THE MEDAL OF HONOR

**RYAN C WALKER**

First published in Great Britain in 2024 by
**PEN AND SWORD MARITIME**
*an imprint of*
Pen and Sword Books Ltd
Yorkshire – Philadelphia

Copyright © Ryan C Walker, 2024

ISBN 978 1 03610 041 4

The right of Ryan C Walker to be identified as the author of this work has been asserted by him in accordance with the Copyright, Designs and Patents Act 1988.

A CIP record for this book is available from the British Library
All rights reserved. No part of this book may be reproduced or transmitted in any form or by any means, electronic or mechanical including photocopying, recording or by any information storage and retrieval system, without permission from the Publisher in writing.

Typeset in Times New Roman 11/13.5 by
SJmagic DESIGN SERVICES, India.
Printed and bound in the UK by CPI Group (UK) Ltd.

Pen & Sword Books Ltd incorporates the imprints of Pen & Sword Archaeology, Atlas, Aviation, Battleground, Discovery, Family History, History, Maritime, Military, Naval, Politics, Railways, Select, Social History, Transport, True Crime, Claymore Press, Frontline Books, Leo Cooper, Praetorian Press, Remember When, Seaforth Publishing and Wharncliffe.

For a complete list of Pen & Sword titles please contact
**PEN & SWORD BOOKS LIMITED**
George House, Units 12 & 13, Beevor Street, Off Pontefract Road,
Barnsley, South Yorkshire, S71 1HN, England
E-mail: enquiries@pen-and-sword.co.uk
Website: www.pen-and-sword.co.uk

or

**PEN AND SWORD BOOKS**
1950 Lawrence Rd, Havertown, PA 19083, USA
E-mail: uspen-and-sword@casematepublishers.com
Website: www.penandswordbooks.com

# Contents

Acknowledgements ................................................................... vi
Foreword ............................................................................. viii
Introduction .......................................................................... x
Terms and Acronyms ............................................................ xii

Chapter 1   Enlisted Submarine Folk Hero ....................................... 1
Chapter 2   Historiography ........................................................... 11
Chapter 3   Pre-Award Life and Career (1900–23) ........................... 27
Chapter 4   Heroism and Recognition (1923–24) ............................ 43
Chapter 5   Post-Award Career (1924–41) ...................................... 56
Chapter 6   'A Pigboat Sailor's Lament': Danger and Discomfort ...... 77
Chapter 7   Family, Friends and Forced Alienation ......................... 92
Chapter 8   'Falls in love with Kate and Jane, then he's
            out to sea again' ......................................................... 104
Chapter 9   Permanent Change of Home Station ............................. 121
Chapter 10  Uniforms, Cigarettes, Pomade and Other Artefacts
            of a Material Identity .................................................. 142
Chapter 11  Henry Breault Reconstructed ....................................... 155

Conclusion ............................................................................. 170
Bibliography .......................................................................... 173
Endnotes ................................................................................ 187

# Acknowledgements

I owe a significant debt of gratitude to several persons and organizations.

To my wife, Brittney, who bore the sacrifice of many nights spent writing this work, because she knows history means so much to me.

To my parents, Manmeet and Joseph Walker. A very surprising culmination of work, isn't it? Thanks for letting me grow up the way I have – that is, very painfully, with lessons from my mistakes. I'm sure it would have been easier had I listened to you both; but then again, that was never quite my style, was it? All's well that ends well.

To my grandmother, Margaret Walker, thank you for helping nurture my love for history by letting me watch the History Channel with you when I was young.

To Vice Admiral Al Konetzni, USN (Ret.), thank you for writing the foreword for a young author that introduced himself during the Sixtieth USS Thresher Memorial Service. It is no exaggeration to state this book was possible due to your efforts.

To my mentors, teachers and professors from all the institutions I attended, but principally Fossil Ridge High School, Southern New Hampshire University and the University of Portsmouth: thank you. I am aware of my difficulty as a student, and I appreciate your patience and mentorship. I must pay particular attention to thank Robert James, Matthew Heaslip, Cathryn Pearce and Mike Esbester of the University of Portsmouth for all of your thoughts and advice throughout this research.

To my first readers (in no particular order), Anthony Doran, John Agostini, Jordan Woolf, Ryan Dicipulo, Chris Spears, Tristan Gilmore, William Damron, Christian Dibenedetto and Phillip Reid Watkins, thank you for your time and feedback. You are part of making this work great.

# ACKNOWLEDGEMENTS

Thank you to Daniel Betzold, James Cerda, Jay Holingworth, Nathan Holmes, George White, William D. Williams, Nathan Huff and James Reilly, my former co-workers, who got to hear all about the research process. Whether or not you enjoyed it, I appreciated the ability to share my research and articulate my argument.

Thank you to Ted Dubay and Kenny Neville, with whom I communicated on social media and who graciously allowed me to use their statements as evidence to support a hypothesis.

Thank you to the Submarine Force Library and Museum for researching and creating the exhibit that continues to inspire aspiring submariners. I feel this work is a continuation of your efforts, and I appreciate the hard work you did before me.

Thank you to the Congressional Medal of Honor Society, specifically Archivist Laura Jowdy, who responded to my enquiry and graciously shared sources.

Thank you to the archivists of the United States National Archives, who digitized Breault's OMPF (Official Military Personnel File). It is no exaggeration to say your work has allowed this research to come to fruition.

Finally, thank you to all of those who helped in my journey to becoming a historian. You may not be called out here for this particular work, but I assure you that you are remembered.

# Foreword

The United States Navy Submarine Force is honored by the eight valiant heroes who have been awarded the Congressional Medal of Honor.

Seven recipients of the Congressional Medal of Honor were Naval Officers who distinguished themselves during combat in the Pacific Theatre of Operations during World War II.

Of interest, the first Medal of Honor recipient, Torpedoman Second Class Henry Breault is the only enlisted man to have been presented this prestigious award.

I became very interested in knowing more about Henry Breault when we dedicated a new submarine pier at Pearl Harbor, Hawaii in his honor in 2000. At the time I was serving as Commander, US Submarine Force, US Pacific Fleet. The genesis of this dedication decision was that we as a service needed to honor those who serve the Nation and their leadership. Petty Officer Breault is a wonderful example of the dedication of the American Sailor. I and all military officers know darned well that these young people are the reason our Nation remains free!

"The Silent Service's First Hero" is not just another military biography. It is truly a "micro history" in that it focuses on one individual's life from birth until his death at the beginning of World War II. It provides a clear picture of life in the service and submarine force in the 1920's and 30's.

As a "micro history" it provides clear insights regarding the thoughts and behavior of a young sailor who risked his life for a shipmate by remaining in the Torpedo Room of the Submarine O-5 when it collided with the steamship SS Abangarez on 28 October 1923. Henry Breault could have escaped the sinking O-5 but closed the Torpedo Room Hatch on himself and his shipmate in order to assist his companion.

Our submariners past and present are very special men and women. Even in peacetime they experience tight quarters, long periods at sea, high pressure systems, a relentless ocean, and today living close to a mobile nuclear reactor plant.

# FOREWORD

This book provides the reader a clear picture of life on submarines and the experiences that form this elite group of sailors.

I don't ever want to take anything away from the actions of the seven Submarine Qualified Officers who were awarded the Medal of Honor for actions during World War II. I sincerely believe that each of them would cherish knowing that "micro histories" were written about the brave sailors who supported their acts of courage under fire!

I do hope that more "micro histories" will be researched and written about our brave Officers and Sailors who serve in the Submarine Force and the US Navy.

"The Silent Service's First Hero" sets a very high mark for such research and studies.

Al Konetzni Jr.<br>
Vice Admiral, USN (ret)

# Introduction

What is the most important history? I believe, and this belief shall be a common foundation underpinning my research, that *the most important history is your own*. Within your own delve into personal historicity, there are no great personages that rise above the rest, but there are certainly impactful people from your own past. Henry Breault, a person with whom I have no ties other than the common service that we were both submariners, is part of my own history. His story shaped my conception of what it meant to be a submariner: decisive, brave and selfless.

Despite the efforts of numerous researchers and institutions, there was relatively little to build upon when I embarked on this research. It came as a surprise that beyond his military award and an outline of his career, Henry Breault was unknown as a person. It simply had not been a primary research focus of previous scholars to find out more about the person and the context of the period in which he lived. Nor was Breault particularly forthcoming himself; he did not seem to aid in uncovering material on his life, to the point, I have come to believe, that his anonymity was a product of his own design. The veneer of anonymity is a difficult one to search past, but sailors foreshadow the bureaucratic identity we now carry in the modern day in the form of impersonal government records.

The monograph you hold in your hands, dear reader, is not a hagiography or a biography – rather, it is a microhistory that follows a single man and explores his interactions with the external world. Due to Breault's prominence, there are ample and accessible records detailing his naval career, though mostly of official documentation. Lacking the close intimate sources that a biographer could draw upon, the work is a construction of his experiences and relationship to the outside world, primarily using those documents, in the hope that his life will grant us special insight into a man who lived both within American cultural bounds and at times observed them as a familiar foreigner. The question 'Who is Henry Breault?' is followed by analysis of how American culture shaped Breault's life. We are thrown into the world; it influences us and dismisses naïve attempts at solely being oneself. Breault's relationship to the world and how he interacted

# INTRODUCTION

through the cultural lenses of submariner, sailor and American can be observed, providing insight as a vehicle, rather than as a subject. The analysis is intended to become a mosaic, one in which each shard may seem insignificant on its own, but when viewed as a whole portrait, creates an artwork with an illuminating insight.

Despite this mosaic description, the research is not phenomenological. While I have great respect for phenomenology, Breault's personal experience is not the primary story; rather, the focus is how American culture potentially shaped his context and experiences. The sources that I employ are impersonal and primarily motivated to satisfy a record that the US Navy (USN) required. As such, the records contained in Breault's OMPF are not authentic sentiments. Rather, they can be viewed as motivated by unknown external sources. Microhistory is built upon a bedrock of clues and hidden meanings behind the documents, rather than relying on Breault to speak for himself. Breault's life becomes a vehicle for historical research, a mosaic microhistory. Breault's life has been constructed from a variety of disparate sources, incorporating knowledge from scholars who never thought their work could be paired with American naval history. That is the beauty of attempting to understand the world through a single individual as an intimate look into the context Breault sought to shape his life within. Sailors are ideal subjects for this type of enquiry because they live both within and spend extended periods of time away from their native culture.

It is no less unusual to use a single person's life as a means to understand history than to attempt to understand a single event. It is a history of the evolution of the person's relationship with the world. While this book is about Breault and attempts to add information to his narrative, this is only a secondary motivator. The primary motivation is to explore Breault's interactions with his culture and how they shaped his actions, his life, his responses, his desires and his relationship with friends and family. Breault was not simply a hero, he was also a person with his own thoughts, motivations and desires, aspects that were likely shared between he and his fellow sailors.

# Terms and Acronyms

Ratings are often shortened and then the rank is added on, such as 'TM2', which is Torpedoman's Mate Second Class. During the period in which Breault served, it was common to add a 'c' for 'class', making the abbreviation 'TM2c'.

| | |
|---|---|
| BESS | Basic Enlisted Submarine School |
| CMDR | Commander |
| CMOHS | Congressional Medal of Honor Society |
| CO | Commanding Officer |
| COB | Chief of the Boat |
| EM | Electrician's Mate |
| GM | Gunner's Mate |
| LCDR | Lieutenant Commander |
| LOC | Library of Congress |
| LT | Lieutenant |
| LTJG | Lieutenant Junior Grade |
| NAVSUBSCOL | Naval Submarine School New London |
| NJP | Non-Judicial Punishment, also informally known as a Captain's Mast. |
| OMPF | Official Military Personnel File |
| QM | Quartermaster's Mate |
| RADM | Rear Admiral |
| RNCVR | Royal Navy Canadian Volunteer Reserve |
| SFLM | Submarine Force Library and Museum |
| SCM | Summary court-martial |
| SUBASE NLON | Submarine Base New London |
| TM | Torpedoman's Mate |
| USN | United States Navy |
| WPA | Federal Writers of the Worker's Progress Administration |
| XO | Executive Officer |

# Chapter 1

# Enlisted Submarine Folk Hero

I arrived at Naval Submarine Base New London (SUBASE NLON) in Groton, CT, in the middle of a blizzard in February 2015. I had just completed Navy Basic Training at Recruit Training Command. Wearing my dress blues, I was picked up from T.F. Green International Airport in Providence, RI, by a duty driver. I arrived on Saturday evening and would begin my time at Basic Enlisted Submarine School (BESS) on Monday, the first of ten months of training to become a Fire Control Technician (FT). One of my first assignments was to visit the Submarine Force Library and Museum (SFLM), located a short walk from my quarters, to conduct a scavenger hunt of the exhibits to learn about submarine history. As my fascination with history was not a new development, I appreciated the opportunity to learn more about the community I was going to join. The very last question on my assignment survey was: 'Who is the only enlisted Medal of Honor recipient in the submarine force?' I then found the exhibit on the first floor of the museum that would shape my perception of what it meant to be a submariner.

**Salt and Steel**

On 28 October 1923, Torpedoman's Mate Second Class (TM2) Henry Breault was underway on the USS *O-5*, a small submarine designed for harbour defence, transiting to the other side of the Panama Canal to participate in fleet exercises.[1] At 0624 hours, the *O-5* was involved in a collision with the SS *Abangarez* of the United Fruit Company and sank rapidly. Most accounts agree that this occurred in less than a minute, with some estimating the *O-5* sank as quickly as thirty seconds after the impact.[2] Breault was in the torpedo room at the time of the collision and managed to make it topside:

> 'Upon reaching the hatch, he saw that the boat was rapidly sinking. Instead of jumping overboard to save his own life, he returned to the torpedo room to the rescue of a shipmate whom he knew was trapped in the boat.'[3]

Writer Julius Grigore adds that Breault secured the hatch as he went back down to find Chief Electrician's Mate Lawrence Brown, who was awake but unaware of the severity of the collision.[4] They attempted to escape back up the hatch, but when that failed, they moved to the Torpedo Room and managed to close the watertight door before the battery compartment caught on fire and the ship had settled underwater.[5] Brown recalled:

> 'Breault and I separated to pound on each of the boat's sides. In this way, the rescuers would know that there were two of us. Breault played a kind of tune with his hammer, indicating to the diver that we were in good shape and cheerful. Neither of us knew Morse Code. We had no food or water, and only a flashlight. We were confident we could stay alive for forty-eight hours.'[6]

Submariners were aware of the potential issues of submarine escape, understanding the risks well enough. They were fully outlined in a 1910 *Scientific American* article, but there was no established procedure to rescue them in a disabled submarine (DISSUB).[7] Brown and Breault were thankfully in shallow water, but their active role ended as the submarine settled on the bottom. They had to wait for rescue from the Panama Canal community utilizing two large crane barges in an attempt to lift them. The rescue took thirty-one hours of nonstop work.[8] This is a story explored in Grigore's articles, his focus is on diver Sheppard Shreaves and the efforts of the Panama Canal community, who worked heroically around the clock to save the trapped men.[9]

Once safe, it became evident Breault's decision to look for his missing shipmates saved Brown's life.[10] When asked why he stayed on board instead of jumping for safety, Breault stated simply: 'I wanted to stay and help, if I could.'[11] Breault uttered this statement while suffering from shock and caisson disease (decompression sickness), a side effect of the pressure while submerged, colloquially referred to as 'the bends' by divers. After about 30 minutes, Breault was whisked away to a depressurization chamber on the *O-7*.[12] Brown did not appear to be in a similar state, so he remained and related the story, as Grigore discovered in several newspapers. Brown's account became the primary narrative in newspapers, with only small snippets from Breault, such as the one above and another newspaper relating a telegram sent to his step-mother:

> 'Just a line to let you know that I am still alive. You have no doubt read about the sinking of the submarine. We were down there for hours and had no food … I sure was a sick boy but am well now.

I have been out helping to raise the submarine. She is all right except the central control room where she was struck. The craft will soon be in condition again. But some of the crew will never go down in a submarine again. Fortunately it did not bother me at all.'[13]

The loss and rescue of the *O-5* was covered by newspapers across the country, enough that Jeanette Maria Collins included five *O-5* articles from various newspapers in her thesis 'Style in the New Story'.[14] Submitted to the University of Wisconsin in 1924, Collins devoted her thesis to analysing the structure of several contemporary stories. For the Breault rescue story, she stated that 'someone's blue pencil got tired', accusing them of sloppy editing.[15] Collins' criticism serves as evidence that newspapers sought to deliver the story quickly, indicating an interest in submarines, the disaster and the rescue of the entombed sailors.

Perhaps no article touches on the reason that Breault's story has such currency among submariners better than the Omaha-based *Sunday Bee* article 'Grim Death Outplayed':

'Simple enough, when told in words, but tremendously important when calmly viewed. It is the real glory of the service, for it was not done in presence of the embattled foeman, but as a routine act when danger and death threatened in an unexpected form. Henry Breault's name goes down with other heroes who have brought honor to themselves and pride to Americans.'[16]

The 'routine act', which defined submarine service, culminated in an award ceremony in Washington DC on 8 March 1924, during which President Calvin Coolidge awarded Breault the Medal of Honor. Photos of the time show a small ceremony, with the President, the Secretary of the Navy (SECNAV) and high-ranking naval officials in attendance.

## *Iconographic Construction*

The narrative surrounding Breault is the result of didactic construction to build his story into a lesson of what is expected of junior enlisted personnel. The early introduction to a story of sacrifice is made, and the incentivisation of an award is intended to make an impression that this was the proper action; one that may be expected of the junior sailor throughout their career.[17] In this selfless decision, Breault embodied the 'ship, shipmate, self' mentality that is instilled in enlisted sailors early in their careers.[18] Breault has become a folk hero for the enlisted submariner, one who represents the essential submariner's duty. As such, Breault has become synonymous with the identity of the submarine community: selfless, courageous and often forgotten.

Throughout my tenure in naval service, I continued to hear and see references to Breault's story. In the building that houses BESS, I would occasionally pass a plaque hanging with an image of Breault and a reprint of his Medal of Honor citation. A nearly identical plaque greeted us when I arrived in Pearl Harbor, Hawaii, at a pier dedicated by then RADM Konetzni. Kenny Neville states a similar plaque hung on his boat, the *Virginia*, commissioned in 2003. Perhaps most memorable for me was the question asked during my board to receive my submarine warfare insignia, informally known as fish or dolphins. I was asked: 'Who is the only enlisted Medal of Honor recipient?' I answered confidently: 'TM2 Henry Breault.' For many submariners who served in the same era as I, Breault is *our* hero. During my research, a response I received from Kenny Neville of a submariner Facebook group highlights this sense of connection:

> 'His service and extraordinary heroism was written down and captured on a plaque that hung on the Torpedo room door on USS Virginia (SSN 774). It was a constant reminder that our service in the submarine community, while seemingly boring, mundane, or ridiculous at times, was of a higher calling than most people could fathom. And it was a constant gut check to keep me going and strive to be a better human being. I honestly can say I read the plaque in it's [*sic*] entirety well over 500 times and never did I think to myself, "Why am I reading this again?" I was not a Torpedoman. I was M-div.'[19]

This book began as a small research project while I attended the University of Portsmouth's Naval History MA programme. I was worried I would not have any original research to add in 5,000 words. At the time, I worked alongside the submarine community supporting shipyard construction activities in Groton, many of my co-workers also being former submariners. I discussed Henry Breault with them and, to my great shock, many of the submariners who had served prior to 2000 greeted me with confusion. I quickly informed them of his status, and they nodded their heads in surprise, stating they had never heard of him. This is not true of all submariners, but those who served prior to 2000 were much less likely to know about his story. I was taken aback at how many submariners of previous generations did not recognize Breault, indicating that his inclusion has been a recent professional movement.

To my further surprise, everything we know about Breault's life and service came from a few newspaper clippings, genealogical records, his Medal of Honor citation and two articles by Julius Grigore.[20] The question evolved to become what potential new sources I could introduce to provide further analysis on Breault's life. The contribution of this book is organizing previous research and then using Breault's previously unutilized OMPF to reconstruct his career, thereby providing a template methodology for microhistorians utilizing other prominent sailors' OMPFs.

## Enshrined but Forgotten: 1941–1999

The end of the Cold War created an identity crisis that affected the submarine fleet as much as the rest of the United States Armed Forces: how were they to define themselves in the absence of an existential threat? A few newspapers within the Submarine Archives of the SFLM located in Groton, CT, and the researcher's personal experience, substantiated with a poll conducted on a US Navy Submarine Facebook group, suggests Breault's renaissance began around 1999 and was fully adopted no later than 2003.[21]

Prior to renewed interest from 1989 onward, there were few pieces that showed interest in Henry Breault's story. Besides Julius Grigore's articles, one indication comes from Mario DeMarco's artwork in the *Navy Times*, as part of a series 'The Highest Honor'.[22] DeMarco's dramatized version of Breault's rescue of Brown was his interpretation and has inconsistencies. Brown was an active participant once he understood the scope of the disaster, and was not unconscious or prone in the water. There are no accounts of the torpedo room being flooded to the extent shown, and they were trapped for over thirty hours, not the three hours the artist mistakenly attributes.[23] Nonetheless, the artist and the publication wished to display the actions of Breault in a high regard as 'The Highest Honor', reflecting the message that Breault's action was worthy of emulation to the audience of enlisted sailors.[24] DeMarco took inspiration from previous periods of peacetime, such as the interwar period, to appeal to an enlisted audience now in peacetime.

DeMarco's Artwork is notable primarily for the inconsistencies. After thirty-three years, Breault's story was not completely forgotten, but when remembered, the details were often misconstrued. It is notable that the artwork was published on 27 October 1956, the date before the thirty-third anniversary of the *O-5–Abangarz* collision. If submariners remembered Breault, they did so in their own circles, and were likely driven by sailors who had served with Breault as opposed to any sort of formal indoctrination.

Explicit mention of Breault's story is lacking in collections of personal accounts of the Second World War and beyond.[25] For 'Cold War Warriors' like Ted Dubay, author of *Three Knots to Nowhere*, Breault was not a part of their identity:

> 'I do not recall hearing about Henry Breault when I attended Submarine School in 1969. In fact, I don't remember any formal presentation on submariner legacy, in sub school or during my time in the Navy. I also think this is true for other submariners of my era. The beginning of my time in the service overlapped the end of the careers of WWII submarine veterans. Breault's incident happened 20 years before WWII. As brave as he was, I believe many WWII submariners performed equally heroic actions during the war. These in turn would have overshadowed what he did. In fact, I think there were so many courageous acts during WWII that they were considered what was expected. In the case of Breault, submarines were still essentially a new phenomenon and an act such as his would have stood out. One other thought. My time in the service was way before the Internet. That means accessing information was much more difficult. Any information about Breault would not have been readily accessible, even for determined individuals.[26]

Dubay is likely correct: if the story had been kept alive by tribal knowledge perpetuated by sailors who had previously known Breault, it would be difficult to rediscover said person before the internet.

After a brief period, the focus of the USN returned to awarding the Medal of Honor to senior officers.[27] The focus on the officers rather than enlisted men is not unusual, as they earned their awards playing an identity-defining role defeating the Imperial Japanese Navy in the Pacific. The disconnect in legacy was exacerbated by the 1963 statute to prohibit the award to non-combatants and the classified nature of submarine operations during the Cold War; by the end of the 1990s, submariners had few active-duty heroes, and a past dominated by officers.[28] Enlisted submariners were proud of their heritage as an aggregate in the Second World War, but as time passed it became more difficult to involve their legacy as part of an enlisted heritage.

## Renaissance

Julius Grigore's articles are the definitive narrative of Breault's story.[29] Both articles mention the collision and Breault, but the primary focus is on the efforts of the Panama Canal community. Grigore's emphasis makes sense, as he was stationed at the now-defunct Panama Canal Zone, but the story of Breault is somewhat underdeveloped. It would take at least twenty years for the articles to reach historians studying submarines, such as SFLM curator Stephen Finnegan. The journals were primarily geared toward an audience of naval officers, who likely appreciated the significance of the topic but did not appreciate the full potential of utilizing Breault's story, likely regarding it as an interesting footnote.

The SFLM initially did not have an exhibit for Breault in its Medal of Honor section; he was included only after Finnegan discovered Grigore's articles in the late 1990s.[30] Finnegan began gathering the genealogical records, creating the exhibit seen above. He introduced the story to a retired submariner, Jim Christley, who was researching submarine collisions. Christley then introduced Breault's story to the wider audience of enlisted submariners, leading to increased interest and knowledge from the submarine community. The introduction was led by senior enlisted men, but submarine officers also began to pay attention. The first indication of renewed interest for the Navy was the dedication of a new pier in Pearl Harbor on 18 June 1999.[31] Shewman McClain reported that the guest speaker, then-RADM Al Konetzni, connected Breault's heroism to the present-day submarine community, stating 'events like this are ways we can shape the future by honoring the past'.[32] The USN has made increasing efforts to connect sailors to their heritage, such as frequently naming buildings and naval vessels after famous sailors. A ribbon ceremony with significant fanfare was conducted. McClain's article was an official Commander, Submarine Force, US Pacific Fleet news release, reflecting a desire to officially condone similar efforts.[33]

Further such efforts were made in Connecticut on 19 May 2001, Hamilton reporting the dedication of the memorial for Breault at Wilkinson Hall in Groton.[34] According to Hamilton, Christley and Senior Chief Petty Officer Anderson were responsible for researching and introducing him to Naval Submarine School New London (NAVSUBSCOL).[35] Then-Captain Arnold Lotring, the CO, made his intentions clear: 'I want our sailors to have a link with their past. And this is a Medal of Honor – this is a big deal.'[36] Christley, echoing Dubay, says this link was lacking during his twenty-year tenure in the Navy.[37] Breault's hometown of Putnam, CT, dedicated a footbridge in his memory on 11 November 2003. Guest speaker Captain Ratte Jr stated during the dedication:

> 'Torpedoman First Class Henry Breault's inspiring and exceptional performance of duty under the worst imaginable conditions, and in the face of seemingly certain death, speak to a selfless courage ... And it was such selfless courage the many Sailors of

our World War II Submarine Force tried to emulate when they were called upon some twenty years later.'[38]

The connection back to Second World War submariners indicates why Breault's story was lost. Seven more Medals of Honor were awarded to submarine CO who served during the war. American fascination with officers in the military has been well documented and reflects greater trends in popular media, a phenomenon that Larry A. Van Meter described as the 'officer fetish'.[39] The dedications present a clear picture of increased interest from 1999–2003, driven by higher echelons of command, with an emphasis on connecting junior sailors to their past. Awareness would eventually manifest in the inclusion of Breault within the curriculum of NAVSUBSCOL and awards named in his honor. One example is known as the 'Torpedoman Second Class Henry Breault Award', which is awarded to the E1–E6 sailor who 'best exemplifies the *traditional spirit* embodied in the Submarine Force' (emphasis mine).[40] Breault's iconographic construction became a connection for twenty-first-century enlisted submariners, particularly those who believe in the oft-repeated navy maxim 'ship, shipmate, self', which Jimmy Drennan explains is the summary of a junior sailor's conduct:

> '[T]he youngest Seaman Recruit swabbing the deck on a Navy warship ... is taught a traditional saying that sailors use to succinctly describe their priorities: "ship, shipmate, self". Like most nautical jargon, the aphorism has a certain graceful ring to it that captures the Navy's mission-first mentality in very few words. It evokes dramatic notions of sailors agonizingly shutting a hatch on shipmates to save the ship from flooding, or sacrificing their own safety to save a shipmate from an engine room fire.'[41]

For those seeking purpose in the mundane life of duty, training and sea time, Breault is representative of those forgotten because they did not have the privilege of rank to be remembered. Breault's commendation became unattainable, yet his heroic action became the duty and expectation of the average sailor qualified in submarines.

## The Forgotten Enlisted Men

The reader now knows the likely sum of possible knowledge surrounding Breault prior to the publication of this book. For the Navy, the sailors who are often forgotten are the enlisted men, who receive little attention while COs garner accolades and glory, personifying the anthropomorphized ship. Breault's heroism came at a pivotal time in the development of the submarine community and during a period of increased focus on awarding the Medal of Honor to enlisted personnel, ensuring the survival of documents that are often overlooked.[42] In a recent professional development for a force that has not seen another Medal of Honor awarded since the end of the Second World War, a renewed focus engrained Breault as an icon within the identity of the enlisted submariner.[43]

To give an idea of how little we knew about Breault's life in the submarine force, we didn't even pronounce his name correctly. While in BESS, I was taught that Breault's name was pronounced 'BRE-ault', likely to assist in spelling his name. We were encouraged to recall 'beautiful Breault' if we were struggling to remember the spelling, as most remembered how to spell 'beautiful'. In my experience, most sailors refer to him with this Anglicized pronunciation, and I thought nothing of it until my visit to the Aspinock Historical Society in Putnam.

I continued to refer to Breault as such until I first visited Breault's headstone, located in St Mary's Cemetery, and swept away the snow from the diminutive original headstone with my bare hands (an unwise move considering the frigid temperature and unforgiving wind). The pennies were placed by others, representing they paid their respects but did not know Breault personally. I paid a moment of respect, knowing the history of this small marker and the larger one to the right of it. The smaller gravestone with a penny was commissioned by Henry Breault's father, Joseph, at a cost of $48 in 1942.[44] Joseph, with legal assistance, filed for reimbursement via correspondence between 5 and 14 March 1942, while the members of the Putnam Veterans of Foreign Wars worked until they could get a Medal of Honor gravestone for Breault in 1988, which is located next to his original headstone.[45]

At the Aspinock Historical Society, I enquired about their 'BRE-ault' collection for the Medal of Honor recipient. The ladies on duty politely informed me of my ignorance in pronunciation, stating they had a 'br-OH' collection, shifting the emphasis to the latter syllable. Unfortunately, comprehension did not dawn on me until they courteously explained, in much plainer terms: 'You are pronouncing his name incorrectly, the Breault family in town pronounces their name this way.' To add further confusion, the census records offer another potential pronunciation. The 1910 US Census indicates that the Breault family pronounced their name 'Br-ALT', as indicated by the census recorder, who likely spelled the given name phonetically. The Breaults, now with three young children, probably did not have time to answer every question with the thoroughness they had in previous years. Considering the likely speaker would have been Joseph or Flora, the family probably pronounced the name in this manner: Brault, like so many French-Canadian names, became the new one with older spelling.⁴⁶ The 'Br-ALT' pronunciation is the most likely one Breault himself would have used, as one of his pages of Medical History in his OMPF confirms; the author had to put an indented correction – an 'e' inserted into 'Brault' to make it Breault – to get the proper spelling.⁴⁷

Regardless of how one elects to pronounce Breault's name, there is a deep well of potential insights contained within Breault's life and those of others like him, their lives acting as a focal point through which to explore interactions of individuals and contemporary society. Breault was an ordinary man who, when given the opportunity, acted in an extraordinary heroic capacity. That heroic capacity ensured the survival of documentation associated with his career. In the egalitarian spirit in which Breault deserved the Medal of Honor, he will be analysed as the subject of a microhistory, exploring his career and life in the context of the time when he served. His prominence ensured official documents would survive, collected in his OMPF. But what can we learn from military records, as impersonal as they may be, about the life and times of Henry Breault?

# Chapter 2

# Historiography

How much can one person's story interact with history? A single person in the sea of history seems to be so small, silent in the middle of the indifferent universe. I hope to prove that the insight that can be gained is surprisingly vast, surpassing any expectations, as part of a mosaic, microhistorical investigation. In Breault's forty-one years, he experienced childhood before the First World War in a dual-language French-Canadian immigrant family, served in the newly formed Royal Navy Canadian Volunteer Reserve, was discharged during the post-war mass demobilization, re-enlisted after post-service disillusionment, served aboard submarines, served near the newly constructed Panama Canal, served in the Asiatic Fleet during the rise of Chiang Kai-shek and Japanese militarism, lived in California and Washington as they grew into their own during the Great Depression, and died an early death likely related to his service. My investigation into Breault's life has convinced me that history is not the domain of those who can afford to pay the salaries of historians, but instead involves understanding the individual who lived in the period.

With the survival and rediscovery of Breault's Official Military Personnel File, we can reconstruct his experience and seek to understand his relationship to the strands and how he could have potentially interacted with them in his life.

**Medal of Honor**

The Medal of Honor is a prestigious American award, on par with the Victoria Cross as the highest military honour the United States can grant. Originating during the American Civil War, 3,530 awards have at the time if writing been granted to recipients, of which 2,074 were granted prior to 1900.[1] The submarine force is unusual in this regard, as of the eight recipients, only one was an enlisted man and the others were Commanding Officers (CO), earning their awards during the Second World War. The award attracts attention in popular culture – such as the video game franchise *Medal of Honor* – popularized in the same span during which Breault's renaissance occurred.[2] This level of attention has been further divided into 'war-winning' and 'soldier-saving', the former largely awarded to officers and the latter frequently awarded to enlisted personnel.[3] For Joseph A. Blake and Suellen Butler, the award was not to honour, but to perpetuate the continued division between enlisted men and officers, reflecting a 'latent' dual role structure in the military.[4]

The Medal of Honor in the interwar period should not be conflated with the same award that is granted today. Today's understanding of the Medal of Honor heavily influences the present-day perception and narrative of Breault's story, falling within a trend that sociologists Richard Lachmann and Abby Stivers identify is in line with more than a 'century of revaluation, clarification, and tightening', in which 'the Medal of Honor has become the principal symbol, and its recipients the highest embodiments, of bravery'.[5] Mears notes that the USN, despite Army prohibitions, rewarded non-combatants' 'extraordinary heroism' throughout the interwar period, making the fifteen USN Medal of Honor recipients an unusually egalitarian sample for the service.[6] Due to the unique motivations of the interwar period, present USN policy and statutory prohibitions preventing non-combatant awards, Breault will likely remain the only enlisted Medal of Honor submariner for actions performed aboard submarines. His distinct case makes him a symbol to the nameless submariners who have performed their duties without the accolades or prestige afforded to him.[7]

The submarine and interwar Medal of Honor samples fit some of the previously identified structures. Blake and Butler primarily rested their analysis on studies of the Vietnam War, arguing that officers were significantly more likely to be awarded for leadership rather than placing oneself in harm's way, and that as recipients increased in rank, their likelihood of receiving an award for leadership also increased.[8] Henry Breault, a junior enlisted sailor, was awarded for a peacetime action that was similar to the soldier-saving awards identified by Blake and Butler, which will be referred to in this context as a 'sailor-saving' Medal of Honor. There were fewer opportunities in a nominal period of peace to receive the Medal of Honor for leadership or war-winning actions, but they were still represented by aviators who flew over the North Pole and divers who saved the crew of DISSUB *Squalus*, the latter of which can be considered sailor-saving and war-winning. Breault's uniqueness stems from his status as an enlisted submariner, the only submariner to come from the enlisted cadre to receive the Medal of Honor.

## The Interwar Navy, The Roaring Twenties and the Great Depression

One of the most important contributions to the USN interwar submarine history is Joel Holwitt's *Execute Against Japan*, which analyses the development of

## HISTORIOGRAPHY

USN submarine doctrine, specifically the question of how the Navy came to a decision to execute unrestricted submarine warfare.[9] His study is a top-down focus, analysing decision-making from the upper echelons of political and naval power. Holwitt seeks to challenge the dominant narrative from previous research on the subject, most of which emphasized doctrinal conservatism, battleship focus and international treaties.[10] The research on this period is sparing from a USN perspective due to its temporal proximity to both world wars, some of the most well-researched periods of history, hence the name 'interwar'. There are few academic works I have been able to identify that focus on the life of a USN sailor during the period, though there are several possible candidates to choose from the 'persons of exceptional prominence' who can provide more information on the unique conditions of the period, primarily from an officer's viewpoint, such as Hyman G. Rickover, who served aboard the *S-9* and *S-48*.[11]

Of all the potential areas that could be focused on, the waters and rivers of China provided the most dynamic environment. The focus on the interwar British Asiatic Fleet could provide insight, the most important recent research conducted into the period being completed by Matthew Heaslip.[12] Heaslip's work still focuses on higher-ranking officials, doctrine, technology and cultural importance of the Royal Navy (RN), but includes considerations of enlisted sailors, such as RADM William Boyle voicing concern that ordinary seamen found raiding villages unpopular and overall damaging to morale, as real and important issues to be resolved.[13] Heaslip even discusses minute matters such as how sailors interacted with Shanghai and its environs, including accounts of the nightlife, showing the full picture of what the China Station meant to the UK and the RN.[14] Analysis of Breault's career can highlight both the USN's role in the region and the role of the submarine in gunboat diplomacy, as Breault was sent by his own request to the Asiatic Fleet from 1925–28 and then again from 1929–32.

While military and naval historians describe 1919–40 as the interwar period, in American history the period is divided and frequently represented as the Roaring Twenties and the Great Depression. The Roaring Twenties is popular for its perceptions as a party era, with the illegal purchase and drink of alcohol, while the Great Depression is primarily remembered for the financial, agricultural and unemployment crises. Breault was not present for much of the Twenties in the Continental USA; while Fitzgerald published *The Great Gatsby*, Breault served in the Panama Canal and Asiatic Theatre. While a naval career was not as rewarding as civilians' jobs in terms of financial compensation, Breault's choice to remain in the USN paid off during the Great Depression, throughout which he was steadily employed. Breault's life does not match the narrative that permeates the popular eras, yet how do we reconcile these grand narratives with Breault's experience?

The answer is not to reject Breault's experience, but instead to examine it through a cultural historical lens. This work will seek to add information to external narratives of history whenever possible, but they will not guide my interpretation of the source material. If the narrative does not fit, then it will not be incorporated into the work. Breault's history is not invalidated because it does not fit into our expectations of the periods he lived within, rather it offers a range of alternatives that existed within those periods. Breault's story is of the forgotten pigboat sailors, most recently observed by Bobette Gugliotta's *Pigboat 39*. Gugliotta writes that all aboard the boat were heroes, and her work offers a surprising level of insight into the personal life of one submarine crew at the end of the interwar period. Breault's account will grant further insights into the period.

## Mosaic Microhistory as Opposed to Biography

My research seeks to fit itself within the framework of historical analyses described as microhistory. A microhistorical approach is controversial, close to biography, but Jill LePore argues that it offers a solution to the 'perils of writing about people'.[15] She relates her experience discovering a historical subject's hair in an archive:

> 'It was coarse, red, and, needless to say, no longer attached to his head. Earlier that day I had come across the catalog entry "Lock of hair" in the finding guide for the Noah Webster Family Papers and had smiled at the quaintness of it, of someone thinking Webster's hair – his hair! – was precious enough to preserve ... I found myself feeling closer to Webster than I had ever felt when reading even his most personal papers. That lifeless, limp hair had spent decades in an envelope, in a folder, in a box, on a shelf, but holding it in the palm of my hand made me feel an eerie intimacy with Noah himself. And, against all logic, it made me feel as though I knew him – and, even less logically, liked him – just a bit better.'[16]

I confess to having the same feeling of intimacy when I found Breault's OMPF. As a former submariner myself, I knew that the USN carried and compiled records on all of its sailors. Searching through the documents and seeing an aged Breault whom few living people had seen since 1941 was a treat, knowing I was likely among the first who sought this record out and saw the picture of an aged Breault, taken in 1941 for an ID card.

LePore says that despite this episode, she found Webster was unsuitable as the subject of a microhistory.[17] She intensely disliked the man, even admitting she found herself tempted to parade his failures, something biographers often deal with, but LePore claims historians try to avoid positive or negative emotions towards their subject.[18] I have withheld any judgements on Breault, but I tend to lean more favourably towards my subject than LePore did. Despite this, I recognize the nuance of his interactions with others and the uniqueness of his motivations as an actor within an unusual period in the USN. How does the microhistorian, which I claim to be, differentiate themselves from the biographer?

LePore offered the following four propositions that distinguish microhistory from biography:

> '**Proposition 1.** If biography is largely founded on a belief in the singularity and significance of an individual's contribution to history, microhistory is founded upon almost the opposite assumption: however singular a person's life may be, the value of examining it lies in how it serves as an allegory for the culture as a whole.
>
> '**Proposition 2.** Biographers seek to profile an individual and recapitulate a life story, but microhistorians, tracing their elusive characters through slender records, tend to address themselves to solving small mysteries about a person's life as a means to exploring the culture.
>
> '**Proposition 3.** Biographers generally worry about becoming too intimate with their subjects and later betraying them; microhistorians, typically denied any such intimacy, tend to betray people who have left abundant records in order to resurrect those who did not.
>
> '**Proposition 4.** A biographer's alter ego is usually the subject of the biography, while a microhistorian's alter ego may be a figure who investigates or judges the subject. For this reason, a microhistorian may be a character in his own book.'[19]

LePore did not write in a vacuum: she was following a model, famously embodied by Carlo Ginzburg writing in a politically tumultuous period in Italian history. Ginzburg discusses the origin of the term 'microhistory' in his article 'Microhistory: Two or Three Things That I Know about It'.[20] Ginzburg identifies that the earliest identified employment of the term 'microhistory' was by American scholar George R. Stewart. Stewart wrote the book *Pickett's Charge: A Microhistory of the Final Charge at Gettysburg, July 3, 1863* in 1959, a focused historical lens that emphasizes Pickett's Charge as one of the most important events in world history. Ginzburg is somewhat dismissive of Stewart's work, arguing that Cleopatra's nose could be a subject of Stewart's microhistory, while offering a contrast to this focused temporal approach by introducing the work of Luis Gonzalez, which Ginzburg utilizes to convey the range of potential microhistorical precursors to his work. If Stewart's work is microhistory, then one could argue all historical analysis is microhistorical, so long as it is sufficiently constrained. A historian seeks to understand the subject and how it is related to the greater subjects.

How, then, do I justify calling this work a microhistory? Ginzburg further emphasizes that the Italian microhistorians, such as Giovanni Levi and Ginzburg himself, sought to create a 'self-portrait' rather than a 'group-portrait', a goal Ginzburg admits that, despite his best efforts, proved too tall an order, calling the boundaries 'porous' rather than distinct.[21] While not one of the Italian microhistorians, Sigurður G. Magnússon attempted a similar study, urging 'scholars to look at the sources they have, and to do their utmost not to be drawn into the grand narrative, which will govern their interpretation of the subject'. Magnússon admits, as does Ginzburg, that divorcing the subject from the group proves to be a difficult task and emphasizes understanding how the self-portrait interacts with the group portrait, rather than focusing on one to the detriment of the other. I believe microhistory can offer original insights into both portraits, seeing how the individual seeks to be a part of the group, as part of a greater mosaic.

A microhistory of Breault will follow the four propositions of LePore whilst simultaneously heeding the warnings of Magnússon. Breault was not likely aware of these greater narratives imposed upon the periods in which he lived, so why should historians fix his account within these narratives? Magnússon utilizes his own research experience to prove the point. After publishing a book based on the lives of two brothers in 1997, an unexpected letter arrived from the reliable (and locally renowned) Guðmundur P. Valgeirsson.[22] Valgeirsson argued that Magnússon's portrayal of Níels Jónsson in his relationship with his betrothed was incorrect, and he related the true story of what occurred, something completely unexpected.[23] This led to a methodological crisis:

> 'My acquaintance with Níels and his people was such that the whole thing seemed inconceivable. I immediately started asking myself whether the sources I had been working with were, by their very nature, simply not to be trusted. I told myself that these events fell outside the scope of my research, since the subject I had actually

been interested in was courtship ... Even so, I was filled with an uncomfortable sense that I had failed to recognize these extreme and violent tendencies in Níels's character. For many years I had pored over the writings of this man and his brother, wondered at their fortitude and perseverance, tried to put myself in their shoes and understand all the intricacies of their thoughts and deeds. And yet, despite this, I had managed to miss such a profound defect of character as the one that had manifested itself here in so macabre a fashion. How could such a thing happen?'[24]

Magnússon concludes that the error was made because he forced an image to fit, 'to serve the insistence of the community of scholars that I must connect my arguments to a bigger picture'.[25] Breault's source documentation is not as personal as the subjects of Magnússon, but I must be wary to not project external analysis onto his life.

During the research process, I divided the surviving documentation into groups associated with specific aspects of Breault's life, exploring his interactions with the Navy, family, friends, women he dated, the material culture, the stations he visited and his own medical well-being. This will not seek to reach into areas that cannot be observed, such as his relationship to greater trends assessed to be reasonably outside of his career, such as his role in interwar Navy development or the Roaring Twenties and Great Depression. If the ties do exist, they will be explored, but within the context of the period from Breault's perspective. The overarching microhistorical investigation becomes, 'how did a sailor interact with American society?' A sailor in the USN occupied a strange position that vacillated between alienation and acceptance, making exploration from their viewpoint a unique opportunity to view American cultural developments from one outside American culture, but simultaneously connected. How Breault continued to live within the self-imposed contradiction will offer insight few other groups can match.

Instead of fully adopting the idea of the self- and group portraits previously espoused by Levi and Ginzburg, I seek to construct an analysis of seemingly different parts and experiences to create a small, focused picture. Due to the lack of personal documentation, I am forced to construct Breault's potential ranges of experience from other scholars' research, which is then substantiated by first-hand accounts or popular culture representations. While some may object to the latter being utilized, as the divide between real life and on-screen life are often considered opposed, I suggest that they are based in the cultural context of the period. While they are not perfect, they do offer potential explanations for how and why Breault reacted as he did in similar circumstances. The final product, Breault reconstructed, is a mosaic, one whose individual portions do not resemble him but, together, reconstruct him. This is a beginning point, a call for new information and others' analysis, rather than an end.

## Local History

Local and microhistory are in some respects intertwined, but the separation is in the nuance of investigation, source material and the subject matter. The seminal local historical work is Carol Kammen's *On Doing Local History*. Kammen defines local history as 'the memory of place', preferring to focus on the local connection of the author to the subject in a manner that straddles biography and microhistory.[26] Kammen offers other guidelines as to what delineates local history from other forms of history:

> 'It is most often crafted by someone who lives in the locality, often someone untrained in historical methodology but who has an idea of what needs to be remembered, what should be celebrated, what it is that is important for residents to know. Many people come to local history following in a family tradition of interest, or because they hold a position that leads them to want to codify what is known, or to understand about the ground on which they live ... Sometimes reverence for a place or a sense of awe of the past drives the local historian; sometimes it is a desire to know what [happened] ... There has never been one way to "do" local history and it has generally been conducted uniquely, although not without motive.'[27]

Kammen's first chapter gives a history of local history, offering the variety of motivations from the Old World to the New, with a particular emphasis on American local history. The key point is that there can be wrong motivations but also no universally accepted methodological process in researching or writing about local history; indeed, in some respects, this lack of methodology can be an asset to the local historian themselves.

I do not meet the qualifications to be a local historian, though I certainly do interact with the work of present day and contemporary local historians. These works are interspersed throughout the analysis but are so wide-ranging in focus and methodology that it would be an injustice to collect them into one single category. Academic history has a place for local historians' works, particularly in reconstructing potential experiences their subjects had in local communities. The Aspinock Historical Society in Putnam, CT, The White Plains Historic Society of White Plains, NY, and the Marysville Historical Society of Marysville, WA, have been in correspondence with me and assisted in research. Kammen's example of Dr Mary Walker, the only woman to receive the Medal of Honor, indicates that Henry Breault's story could contain similar currency to the communities he was associated with. I hope the research adds to the local historical quilt of the respective communities with which Breault interacted in his lifetime.[28]

## French-Canadians in New England

While important to the overall development of New England, Joseph E. Price observed that French-Canadian communities in the region are relatively unknown popularly as part of the cultural makeup.[29] French-Canadian immigrants in the United States occupied a unique position during the waves of immigration that characterized late nineteenth- and early twentieth-century American demographics. They came for employment, like many other groups, but unlike those that came from Europe or Asia, they could return to their birthplace when opportunities dried up or they fancied a change of scenery. As such, many primarily sought to emigrate to New England for its close geographic approximation, affording them a pragmatic relationship to the communities they engrained themselves within. Such circumstance brought Joseph J. Breault and Flora Breault to Putnam, CT, and many other French-Canadian families to the North-east. By 1898, analysis of the 1890 census revealed that 331,804 French-Canadians lived in New England.[30] While that number seems small in the total aggregate of migrants to the United States, the influence of French-Canadians in New England could be felt in local politics.[31]

The primary consideration that brought French-Canadians to the USA was employment. Claude Bélanger argues that a combination of internal factors such as demographic pressures, rural poverty, agricultural crises in Québec, relative lack of industrialization and external factors of higher average wages in the USA and remarkable improvement in rail transportation 'fuelled migration'.[32] Despite this, the exact experience of a French-Canadian family in New England has been difficult to pin down, though not for lack of research.[33] Jason L. Newton argued that the French-Canadians, particularly rural groups, were systematically oppressed by both the American and Canadian authorities as part of the greater American emphasis on racial hierarchy, but Jean-Philippe Warren claimed that French-Canadians assimilated easily and rather willingly, particularly when compared to German or Jewish American groups, as evidenced by the decline in readership of French newspapers.[34]

For research into Breault, Warren's interpretation may be closer to the mark; despite Newton's assertion that French-Canadians were settled in the nativist hierarchy that dominated American thinking, the community also exercised a remarkable amount of political power. By 1914, in Norwich, CT, a third of the voters were French-Canadian, indicating a salient group that understood there was strength in numbers in local communities.[35] Similarly, Jason Peters discovered that 51 per cent of voters in 1924 Woonsocket, RI, were French-Canadian, which spurred a reactionary 'English-only' policy in schools. Peters focuses his analysis on the subsequent process of assimilation to American culture.[36] Neither of these points invalidate Newton's claim, however, as he primarily focused on a rural community of loggers, rather than the more urban centres that contained *le petit Canadas*. Breault would continue to be proficient in French throughout his life, indicating he likely still identified as both American and French-Canadian and was part of the struggle, at least internally at times.

As a sailor who served in both the RNCVR and the USN, the balance of identity was a real and sincere problem for those like Breault and their families. The question for this strand of historiography will be explored throughout the investigation: did Breault receive any unusual treatment for being French-Canadian throughout his life, or was he able to rapidly assimilate while reconciling his linguistic and religious ties?

## Gender, Sexuality and Family History

Sailors are remarkably malleable symbols. They frequently represent a masculine figure, as represented by Hetty King's 'Ship Ahoy! (All the Nice Girls Love a Sailor)':

> 'All the nice girls love a sailor,
> All the nice girls love a tar –
> For there's something about a sailor,
> Well, you know what sailors are!
> Bright and breezy, free and easy,
> He's the ladies' pride and joy!
> You can hear the people shout,
> As the ship comes full about:
> Ship ahoy! Ship Ahoy!'[37]

Yet the contradiction is implicit in the nature of the person who initially sang the song. Hetty King was a 'drag-king', a woman who dressed in male garb on stage, representing the fluidity of male and female sexuality within the era.[38] The song also changed over time to reinforce the idea of the sailor as a heterosexual male, when lines seven and eight were replaced with 'Falls in love with Kate and Jane / Then he's off to sea again'.[39] The departure from the original lyrics indicates the maturation of the sailor as a ladies' man: one who was expected to pursue women ashore.

*Uniformed* sailors in Western societies became a sex symbol, one which could appeal both to men and women,[40] as Michel Imbert describes in his analysis of Billy Budd the Sailor, a literary character created by Herman Melville:

> 'The miracle performed by military service, almost like a religious sacrement [*sic*], consists in erasing vulgar sexual fantasies, sublimating them and raising them to the sublime heights of military or/and religious glory. Same-sex Eros is thus transfigured into a collective ethos and this military *Aufhebung* of ordinary lust by a kind of relief of the guard is converted into a latter-day avatar of the Christian miracle of Incarnation.'[41]

Perhaps even more surprisingly, the idea of a sailor as a sex symbol, particularly for male groups, is ubiquitous in numerous cultures in the same period that Breault was a sailor, Andrew Stephenson discovered that British and French subcultures embraced the sailor and his uniform as a sex symbol.[42]

The challenge that industrialization had on traditional gender roles manifested itself in pressures on the traditional nuclear family. Breault was frequently estranged from his parents, in part due to his profession and in part to his own preference.[43] When Breault did establish a family, he elected to marry a woman who already had a child, adopting Pearl's daughter as his own child. In this case, creating a family also entailed breaking up a nuclear family to create a blended family. There is a certain contradiction in a sailor being a family man, one that was recognized in the contemporary literature. In Edward Ellsberg's *Pigboats*, one of the sailors recalls to the narrator in touching detail his family in Colorado. As he realizes the likelihood he would ever see them again was rapidly decreasing due to his current situation on a DISSUB, he kills himself due to his anguish. In response to the death of his shipmate, sailor Biff Wolters proclaims: 'It oughta be agin the Regulations fer a sailor to git married 'n have kids. They just don't jibe with goin' to sea.'[44] Breault likely felt the same early in his career, but he was still a man and subject to American cultural norms surrounding masculinity. Part of manhood was becoming a father, and he was not immune to the temptation when it presented itself. Breault's account illustrates the delicate cultural boundaries sailors had to live within, particularly when they also had a family.

## Material Identity, Consumer Culture Theory and the Foundations of Hyperrealism

Friedrich W. Nietzsche stated, foreshadowing Charles H. Cooley's 'looking glass self' theory, that identity has a more external realm:

> 'What we know about [ourselves] and remember is not so decisive for the happiness of our life as people suppose. One day that which others know about us (or think they know) assaults us – and then we realize that this is more powerful. It is easier to cope with a bad conscience than to cope with a bad reputation.'[45]

Nietzsche observed that we would rather be seen as something than act in a manner consistent with one's own desires. Industrialization and the introduction of mass-produced products changed the average American's access to consumer goods. The subsequent branding led to an emergence of subcultures organized by a material identity associated with the products produced. Automobiles, watches, houses and uniforms fit into this study, but there are some methodological discussions. There are two approaches with a consumer culture theory that emphasizes the rather centralized efforts of branding and marketing at the expense of choice, but also seeks to understand how the audiences rework the product to match their conceptions.[46] Eric J. Arnould and Craig J. Thompson explained:

> 'More broadly still, [consumer culture theory] research has emphasized the [productive] aspect of consumption. Consumer culture theory explores how consumers actively rework and transform symbolic meanings encoded in advertisements, brands, retail settings, or material goods to manifest their particular [personal] and social circumstances and further their identity and lifestyle goals … From this [perspective], the marketplace provides consumers with an [expansive] and heterogeneous palette of resources from which to construct individual and collective identities.'[47]

This explanation may appeal to an idea of consumer goods being able to help communities, the works they cite appearing to originate from a marketing field.[48]

In their conclusion, they note that the theory aims at 'fulfilling the recurrent calls of consumer research's thought leaders for a distinctive body of theoretical knowledge about consumption and market-place behaviors'.[49]

The focus on marketing alienates the very people whom consumer culture theory seeks to understand. As Penne Restad observed, the 'disquieting sense that the consumer might not be entirely human further separates it from other historical actors'.[50] Restad further argues that the revival of the consumer's role, not as a consumer but as a person, has been forwarded by scholars in the field who recognize that 'Consumer, after all, is not a stable identity'.[51] Is there an alternative model that could help seek understanding in Breault's relationship with the physical objects he made a part of his identity? Breault did purchase goods that defined him, foremost among them naval uniforms, and Breault's perception in the present day is due to his status as a Medal of Honor recipient. Fundamentally, therefore, Breault's story comes with some sort of identity sculpted by material goods.

Access to and the ability to afford consumer goods represented the developing desires of the American middle class during Breault's life. Heike Paul argues that the idea of 'Rags to Riches', or 'Self-made men', are *the* defining American myth or fairy tale in modernity.[52] Fundamental to the idea is that hard work leads to 'earthly rewards', or the hope for material desires that only a rich person could afford.[53] Thus, what Breault could afford in some manner defined his ability to exercise his status as a self-made man in American culture. The material in his life defined him, creating the foundation for what Jean Baudrillard would later term hyperrealism.[54] Baudrillard argues:

> 'Whence the characteristic hysteria of our times: that of the production and reproduction of the real. The other production, that of values and commodities, that of the belle epoque of political economy, has for a long time had no specific meaning. What every society looks for in continuing to produce, and to overproduce, is to restore the real that escapes it. That is why today this "material" production is that of the hyperreal itself. It retains all the features, the whole discourse of traditional production, but it is no longer anything but its scaled-down refraction (thus hyper-realists fix a real from which all meaning and charm, all depth and energy of representation have vanished in a hallucinatory resemblance). Thus everywhere the hyperrealism of simulation is translated by the hallucinatory resemblance of the real to itself.'[55]

Baudrillard claims that this new hyper-reality replaces actual reality, but that this was a process that occurred over time. Andreas Wirsching connects this idea to more mature Baudrillardian works and compares them to the 'optimistic American attitude' towards consumerism.[56] Wirsching argues that the ideological triumph of American consumerism was a paradigm shift:

> 'Truly has it been said that "the emergence of a consumer-oriented society is becoming the narrative of the age". As teleology this has been disputed, but there is no denying that the new narrative contains a normative, historically rooted developmental trend linking it to a model of Western mass consumption society that is outwardly irenic and inwardly at peace.'[57]

Breault was a part of the American culture that emphasized building a personality through the materials accessible to a member of particular subcultures. Thus, in certain respects, Breault constructed his identity by purchasing material goods that adhered to the image he sought to project. Breault didn't just wear his naval uniforms, the uniforms defined Breault's relationship to American society. Breault didn't just buy an automobile he couldn't afford, he also sought to buy the social status associated with that vehicle. These are problems faced in the present day, and finding the origin of them could potentially provide insight into the process of constructing identity from material goods.

## Methodology

Sailors, even those less famous than Breault, provide an ideal subject for future microhistories. They have a wealth of impartial documents in their surviving military documentation. These documents are akin to legal documents, with the subject's personal life bleeding in bits and pieces, requiring a greater knowledge of the period in question to fill the gaps. The connections can be further substantiated by census records, newspapers and of course personal documents, whenever available. Unfortunately, there are no known surviving personal accounts on Breault, written either by him or people who knew him. Even the physical artefact, Breault's Medal of Honor, has been lost. Chapter 1 has outlined the research that has already been conducted and reflects the possible extent of what the most knowledgeable person could reasonably be expected to know prior to the publication of this work. As has been established, my relationship with Breault is through common association with the USN Submarine Force. A submariner in the company of another submariner shares a shibboleth that has the potential to transcend bonds of nationality or individual enmity. This association has its own dangers for a researcher, ones I have taken precautions to divorce myself from. Henry Breault, although constructed into a professional icon, was still a man, so his life will be established as a vehicle, rather than as a subject or object, particularly in analytical chapters. This study is partially to reconstruct Breault's life, but also to explore how he interacted with the world around him, while avoiding determinations of praise or condemnation.

The first layer of this book, Chapters 1 and 2, establish the previous research, major stands of historiography and my relationship to the subject. After reading these chapters, the reader should have a sufficient level of knowledge one would have access to prior to publication of this research, strands of research the subject touches and an understanding of the methodology that guides successive chapters. I also stress the importance of understanding that Breault was a hero to me, and to many others in the submarine force. This relationship allows me to understand certain fears associated with being a submariner, but also puts me at risk of allowing too much of a sympathetic treatment of the subject. In this case, exploring the subject's relationship to the external world will minimize the risks of being too close, a line that prevents my work from being a biographical entry.

The second layer is based on the documentary *corpus*: the bulk of the information we have on Breault's career in the USN in the form of his OMPF, newspapers and any other documentation previously found in institutions such as the Aspinock Historical Society, the SFLM and the CMOHS. As a result, the documentation emphasizes his career prominently. As a career is a pillar of a man's self within traditional American ideas of identity, Breault's desire to remain a sailor was also likely how he defined himself. The exploration of these documents seeks to give a baseline of Breault's career as divided into three periods: pre-award career and life (1900–23), heroism and recognition (1923–24) and post-award career and death (1924–41). This will be the *self-portrait* of the microhistorical investigation, seeking answers as to how Breault's career developed as it did and reconstructing his career as he lived it.

The third layer will analyse Breault's interactions with the world, reconstructing the *group portrait* described by Levi and the fulfilment of propositions one and two from LePore. Breault's relationship to greater society will be explored. While not done through first-person accounts or sources, these chapters will attempt to use Breault's experiences to highlight the relationship between Breault, his family and friends, the women in his life, the communities in which he resided, the portrayal of masculine sailors in popular culture and his participation constructing a material identity. The overall goal is to explore the commerce between the constituent portions of the mosaic and uncover how Breault would have likely seen himself and interacted with American society through these focused avenues.

The fourth and final layer will attempt to reconcile the group and self-portraits and to offer future avenues for research. Breault, like all of us, found himself thrown into the world. His facticity will be explored throughout the interactions, seeking explanations as to what he likely identified as, what his temperament was, why he adopted these as pillars of his identity and what the realms of self-identity can tells us about contemporary American society. Once fully reconstructed, the hope will be a greater insight into both the self and group-portraits; that we will have a better idea as to who the real Henry Breault was and how an individual living in America from 1900–41 would have understood his world. The work will be the pinnacle of the research achieved thus far – but it will not be the end. The research must be continually surpassed as new evidence surfaces; it is the curse of a short life. I have created a skeleton and displayed it in a museum, stating this is what we know of Henry Breault. I will continue to seek the flesh, but others will likely be required, long after my time, to fully uncover his story.

# Chapter 3

# Pre-Award Life and Career (1900–23)

Sources for Henry Breault's early life and pre-award career are scarce. Census records, SFLM archives and Breault's OMPF all contain small pieces of information, through which we can reconstruct how he advanced through his early life and career. I do not seek to intimate that Breault was a special youth, one destined for greatness. Breault was not a Victorian hero or a literary figure rising above the mediocrity of the populace to serve as beacon of respectability.[1] This chapter will seek to understand how Breault became the sailor who was willing to risk his life in a moment's notice, rather than to aggrandize him unnecessarily.

## Early Life: 1900–16

On 26 June 1900, a census-taker for the US Census Bureau's twelfth census, Patrick O'Leary, walked along Allen Street in Putnam, CT. O'Leary knocked on doors throughout Putnam, asking several questions associated with:

1. Location
2. Name of persons living in the abode
3. Relation to the head of the household
4. Personal description of each person
5. State or country born in
6. Citizenship
7. Education
8. Ownership of home

O'Leary had just finished recording the extended Breault family staying at 669 Allen Street in the household of Henri Breault. O'Leary then visited 670 Allen Street and met Joseph J. Breault and Flora Breault. They were 25 and 24 years old respectively, Joseph being born in January 1875 and Flora in April 1876. Although Flora indicated she had no children, O'Leary likely noticed she was pregnant with Henry Breault, who would be born on 14 October

1900.² Joseph and Flora had lived in the United States for sixteen years, but had emigrated from Canada, where their parents had lived. Joseph was employed as a 'woodchopper' and indicated he had never been unemployed, while Flora did not indicate whether she was currently employed or was seeking employment. Joseph and Flora rented their abode, as did their relatives next door.³

Henry Breault was born in Putnam, but it is unknown how long the growing family remained in the town. By 18 April 1910, Ray St Blackmore, census-taker for the thirteenth census, recorded that the Breault family had moved to 97 Oakley Avenue in White Plains, NY. The move occurred sometime between the births of their second and third children, Diana and Beatrice. Diana was born in Connecticut and Beatrice in New York state. Beatrice was only a year old at the time of the census, indicating the move was a very recent one, likely for Joseph's employment as a carpenter. They recorded that French was the primary language spoken in the household, though Henry and Diana both attended school, likely an English-speaking establishment. Their home was still rented, which was to be expected for a family that had only recently moved.⁴ The most important indication in this record is the pronunciation of their surname: 'Brault'.

Sadly, Breault would lose his mother, Flora Breault, on an unknown date in 1913, the only indication being the Breault family headstone in St Mary cemetery in Putnam.⁵ Before she died, Estelle Breault had been born, with the 1921 sixth census of Canada identifying her birthplace was Canada. This appeared to have been a correction on the part of the recorder, who had likely assumed the whole family was born and raised in Canada. Joseph would remarry at an unknown date, Marie Breault being thirteen years his junior and likely French-Canadian herself. The Breault family lived in Canada throughout the war, likely travelling for employment in war industries, as both Breault and his father appeared to be employed in factory work.

From the census records, it can be gathered that Henry Breault spent his childhood primarily in Connecticut, New York and Canada as part of an immigrant family that preferred speaking French at home. Breault likely favoured speaking in French in his home, but lived in an American or Canadian society that primarily communicated in English in public institutions. Breault was a bilingual citizen in an American society that had many families seeking to become American while simultaneously maintaining their old cultural ties, a condition that is not unique to French-Canadians immigrants in the period. The likely fact that Breault was not a native English speaker may have interfered with his education; he professed to have a grade school education, claiming it was fourth or fifth grade at varying points in his enlistment paperwork.⁶ Breault's bilingual (though favouring francophone) background may have prevented him from achieving academic success early in life.

A major question of the nature of his early life outside of these details is whether Henry had a place he considered home, or did he move with Joseph to wherever work was available? The latter possibility is more likely, but due to his initial willingness to return to Putnam post-RNCVR discharge and future references to White Plains, the two cities can be considered his home for his formative years. One major issue with using newspapers is the relatively common names of Henry and Joseph. Complicating the matter further, there was another father-son pair from Putnam named Joseph A. Breault and Henry J. Breault; when local newspapers refers to Joseph and Henry Breault, they frequently referred to this father-son duo and not that of interest to us. Their records are commented upon, as they were called for Connecticut court cases and military service in the Canadian Expeditionary Force. In an era where visiting a town entreated a section in the personal section of the local newspaper, the scarce mentions are likely due to the lack of movement outside of places they considered home or had family in the community.

In Breault's OMPF collection, he would make infrequent references to his youth in paperwork, primarily medical and enlistment documents. In later medical records, Breault revealed he did not suffer from measles or mumps, explaining that he did not contract any 'significant' illnesses as a child, such as polio or typhoid.[7] Breault would give infrequent and inconsistent indications of his highest achieved level of education, though it is consistently declared as no higher than a 'grammar school' education, which was enough to gain a passable level of literacy.[8] Whenever he had an academic obstacle, such as a naval school or advancement exam, he was not confident in his ability, potentially stemming from this lack of formal education during childhood. Breault's relationship to Putnam, White Plains and Montreal, and other aspects of his early childhood, could be promising avenues for future research. Here, I call upon local historians to add to the story.

## Enlistment in the RNCVR

Henry Breault enlisted in the RNCVR on 24 July 1917, lying about his age on the application to gain a year, indicating he was born on 14 August 1899.[9] As researcher Eric Brown discovered, minors lying about their age – and even assuming false identities – was not an uncommon practice to circumvent parental permission to enlist.[10] Joseph may have even played an active role in the subterfuge, as Breault indicated on the official paperwork that he lived at his father's household at 34 St Phillip St Ville de Laurent in Montreal, Quebec. A month later, on 24 August 1917, ten days after his alleged 18th birthday, Breault was promoted to ordinary seaman, being part of the boy's mess for a shorter period than if he had enlisted at his actual age.[11] Breault had an amendment made in pen ink to his requested location of service, the form stating that the request was for 'Overseas' service, but he expressly desired service in the Atlantic, indicating his intent on his application. Breault's application also contains his first physical description. He was 5ft 4in tall, had brown hair and blue eyes, and had no distinguishing marks upon his entry into the service, which would change by his enlistment in the USN as he gained scars or tattoos.[12]

An early question that was raised, and has previously been addressed in the SFLM exhibit, is why Breault elected to enlist in the RNCVR and not the USN. The SFLM exhibit claims this was due to being turned away at the USN recruiting office, so he went to Canada to enlist somewhere they were not as discriminatory in the middle of a war that demanded more from young men than ever before. Breault was likely no stranger to hunger, weighing only 126 pounds at his enlistment in 1920, and this is only after he likely had access to consistent meals, something that could have disqualified him from peacetime service in the USN but would not matter in a wartime force that needed manpower.[13] The pay of the RNCVR at the time of Breault's discharge as an able seaman was comparable to that of his first enlistment in the USN, so pay or glory were not likely primary motivators in choosing either the RNCVR or USN.

Despite this supporting evidence, the SFLM explanation is still evaluated as unlikely. Breault lived in Canada at the time of his enlistment, and it is possible that the RNCVR was his first choice and he understood what he needed to do to go underway as a full sailor and not a boy sailor, restricted to certain vessels that would not see significant time at sea.[14] Furthermore, Canada may have lacked documentation of his true birthdate, as Breault was born in the USA, which would likely have appeared and disqualified him in a USN background check. Breault indicated in his paperwork he had previously been employed as a 'Nickel Plater'. Considering his rudimentary education and large family, he was probably needed as a second income for the household at a young age and took on significant roles raising his younger sisters.[15] Breault likely acted older than his 16 years, as did so many of his peers. When viewed as a potential employment to help support his family while seeking independence in a coming-of-age story, Breault's service meets several requirements. With service in the RNCVR, he could live on his own, earn a paycheck, receive free room and board, learn a seafaring trade and seek adventure greater than industrial or physical labour during a war that would define the young men of his generation.

## PRE-AWARD LIFE AND CAREER (1900–23)

Breault served aboard HMCS *Niobe*, an older, 9,980-ton Diadem-class cruiser built in the UK that was one of the first ships (along with HMCS *Rainbow*) of the budding Royal Canadian Navy. The *Niobe* had required augmentation from a group of the Newfoundland volunteers of the RNCVR to bring the ship to its full complement.[16] It was not as seaworthy as it had once been and primarily served as a mothership for sailors who were assigned to the unceremonious task of serving on board commandeered trawlers, which in turn allowed the reservists to be paid at the same rate as their RN compatriots.[17] The *Niobe* was home for Breault, and it was likely the ship he spent the most time on as it was the only one mentioned on his service record. Breault in all likelihood trained, received assignments, mustered and overall resided on the vessel. If he went out to sea, it was doubtless on other vessels. With this qualification in mind, the *Niobe* is potentially the largest ship Breault would serve on as a primary duty station throughout his seagoing career.[18] His duties both on and outside of the *Niobe* are currently not recorded in available documentation from the SFLM.

Despite Breault's otherwise innocuous lie regarding his age, his first rank as recorded by his service record was 'Boy' on 24 July 1917. If the purpose of the lie was to minimize time as a rated Boy, it was successfully executed, as he was advanced on his alleged 18th birthday, 14 August 1917, to ordinary seaman, moving him from the Boy's Mess to the Crew's Mess.[19] The tradition of having underage seamen in training stationed aboard ships was a longstanding RN tradition. This advancement afforded Breault an increase in pay while he remained in a training status. On 1 October 1917, he completed training and attained the status of an able seaman, the highest rank that he would achieve during his tenure with the RNCVR, and which accorded him a pay of $1.10 (Canadian Dollars) a day.[20] In the service record document, one can make out another rank which Breault held from 14 August to 31 December 1917, which appears to be 'Spec A'.[21] According to David J. Freeman, there was no enlisted 'specialist' rank, only leading seaman and petty officers prior to the rank of chief petty officer, leading it to be believed that 'Spec A' was either an indication Breault was a stoker or his cumulative service for RNCVR record keeping.[22] There is no surviving indication that Breault was a stoker, which would have gained him an extra 10 cents per day, so the latter possibility of cumulative service is considered more likely.

Breault's inclusion as a French-Canadian in the RNCVR is unusual. His ship was likely comprised mostly of sailors of Anglo-Saxon descent, as indicated by quantitative analysis conducted by Mark Richardson, who analysed 1,875 names of service members from 1918–39. Richardson's study indicates 94.5 per cent of RNCVR service members had an Anglo-Saxon origin, and only fifty-six French names were observed.²³ Despite the wide range of source data, of which only 1918's is applicable to Breault's career, Richardson substantiated his statistics with qualitative evidence from several sailors. Richardson's analysis is not alone in observing French-Canadians' lack of representation in Canadian military service during the First World War. In an excellent analysis of labour statistics in the largest company in Canada, the Canadian Pacific Railway Company, Mary MacKinnon observed that Anglophone citizens volunteering for the war influenced the dynamic composition of the workforce, as Francophone citizens volunteered at a much lower rate due to a variety of demographic factors.²⁴ MacKinnon concluded that the aggregates supported the thesis that French-Canadian workers replaced Anglo-Saxon workers who went to war:

> 'In the years just before the war, only about a third of the sampled employees in Québec were French-Canadian. By 1916, about half were. This shift highlights the absence of French-Canadian volunteers ... The increased FrenchCanadian presence within Québec was maintained after the war – in the mid to late 1920s about 45 percent of sampled Québec employees were French-Canadian.'²⁵

As French-Canadians did not seem to have the same social pressures exerted on them as English-speaking Canadians, what motivated Breault to join at all?

The most likely influence that Breault had on his life was that of his father, Joseph, who had previously served as a soldier in the 3rd Connecticut Volunteer Infantry during the Spanish-American War.²⁶ At the onset of war, Joseph had been a corporal, but was promoted to one of the sergeant positions in Putnam's own Company G.²⁷ While Joseph did not see combat service, he was likely transferred via ship at some point, which explains why Fred St Onge misremembered that Joseph had once been a sailor himself.²⁸ Although Joseph had not been a sailor, he probably remembered his time serving in Company G fondly, as so many do from all services and branches. One can almost imagine a young Breault captivated by these stories, perhaps fixating on a particular tale of his father's that occurred when out to sea or waiting along the coast for the Spanish invasion that never came.

For Henry Breault, life on the *Niobe* may not have been perfect, but it could have felt liberating to be a part of the service, particularly in the days he could wander around Halifax with his fellow shipmates. As American visitor B.H. Nye noted, sailors in uniform were wont to travel in pairs and gaggles during his visit in 1916, enjoying their time ashore in good company.²⁹

## PRE-AWARD LIFE AND CAREER (1900–23)

Breault joined the *Niobe* in time to be a likely witness and participant during what became known as the Halifax Explosion on 6 December 1917, and the resulting disaster recovery. The Canadian War Museum offers the following summary on these events:

> 'On 6 December 1917, the *Mont Blanc*, a French vessel loaded with 2.9 kilotons of explosives, collided with the Belgian relief ship, *Imo*, in Halifax harbour. A fire broke out on the *Mont Blanc* which local firefighters tried unsuccessfully to extinguish. When the flames reached the *Mont Blanc*'s volatile cargo, the resulting explosion devastated a large part of the city. The Richmond district in the city's north end and the Dartmouth region across the harbour were all but wiped out. The official death toll was 1,963, with another 9,000 injured and 6,000 left homeless.'[30]

Lambert 'Bert' Griffith, a shipmate of Breault's on the *Niobe*, wrote several letters that allow us to relive the explosion as a member of the crew experienced it. Griffith had joined the RNCVR a few months before Breault and was advanced to able seaman in July 1917.[31] John G. Armstrong reconstructed Griffith's account as best he could while editing his grandfather's letters for publication, but notes:

> 'Bert's actual duties during the summer and fall of 1917 cannot be precisely defined but some information can be gleaned from his letters and his service records. Both he and Walter Webb were employed on the "boom" (either the inner or outer anti-submarine nets) where they might remain for as much as two weeks before being brought back to *Niobe*. Aboard the depot ship they appear to have been utilized more in those general duties peculiar to the Navy, including painting, scraping and that particularly beloved task of "coaling ship". Bert was rated Able Seaman in mid-July and his records show assignments to the *Wilfred C.* and the *Nereid*, armed tugs which served turns as gate vessels on the nets, opening and closing the "gates" for passing ships through in daylight.'[32]

Breault, working at the same rank for much of his career, was in all likelihood employed in a similar capacity. For the hands aboard, the morning of 6 December 1917 consisted of an 0620 hours muster, cleaning and then breakfast of 'bacon and fried tomatoes, bread, butter, and jam, and tea that you could stand a knife up in', which they 'scoffed down' quickly to have time to smoke before divisional muster.³³

Griffith recounted that the explosion happened almost immediately after breakfast was concluded at 0730 hours. Armstrong notes the discrepancy between the account and the actual time of the collision, which occurred at 0854 hours, with the *Mont Blanc* erupting at 0904 hours. Armstrong attributes the discrepancy to disorientation caused by stress, fatigue or any other number of potential issues that come with recollection after a traumatic event.³⁴ Griffith recalled being among sailors who were topside to catch a glimpse of the ship on fire 500 yards away when it exploded:

> 'All at once there was a most hideous noise & I saw the whole boat vanish, a moment after I saw something coming [but I] can't describe it. I was hurled on the deck & there was an awful noise going on. I got to my feet & ran with a whole lot of fellows. My one fixed idea was to get below. We all tried to get down the one ladder without any success. I had presence of mind enough to dig my head in between all kinds of legs & c. After that I ran along the deck & heard all kinds of things falling. It was shrapnel & bits of the side of the ship. I did not know this at the time.'³⁵

The explosion emanating from the *Mont Blanc* generated a large swell which then struck the *Niobe*. In the aftermath, the *Niobe* was damaged but still afloat, with a crew that was badly shaken. Gunner William O'Reilly calmed the enlisted men and put them to work operating the ship's cutter in rescue efforts, retrieving the wounded, reburying the port anchor, moving ammunition from the rapidly burning dock and then fighting the fire that threatened the dock.³⁶ Griffith recalled the long hours, while Armstrong noted that naval manpower helped civil authorities when it could be spared.³⁷ Fred St Onge stated that Breault was employed searching for survivors, though St Onge had considerable temporal distance between the conversation and the interview.³⁸ Breault was likely employed in many of these tasks, working on a shattered ship alongside the shattered city.

Another sailor who served aboard the *Acadia*, Frank Baker, recorded the day's events in his diary and substantiates Griffith's experience:

> 'There are no ships in for examination today, so we again proceed to cleaning stations and had just drawn soap and powder and the necessary utensils for cleaning paint work when the most awful

explosion I ever heard or want to hear again occurred. The first thud shook the ship from stem to stern and the second one seemed to spin us all around, landing some under the gun carriage and others flying in all directions all over the deck. Our first impression was that we were being attacked by submarines, and we all rushed for the upper deck, where we saw a veritable mountain of smoke of a yellowish hue and huge pieces of iron were flying all around us. A shower of shrapnel passed over the Forecastle, shattering the glass in the engine room and chart room to smithereens, which came crashing down into the alleyways. It was the greatest miracle in the world that we were not all killed. God only knows how we escaped. The fires all burst out on to the floor of the stokehold and it was a marvel that the stokers were not burned to death, but all of them escaped injury as did all the other of the ships company. A tug was alongside us at the time and part of her side was torn completely out and three of the crew were injured, one of them getting a piece of flesh weighing nearly 2 pounds torn off his leg. A hail of shrapnel descended about 20 yards from the ship, this came with such force that had it struck us we should certainly have all been lost, it was so terrific. This was the last of the explosion, the whole of which had taken place inside of five minutes. We were fully impressed [at] the time that we were being attacked by submarines and we were expecting our turn to come at any moment. Then came a lull of a few minutes and when the smoke had cleared sufficiently, we saw clearly what had happened.'[39]

Unfortunately, the disaster happened in December, just before a bitter blizzard, making the efforts to help the city even more difficult.[40]

Did Henry Breault's experience on the *Niobe* during the Halifax Explosion allow him to keep calm under pressure while the *O-5* was sinking six years later? Did he see O'Reilly's coordination of rescue efforts as something worthy of emulation? Six sailors from the *Niobe* perished during the explosion, all aboard a steam pinnace that went out to scuttle the *Mont Blanc* in a failed attempt to prevent closure of the harbour.[41] Was Breault friends with any of these sailors? Did Breault suffer from any lingering ailments directly correlated to the aftermath of the disaster? Griffith would go into a steady decline, admitting he was affected by the disaster and a sickness that swept through the crew of the *Niobe* after the explosion.[42] Would Breault have been sick from this same illness, and was it part of the greater spread of influenza cases that would affect the world from 1918 onwards?

There are no surviving documents indicating what acts Breault performed in the *Niobe*, other than Fred St Onge's remembrance seventy years later, but it is likely his experiences were similar to those of Griffith and Baker. Breault would not remain in the RNCVR, being discharged as part of the normal demobilization that occurred post-war on 31 December 1918.[43] From all known accounts, he performed satisfactorily in his duties.[44] A major unresolved question is that of Breault's agency: did he have the option of staying in if he chose? The answer in this case is likely 'no', as Breault indicates on his final discharge form that he would like to remain in the RNCVR after discharge.[45] The treasuries of the victor and the vanquished were in similar states upon the end of the Great War, and the RNCVR would not have the luxury of a wartime budget. Demobilizing the reserves who were no longer needed would be among the first cuts.

## Civilian Life and a Return to Putnam

Six days after Christmas, on 31 December 1918, Henry Breault was discharged from the RNCVR after almost a year-and-a-half of service. The reason given was simply 'Demobilized'. Breault reported that the address he intended to return to was not his father's residence, but 22 Mill Street in Putnam, CT, the home of his relatives – the St Onge family.[46] His time in Putnam provides us with the only known personal account about Breault, which came from his cousin, Fred St Onge. Fred's account has some inconsistencies, but he recalled that Breault was 'an average fellow, good natured, very sociable and a person with an open mind'.[47] Apparently, Breault was fond of smoking 'Turkish Drophies' (believed to be a misprint for Turkish Trophies) and English Oval cigarettes, and enjoyed ocean air, claiming that he 'never felt well unless he was on the water'.[48]

Envisioning the scene of a returning war hero, likely still clad in his RNCVR uniform, revisiting his family and regaling them with tales of his time in the service is not difficult to imagine. The family, being of Canadian descent, would have been very interested in the events of the Halifax Explosion and the subsequent reconstruction efforts. His relatives, including Fred St Onge, would have listened to Breault speak while he smoked an Oval or Trophy cigarette, sharing a sanitized version to spare his relatives the worst while simultaneously giving them a taste of what he had experienced. As all sailors wish to portray their livelihood as masculine, worldly and eminently different from that which land dwellers could understand, Breault would then wax poetic lines to the best of his ability, stating confidently he belonged on the water to the point he felt unwell if off it for too long.

## PRE-AWARD LIFE AND CAREER (1900–23)

It is the kind of rubbish that would be laughed at if spoken amongst sailors, yet the rules were different when speaking to family and friends who simply could not understand the world they were a part of. Scenes of the same ilk are common in movies that show enlisted sailors. While not of the same period and context, Jack Nicholson's character, Billy 'Badass' Buddusky, has a scene in the movie *The Last Detail* in which he appeals to the same sort of masculinity to pick up a female companion at a party:

> 'There ain't nothing better in the world than being on the sea – even in the navy – being on the bridge – talking to ships – across miles and miles of liquid real estate ... I tell you when you're on deep water and doing a man's job on the bridge or when it's rough weather and you lash yourself to the rack [bed] and get rocked to sleep like a baby and you wake up and it's calm and for miles and miles the water's like fucking glass and there's porpoises off the bow, well then you're talking about deep water and there's nothin' like it.'[49]

The film director makes it clear in the reception of the woman to whom he is speaking that Buddusky's attempt is part of a tired routine that is literally boring his target to sleep. Buddusky, not catching the social cues, privately tells Randy Quaid's character, Larry Meadows, 'kid ... I'm handing this girl such a line of shit it is unbelievable ... She loves it, she loves it.'[50] Breault may not have believed what he was saying, but simultaneously it was an almost stereotypical and expected monologue from a man returning from sea service. These interactions recalled by Fred St Onge must be given their proper context: Breault was portraying himself as the salty sailor finally returning home. And St Onge's fond remembrance indicates Breault's bearing had a positive, endearing impact, unlike Buddusky's routine.

St Onge further remembers that Breault left Putnam at some point and relocated to Bristol, CT, to work with the New Departure company making coaster brakes for bicycles.[51] At first, the break from naval discipline was likely welcome, regardless of whether the decision to leave was his or not. While staying with the St Onges, Breault was probably have been able to wake up as he wished, having a cup of tea or coffee in the morning at his leisure. The honeymoon period must have felt like a relief, but simultaneously induced a sense of insecurity or anxiety. The reality of life would set in shortly: he had to find a job, just as many of the demobilized men and women in the post-Great War era had to.[52] This may have been a major reason why Breault, and eventually his immediate family, would move back to the USA from Canada, seeking employment as the war industry that had initially attracted them slowed down.[53]

When Breault found a position, he appears to have been unsatisfied with the work. The only other location in this inter-service period where we know Breault spent time is Grand Isle, Vermont, where he worked at L.R.B. Hale's farm, though his enlistment record states he was an 'Electric Plater', indicating he did travel to new locations and employments seeking suitable work.[54] From St Onge's conversation, enlistment in the USN and request for British medals years later, it is clear that his time in the RNCVR impacted Breault tremendously, in a largely positive manner.

There are many questions that cannot be addressed with the current source material. For instance, why did Breault visit Putnam instead of going home? The lack of contact and unwillingness to see his immediate family suggest that Breault was estranged from them. Their home in Canada could have been a stop for him in his search, but there are no known records of such a visit. On his initial enlistment paperwork, Breault did not utilize a family address, opting to put his 'friend' in Grand Isle, L.R.B. Hale, as his next of kin.[55] Did Breault overstay his welcome in Putnam? Did the family make the decision, or was it mutual? And did Breault elect to sever ties voluntarily during his time in the RNCVR? Any number of possibilities could explain this estrangement, but there is no clarity beyond suggesting that it existed.

As to why Breault elected to enlist in the USN, an educated guess is that he craved a return to the sense of purpose and identity he once had, as so many veterans do today. From experience, I can confirm that transitioning from sailor to civilian is difficult in the present day, and many of the services now provided by the government to ease the transition were not then available. Furthermore, the mass of demobilized men made the advantages of prior service seen today much less endearing, as so many returning home made it less of a competitive advantage. In a disillusioning realization, Breault could only look forward to a future of manual labour, divorced from any feelings of purpose that he had experienced in naval service. Meaghan C. Mobbs and George A. Bonanno, who primarily researched the effects on soldiers in the present-day transitioning from military to civilian, have commented:

> 'During this [transition] time they may struggle with any number of interrelated concerns, including unresolved or prolonged grief and bereavement over fallen comrades, loss of their previous military identity, nostalgia for the order and purpose that characterized their service experiences, a sense of moral injury, confusion about military-civilian differences, and changing masculine roles.'[56]

## PRE-AWARD LIFE AND CAREER (1900–23)

Breault's decision to enlist in the USN could have been motivated initially by a desire to return to the RNCVR. He may have heard rumours as early as mid-1919 that the service was struggling to man its small fleet.[57] This could explain why he was in Vermont; perhaps he was making his way north to re-enlist in Canada's service when he was convinced to enlist in the USN instead, attracted by more opportunities, better advancement, similar pay and the need for a job.

Breault enlisted with the USN in Manchester, New Hampshire, on 14 July 1920, for an initial two-year tenure. Now 19 years old, he had no need to lie about his age and elected to give his real birth date. His enlistment was credited to Vermont, not Connecticut, which would have future implications in recording his Medal of Honor. His physical appearance did not change much between his service, though of interest was his ruddy complexion (instead of the previous dark) and the addition of numerous scars. On his right breast, he had a small half-inch puncture mark, a half-inch scar on the base of his left-hand little finger, a large scar on his back that measured three-quarters of an inch by a quarter of an inch, a large mark on his right buttock and a smaller scar on his right-hand third finger. Did these scars come from the Halifax Explosion, regular naval service or a long period of manual labour? A likely combination of each can be safely assumed, but one can imagine the rain of shrapnel causing the large scar on his back as Breault ducked for cover and attempted to go below decks on the *Niobe*. Breault now weighed 126 pounds and still only stood at 5ft 4½in.[58]

Breault was shipped from Manchester to Newport, Rhode Island, for basic training at Recruit Training Command (RTC) Newport.[59] RTC still exists today, though in Great Lakes, Illinois. The training was designed to rapidly acclimatize, indoctrinate and socialize prospective sailors. Further, it sought to teach sailors essential skills, such as boat drills, rank structures, swimming, deck seamanship known as Marlinspike and other general skills needed in the fleet, as recorded in several pictures taken by Bain News Service.[60] For an experienced sailor, one who was already accustomed to naval discipline and routine, Breault would not have struggled through any aspect other than learning the nuances of becoming an American sailor, such as learning new ranks and traditions. It was likely slow and tedious, though the guarantee of three meals a day could have been a welcome relief if Breault had been struggling to obtain sufficient food during his inter-service life.

Breault did not have a rating guarantee in his contract, but he stayed in Newport after his graduation from RTC on 27 October 1920, likely for Torpedoman 'A' School training at Newport Naval Torpedo Station.[61] The duration of the school appeared to be just over seven months of instruction, meaning Breault was in training for nearly a full year, a much different style of training than he had experienced in the more hands-on RNCVR in the boy's mess. The change in training was due to the progressively technical fleet that required an increasingly specialized crew, a need that perseveres in the present day. The rating education had been reformed by Secretary of the Navy Josephus Daniels, who claimed he sought to make the USN 'a great university', recognizing the value of educated and well-trained men to the Navy and the civilian sector.[62] Further aiding this was the perception of enlisted men, who saw the Navy as a steppingstone into another career, a mentality that continues to this day.[63]

After Breault graduated from Torpedo School, he advanced from Seaman Second Class to Torpedoman (TM) Third Class on 1 July 1921, about a month after his transfer to USS *Eagle* and USS *O-5*.[64] The *Eagle* was probably just a receiving ship on his way to an assignment, but the SFLM has a small card indicating this was Breault's short acclimation in Naval Submarine School, which is likely how they filled his time from 5–8 June 1921.[65] The USN Submarine Force was already an all-volunteer force, though there is no evidence in Breault's OMPF of when or why he made the decision to volunteer. As a TM, Breault potentially could have had a limited choice of platforms on which he could serve, or it could have been understood that volunteering for submarines was necessary to become a TM.

## Submarine Service

Unusually, the Navy press memorandum in the aftermath of the *O-5–Abangarez* collision states that Breault was rated as a QM3, skipping Seaman First Class, and then rated a TM3 on 1 July 1923.[66] While rating transfers can and do happen, there is no other record that exists indicating Breault was ever a rated QM. It is assessed to have been *errata*, a typo for GM3, as indicated in his service record on the same date in the memorandum.[67] Considering the timing of TM becoming a formal rate, Breault was likely among the first TMs in the USN, but was initially rated as a GM who specialized in torpedoes. Further, his advancement in the USN was impressive when compared to the RNCVR. In wartime, when promotion is notoriously rapid, Breault never advanced past Able Seaman during his tenure in the RNCVR. Yet in peacetime, only having spent a year in the Navy – most of it in training – Breault was now a rated TM3, with significantly more pay! With another year under his belt, Breault would voluntarily extend his initial enlistment by two more years on 13 July 1922, with the confidence that his decision to enlist in the USN was the correct one.[68]

Breault reported aboard USS *O-5* on 10 June 1921. The *O-5* was a submarine of the O class, designed as an improvement over the previous class and built under

## PRE-AWARD LIFE AND CAREER (1900–23)

Electric Boat and Lake Torpedo Boat designs in five different shipyards. The *O-5* was laid down by Electric Boat on 8 December 1916, and built throughout 1917 by Fore River Shipbuilding Company in Quincy, Massachusetts, until launched on 11 November 1917. The boat was commissioned on 8 June 1918, with Lieutenant G.A. Trever in command. The *O-5* had just narrowly missed service in the Great War, being part of a fleet headed for service in the Atlantic when the Armistice was signed.[69] Sadly, the *O-5* still lost two members of its crew on October 14 1918 (Breault's 18th birthday coincidentally), Lieutenant George A. Trevor and Ensign W.J. Sharkey, who were killed in a battery explosion, while an electrician named Still (rank unknown) was also injured.[70] It is unknown if Breault was aware of the tragedy, but it is considered likely and may have even created a negative stigma associated with the *O-5*.

Even during peacetime, the *O-5* was underway frequently during Breault's tenure. Shortly after reporting, on 7 August 1921, *The Pittsburgh Press* reported on the boat's participation in a naval exercise conducted as a part of the 8th Submarine Flotilla.[71] During this time, Breault lived in Groton, Connecticut, either aboard ship or in the barracks on New London Submarine Base. A picture of the *O-5* shows that on 16 August 1921 it had transferred to the Boston Navy Yard in Charlestown, MA, likely after the crew experienced liberty in Boston following the exercise.[72] The boat likely returned to New London for much of 1922, but the 8th Submarine Division was transferred to Coco Solo Submarine Base in the Panama Canal Zone by 23 January 1923.[73] The submarines seemed to travel in groups with a mothership, referred to as a submarine tender. Breault presumably knew the men aboard the other submariners in his division, and the accompanying tender, as they travelled together.

Breault would have immediately set out to learn the systems of the submarine. The crew of the submarine had no more than thirty men at any given time, with space at a premium and every hand needed to operate at peak efficiency. MM3 Robert E. Fretz's week-one qualification notebook indicates how comprehensive the training was, including a full diagram of the boat traced and labelled by Fretz.[74] The Torpedo Room where Breault would spend much of his time was a maze of valves surrounding four tubes. O-class submarines were not designed to operate at sea for long periods, so there were no showers and only limited habitability measures were offered. Breault's underway periods were brief, uncomfortable and unhygienic, the same as any submariner who served in the numerous tropical regions would have experienced, for example the crew of the *S-39* being forced to suffer such conditions during the Second World War while serving on the Asiatic Theatre.[75]

The *O-5* was an improvement compared to the previous classes, but was designed for short coastal patrols. It lacked features that even the S-class vessels would have, boats notorious for their spartan living conditions, that made crew habitability slightly more tolerable. Later in his career, serving aboard the *O-5* probably allowed Breault a certain measure of pride that he served on a harder, older-class submarine like the S-class, when compared to the fleet boats of the Second World War. Though the 'fish' or 'dolphin' insignia to indicate a submarine sailor was an expert had not yet become a formal award for either officers or enlisted sailors, Breault was 'qualified' on 27 February 1922, but would not wear the warfare device until after his Medal of Honor award ceremony, when it was added into the uniform regulation.[76]

The *O-5* frequented New London and the Coco Solo submarine base, but it also visited New York, Boston, the Virgin Islands and Guantanamo Bay.[77] The *O-5* was likely part of the Caribbean exercises that included the 8th Submarine Division, but the only indication of a port call in Breault's OMPF is his small arms qualification record which specifies that Breault was on the Guantanamo Bay Range on 15 February 1922.[78] The conditions must have been tolerable enough, or the advantages of service so greatly outweighed other opportunities, that Breault would extend his enlistment for two more years.[79] A year later, Breault would advance to TM2 on 18 June 1923, after taking the rating exam a second time.[80] Having spent time in Newport, New London, New York, Boston and the Panama Canal, and port calls in the Caribbean such as Guantanamo Bay, he presumably got the chance to become more worldly and seek adventure. Breault's greatest feat was yet to come, but he must have felt increasingly accomplished and confident. He became one of the senior enlisted sailors in this timeframe, on whom many would have depended in numerous situations.

Unfortunately, this pre-award period of Breault's life is the least documented. New sources will be required to further the story, particularly those of a personal nature, to increase our understanding of his early life. Indirectly, clues as to how Breault remembered his early career are present in Benjamin L. Fairchild's letter requesting Breault's re-enlistment.[81] While many of the dates are inaccurate, such as his time in the RNCVR and the date of the *O-5*'s time in the Virgin Islands, Fairchild's letter itself is probably a summary of one Breault wrote himself. However, unlike many sailors, while Breault likely told these stories that were common, the first question his family would have asked was about his Medal of Honor and how he received it.

# Chapter 4

# Heroism and Recognition (1923–24)

The trajectory of Henry Breault's career would change, largely for the better, in the aftermath of the sinking of the *O-5* and his subsequent rescue. If it was possible for any man to look back at a single turning point in his life, a more obvious choice cannot be found for Breault than the action that saw him awarded the Medal of Honor. The dominant narrative belongs to Julius Grigore, which has been repeated in numerous volumes and websites and currently stands as the major contributor to Breault's story. While this provides an excellent start, the lack of primary sources surveyed by Grigore and the emphasis on the rescue make Breault-related details scarce in the articles. This chapter will be devoted to understanding Breault's actions, the construction process of the actors within the story and the procedure through which the Medal of Honor was approved.

## Henry Breault

Surprisingly, there is little evidence to suggest Breault had agency within the telling of his own story. No official statements on the subject were recorded in his OMPF, and only one letter was identified as being from him. The only reason this letter is available today is its publication within the *New York Times*:

> 'Just a line to let you know that I am still alive. You have no doubt read about the sinking of the submarine. We were down there for hours and had no food. There was water in the lead tanks, but we did not dare to use it because it had been there for months and we were afraid of lead poisoning. I sure was a sick boy but am well now. I have been out helping to raise the submarine. She is all right except the central control room where she was struck. The craft will soon be in condition again. But some of the crew will never go down in a submarine again. Fortunately it did not bother me at all.'[1]

Should the letter be treated as authentic? Another newspaper suggests it may have been an embellishment. According to *The Daily Argus*, the White Plains local newspaper, the Breault family reported they received a 'message' (likely a telegram response) from Breault that stated simply: 'I am safe and well.'[2] Why would the local newspaper have less information than a nationally syndicated one, particularly from the town the recipients resided within? The *Argus* article was written at least two weeks before the article containing the *New York Times* letter, so it could have been a telegram informing the Breault family that he was alive and well, with the follow-up information in a more detailed letter.

There is little other surviving evidence to suggest Breault spoke much of the events surrounding the sinking or made any official statements, meaning there are no potential sources to cross-reference. One of the few snippets comes from the *United Press Association*, which asked why he stayed on board instead of jumping overboard for safety.[3] According to the *UPA* reporter, Breault stated before losing consciousness: 'I didn't know whether there was anybody inside or not, and if there was, I wanted to stay and help, if I could.'[4] This statement, though seemingly characteristic of the brand of selfless heroism Breault espoused in his actions, is uncorroborated by any other account. Even if he did say this, Breault was surrounded by people asking numerous questions; this report should thus not be considered inviolable as the statement was conveyed second-hand and reported by a newspaper while he was dazed, dehydrated and afflicted with caisson disease.[5] Again, the possibility that the quote was an embellishment to further sell a story of bravery and heroism should be considered. If this statement was uttered by Breault, however, it indicates a selfless individual. Considering Brown's statement, it can be considered an authentic sentiment, if not a completely faithful rendering of diction. Considering Breault's potential experience in the Halifax Explosion, he understood decisive action was required and acted on that impulse. Breault's action may even have been inspired by the heroes of the Halifax Explosion.

While I ultimately made the decision to work under the assumption that these were authentic letters, statements or at least sentiments that Breault would have agreed with, this may be a difficult sell, considering errors seen in other newspapers. Press mistakes included misreporting Breault's age (19 instead of 23), misspelling his name (Berault as opposed to Breault) or even accusing him of being three days late to his own award ceremony, so the story suffered from no shortage of error or embellishment.[6] In a contemporary analysis, Jeanette M. Collins included five of the *O-5* articles from various newspapers in her thesis 'Style in the New Story'.[7] Submitted to the University of Wisconsin in 1924, Collins accused many of the newspapers of sloppy editing.[8] Collins' criticism serves as evidence that newspapers sought to deliver the story quickly, indicating an interest in submarines, the disaster and the rescue of the entombed sailors, and that every paper wanted to be the first to report on or have the most interesting piece of the story.

Without the original letter, it is impossible to know with absolute certainty that the *New York Times* letter was unabridged or written by Breault. The letter was allegedly provided by his mother to the newspaper, which raises further questions of authenticity.[9] Breault's biological mother died in 1913, so it is unlikely the letter was addressed to her. His father, Joseph J. Breault, married Mary Breault, so it is possible this letter was addressed to his stepmother and indicates a healthy relationship between the two, but this presents a potential issue.[10] There are a few indications to suggest Breault was estranged from his immediate family prior to enlisting. On Breault's initial enlistment paperwork, he named his 'friend', L.R.B. Hale from Grand Isle, as his next of kin, and as such the Bureau of Navigation sent most status reports to her, rather than to the Breault family.[11] Hale's inclusion is unusual, as most people tended to name a close family member as next of kin, and it would be the only time in his enlistment paperwork that a member of his family was not thus named.[12] In the immediate aftermath of the accident, many wrote to the Bureau of Navigation asking if Breault could have been their lost loved one, one of these by his father, identified as 'J.J. Brault', who sent a telegram requesting: 'Please wire whether Henry Breault on Submarine O 5 reported sunk canal zone is safe and if injured what extent.'[13] This could be used as evidence to support the authenticity of the *New York Times* letter, as a month-long turnaround time would not be unusual, nor would it be surprising if Breault wanted to reconnect with his family after a near-death experience. *The New York Times* letter also supports the estrangement thesis by suggesting he had little or no prior correspondence with his family, whilst simultaneously explaining why Breault would have written the letter.

Another point in favour of the authenticity of the letter is the identification of the location of the most damaged area from the collision being the central control room. From two pictures in the collection of Ric Hedman, the main damage does correspond to this location.[14] Another point is Breault's belief the *O-5* would return to service. It wouldn't be until 1924 that the USN would decide to sell the *O-5* for scrap.[15] It was difficult, though certainly not impossible, to return a ship to service after it was recovered from a DISSUB situation, but the investment would be considerable in an era when the sub was no longer needed and naval budgets were tight. The published letter thus appears to be authentic, and the assumption moving forward will be that Breault indeed wrote the letter, and it was unabridged by Breault's family and the *New York Times*. While this is a leap of faith, it is one that is merited until proven otherwise by new information.

I was hoping that an official statement by Breault could be found within his OMPF, but there was nothing from him. It does contain several documents suggesting the USN was aware of the newspapers' ability to influence public opinion and sought to make timely news bulletins via Navy press releases.[16] As a large organization, the USN was often reactive, only influencing the news proactively during the award ceremony. Because of this, any official statement by Breault was likely retained for the command and the squadron; if it has survived, it could be fruitful to discover whether Breault gave a much more detailed observation of the situation, though that document currently remains elusive.

Despite this interest, or perhaps even because of this interest, there is little to suggest that Breault had a major role in promoting his story, either before or after his award. So how was Breault's story conveyed, and how did it lead him to becoming a Medal of Honor recipient?

## Lawrence Brown

The primary account of the rescue did not belong to Breault, but the other sailor trapped underneath the waves whom he rescued: Chief Electrician's Mate Lawrence Brown. Brown did not suffer from caisson disease, so he stayed to recount the story to the *United Press Association*, whose story was then reprinted by other newspapers.[17] Grigore summarizes this well, but it was the primary reporter for the *United Press Association*, Paul Seymour, who conveyed Brown's story.[18] Brown states that he was resting before his watch when he felt the crash from the *Abangarez*, but despite knowing it was a serious incident, he stayed in his rack until Breault woke him up: 'We both went into the torpedo room, closing the door behind us. The boat sank in thirty seconds, settling in forty feet of water at an angle of 70 degrees to starboard.'[19] It is surprising that Brown did not hear any communications, but the only known order was reported by Captain Card of the *Abangarez* just prior to the collision Card heard an order given verbally topside or from the bridge.[20] Since Brown was sound asleep, it is possible he may not have heard the verbal order to abandon ship.

Finding themselves trapped in a compartment with 12in of water, holding fast to a ladder with only a flashlight for vision, Brown recalled that 'the first hour was the hardest'.[21] Forty-five minutes after the crash, the *O-5*'s batteries caught fire, heating the compartment.[22] With no food or drinking water, the pair remained optimistic they could survive forty-eight hours and that a crane would be able to lift them before that time limit expired.[23] After three hours, it became clear once they heard outside activity that the Panama Canal community was working to rescue them. The pair then split up, Breault moving the furthest aft he could go while Brown went forward, using a hammer or blunt object to bang at the hull, alerting their rescuers that they were still alive. Brown recalled: 'Breault played with the hammer to indicate we were in good shape.'[24]

The first attempt with the hoist was estimated to have occurred after twelve hours. While the attempt failed, it did level the boat from the awkward angle at which it had settled, allowing for easier movement and comfort. As they rose on the fourth and final attempt, Brown recalled that the last twenty minutes were 'terrible', Breault estimating that the pressure was between 25 and 50lb.[25] The doctors treating him disputed these numbers, deciding they were unlikely, but agreed those trapped in the compartment were subject to high pressure.[26] The ship finally broke the surface, and the workers rapidly opened a hatch to let the men escape. Brown continued: 'Then we heard the water splashing over the top, and our comrades walking on the deck, and we knew we were up. Breault opened the hatch and the light was so bright I could not find my way up.'[27]

Brown 'seemed no worse for wear', according to a reporter, and was in a lucid-enough state to retell the story.[28] Brown's account became the primary account by chance, because he was the only one of the duo who was unafflicted and conscious enough to answer questions. Brown's decision to focus the spotlight on Breault is indicative of the quality of his leadership, being unsparing in praise when merited. Brown fully credits his rescue to Breault and diver Sheppard Shreaves, offering only his viewpoint and eschewing any self-aggrandizement; he should serve as an inspiration for all chiefs. It is likely that among the audience listening was the *O-5*'s commanding officer, Lieutenant Harrison Avery.

## Lieutenant Harrison Avery

It was LT Avery who began the award process, initially recommending Breault for a Navy Cross. After dealing with the aftermath of the collision and likely conducting an investigation, Avery submitted his recommendation on 19 November 1923, citing Article 1709 of the 1920 *Navy Regulation Book* as a reference.[29] Avery argued that Breault's complete disregard of his own safety displayed his devotion to duty, which he believed to be in accordance with the 'best traditions of the Navy'.[30] Avery's recommendation contains much of the original language used to describe Breault's actions and should be considered the closest to the true retelling of events. Avery was a first-hand witness to the rescue events, likely interviewed Brown and Breault in the immediate aftermath and must also have had good knowledge of the trustworthiness of the pair under his command. The recommendation reads:

1. In view of the extraordinary heroism displayed by Breault, H., TM2c, when the O-5 was sunk in collision with the S.S. ABANGAREZ, it is earnestly recommended that the above named man be awarded the Navy Cross.
2. The following is a history of the extraordinary heroism displayed by Breault:

    At 6:24 on the morning of October 28, the O-5 collided with the S.S. ABANGAREZ, and sank in less than one minute. Breault at the time of the collision was in the torpedo room. As soon as the collision occurred he went up the torpedo room hatch and looked out on deck. Upon his arrival at the top of the hatch he saw the boat was sinking very fast and instead of jumping overboard as a number of the crew had already done, thereby trying to save his own life, he went back to the torpedo room, closed the torpedo room hatch on himself, and then assisted Brown, another member of the crew who had been trapped in the boat, to close the water-tight door between the forward battery compartment and the torpedo room. By the time this door was closed the boat had sunk in forty feet of water with every compartment flooded except the torpedo room. Breault and Brown remained trapped in this compartment until they were rescued thirty-one hours later by the salvage party. During this time their efforts were concentrated on stopping leaks between the forward battery and the torpedo room.
3. The conduct displayed by Breault by casting all personal safety aside when he saw that the O-5 was sinking fast and going below to close the torpedo room hatch and even closing same while water was coming into the compartment showed that his devotion to duty was of the highest order. The Commanding Officer therefore earnestly recommends that he be awarded a Navy Cross in recognition of this action, so in keeping with the best traditions of the Navy.

H. Avery (Signed)[31]

Avery's award recommendation probably occurred after an investigation was conducted to ensure that an accurate retelling of events was provided. Avery would have known the men under his command well enough that he believed their story, so any doubts as to the reason Brown stayed in his bed were likely chalked up to miscommunication and him not hearing the verbal order. If Avery had any doubt, who was a witness other than Breault and Brown? If he was wise

# HEROISM AND RECOGNITION (1923–24)

enough, he may have even recognized the utility of the story to shift focus onto the positive aspects of rescue. If that was the motivation, I believe it was at best a secondary one, as Avery appeared genuinely impressed with Breault's conduct and desired to see him awarded for his actions.

Why did Avery select the Navy Cross and not the Medal of Honor? Avery may not have been authorized to recommend the higher award, while he was the commanding officer, he was still a relatively junior officer. Regardless of the reason, the Navy Cross is still an incredibly important medal, and Breault would have been excited to hear he was recommended for such an award. Avery's recommendation report built on Brown's account of events, meaning the story of the *O-5* was no longer one restricted to the Panama Canal community or submariner circles, but was now in the hands of high-ranking officers as they gave their concurrences or further recommendations.

## Rear Admiral (RADM) Montgomery M. Taylor

Avery forwarded his recommendation to the Commander of the 8th Submarine Division, Lieutenant Commander Robert H. English. English reviewed it and passed it on to the Commander of the Submarine Force, Captain Amon Bronson. They both concurred with Avery's assessment on 23 November 1923, and forwarded their recommendations to the Control Force Commander, RADM Montgomery M. Taylor. These officers, in agreeing with the initial assessment, showed faith in Avery's ability to commend the men in his command appropriately, something the young officer likely needed as affirmation in the aftermath of the collision. The officers were likely already aware of Breault and Brown's rescue from official reports. They were stationed on the flagship in the area and would have received reports the entire time, making their own judgements. They did not choose to dissent, giving their recommendations to continue the award through the chain of command, which allowed Taylor to receive the award recommendation.[32]

Taylor agreed with the sentiment, but felt the Navy Cross was insufficient. As the final person in the chain before reaching the Secretary of the Navy, he was the last opportunity on the military side to change the award. Taylor's recommendation reads:

1. Forwarded.
2. The Commander Control Force is of the opinion that the unusual heroic conduct of Breault and his devotion to duty, particularly in that he almost surely saved Brown's life at the risk of his own and in that his devotion

to duty saved a [considerable] loss of Government property, deserves recognition. Accordingly, it is requested that Breault be recommended for the Congressional Medal of Honor.

M.M. Taylor (signed)[33]

While Taylor was not the originator, his recommendation to award the Medal of Honor superseded all other recommendations and changed the nature of the award. If Breault had received the Navy Cross, he would surely not be remembered with the same level of vigour he is today, as that award does not command the same level of attention as the Medal of Honor. While seldom done, overriding subordinate officers is judiciously employed, though it is unlikely Avery would object to a higher award for Breault. The impression Breault's story made on Taylor is evident, as he was willing to upgrade the award and would also be in attendance at the small ceremony on 8 March 1924.[34] The Secretary of the Navy concurred with the assessment that awarding a Medal of Honor was merited and in accordance with drafted General Order No. 125.[35] Breault's award was now a reality, one that only needed to be fleshed out in ceremony, in accordance with the regulations, which required that the award 'shall always be made with formal and impressive ceremony'.[36] Four pictures survive of the 8 March 1924 event, taken by an unknown photographer.[37] Taylor smiled almost as widely as Breault in the pictures, understanding the bravery of the man before him.

## Breault's Medal of Honor in Newspapers

The first indication that Breault would receive a Medal of Honor was in the *Baltimore Sun* on 20 February 1924.[38] The Navy Board announced his award but gave no date; they likely did not know when he would show up as they organized transportation. A surprising detail appeared in some of the newspapers, that Breault was allegedly late to his own award ceremony. Several newspapers reported that the award ceremony was scheduled for 1215 hours on 5 March, with naval officers and the US President waiting. Memphis-based *The Commercial Appeal* reported:

> 'A sailor of the United States navy broke an important engagement with President Coolidge today. Henry Breault, a torpedo man, was to have appeared at the White House at 12:15pm, after a long voyage from Coco Solo, Panama Canal Zone, to receive from the hands of the chief executive a medal of honor for bravery. High naval officers, movie men and others were on hand with their presence

## HEROISM AND RECOGNITION (1923–24)

and extensive [preparations] for the occasion. Henry did not show up. The [reason] assigned at the Navy Department was that he had missed his ship at Norfolk. He is due to explain when he arrives.'[39]

Several newspapers offered an alternative reason, the *Brooklyn Daily Eagle* suggesting the delay was due to Breault's need for a new uniform, which makes sense in the aftermath of the loss of the *O-5*, for which Breault filed a property claim, indicating he may have lost many of his uniform items.[40] The only thing close to a reason or excuse given by Breault himself was in an interview with a reporter from the *New York Evening Post* on 15 March 1924. According to the reporter, Breault gave the justification that 'he could see no reason to hurry'.[41]

In the era before rapid transit via air travel, ship or rail were the primary methods used. Movement by ship was reliable, but it was not perfectly punctual. While the newspapers would jump on the story of a simple seaman snubbing a presidential appointment, the most likely explanation is that Breault's ship was late through no fault of his own, as indicated by his lack of punishment. The newspapers thus simply took the opportunity to spin a yarn that would have made a sailor blush. It's certainly humorous to imagine the conversation between Breault and his chain of command, with a chief telling Breault to have an SAT uniform or 'don't bother showing up'. No mention of his tardiness can be found in his OMPF, indicating Breault was not punished for any infraction of decorum and that there was a valid reason for his late appearance. Still, it seems Breault thus shares another first, being the only Medal of Honor recipient to be late to his own ceremony. Even if Breault was not at fault for his tardiness, for a service that revelled in displaying an independent streak and a tendency to being non-regulation in the period in question, Breault's lateness likely added to his legend in his lifetime, rather than detracting from it.

When the award ceremony did occur a couple of days later on Saturday, 8 March, a sharply dressed Breault met the naval party organized to recognize him on the lawn of the White House. Four photos of the event are available in the Library of Congress. Several of the people in the audience were identified in contemporary newspapers. President Calvin Coolidge himself presented the award and granted effusive praise, likely proud of a Medal of Honor to his home state of Vermont.[42] Secretary of the Navy Edwin Denby was also present, in all likelihood acting as master of ceremonies during the last award ceremony before his resignation due to his role in the Teapot Dome bribery scandal.[43] We also know two of the identities of the officers in the audience. One was Rear

# THE SILENT SERVICE'S FIRST HERO

Admiral William A. Moffett, Chief of the Bureau of Aeronautics. Moffett also held a Medal of Honor, awarded for bravery during a night landing in Veracruz, Mexico:[44]

> 'For distinguished conduct in battle, engagements of Vera Cruz, 21–22 April 1914. Comdr. [Commander] Moffett brought his ship into the inner harbor during the nights of the 21st and 22d without the assistance of a pilot or navigational lights, and was in a position on the morning of the 22d to use his guns at a critical time with telling effect. His skill in mooring his ship at night was especially noticeable. He placed her nearest to the enemy and did most of the firing and received most of the hits.'[45]

Rear Admiral Montgomery M. Taylor was the other senior officer present. He is not mentioned in any newspaper, but his distinctive moustache and facial features can be seen in a photograph from 1927, and he looks remarkably similar. While not a guarantee, it makes sense that the senior-most person in Breault's command would be present.[46] It would also not be unusual for others who recommended Breault for a Medal of Honor to be present, which would explain the identity of at least some of the other unidentified naval officers in the photographs.

Award ceremonies generally begin with the master of ceremonies calling the party to attention. Breault would have been called 'front and centre', likely by Secretary of the Navy Denby. Breault would have proceeded to the centre, facing the President. If required, Breault would have saluted once he heard the order 'hand salute', dropping his hand only when given the order 'two'. Denby, who can be seen holding a portfolio, would have announced the citation:

> 'For heroism and devotion to duty while serving on board the U.S. submarine O-5 at the time of the sinking of that vessel. On the morning of 28 October 1923, the O-5 collided with the steamship Abangarez and sank in less than a minute. When the collision occurred, Breault was in the torpedo room. Upon reaching the hatch, he saw that the boat was rapidly sinking. Instead of jumping overboard to save his own life, he returned to the torpedo room to the rescue of a shipmate who he knew was trapped in the boat, closing the torpedo room hatch on himself. Breault and Brown remained trapped in this compartment until rescued by the salvage party 31 hours later.'[47]

## HEROISM AND RECOGNITION (1923–24)

As the citation was read, Coolidge would have approached Breault and slipped the Medal of Honor over his head, offering brief congratulations and a handshake. Perhaps Breault had always dreamed of meeting a President and he finally received his opportunity.

Once the award was granted to Breault, Coolidge may have spoken. Notoriously a phlegmatic man of few words, Coolidge likely kept it simple with a few comments of praise. Breault would also have had the chance to speak, but unfortunately no newspaper recorded exactly what any of the participants said. Breault would have had the opportunity to converse with any of the participants in the ceremony, perhaps asking a favour to go home to New York to visit his family before returning to Panama.

Several newspapers included the pictures taken during the ceremony.[48] The most important to note is the *Brooklyn Daily Eagle*, which on 10 March featured a (relatively) high-fidelity portrait, meaning Breault would be immediately recognized when he arrived in New York on 13 March for a brief period of leave.[49] Even though the news was not as urgent, there were still several errors in the newspapers, such as in Memphis' *Commercial Appeal*, which claimed Breault earned his award for actions while serving aboard the *S-5*, not the *O-5*, perhaps remembering the other submarine that had sunk with survivors in 1920.[50] Many details were also exaggerated, such as the depth from which Breault and Brown were rescued, the *Buffalo Evening News* reporting the pair were rescued from 240ft, instead of the actual depth of approximately 42ft.[51] Collins likely would have found numerous faults in the reporting, as she had previously found in the initial reporting of the rescue.

Immediately after Breault received his award, he was granted leave to New York by A.T. Long, chief of the Bureau of Navigation, who also authorized his passage aboard the New York Receiving Ship, where he was authorized leave until 15 March 1924, when he would be shipped on the Panama Canal Railroad Line back to the Panama Canal Zone.[52] Breault probably requested the time to go on leave and was granted passage through official channels under the guise of official transportation back to his duty station. Breault likely sought to reconnect to his family, who were in White Plains and had reached out to him.[53] White Plains was only a short, thirty-minute train ride from the city. Breault's inclusion in the newspapers had helped his immediate family locate him by writing to the Bureau of Navigation.[54] Potentially, Breault's time in New York was the first time he saw his family since enlisting in the RNCVR.

Were his father, step-mother, and sisters waiting for him when Breault arrived on 12 March?[55] Or did he have to contend with similar crowds to those faced by fictional submariner Scotty McClenahan in the movie *It's Tough to be*

*Famous*?⁵⁶ No current record has been identified, but the circumstantial evidence of his address upon discharge and subsequent enlistments indicates that he had a reunion with his family and ended the estrangement that had plagued their relationship. On 15 March, Breault set sail on an unknown vessel commissioned by the New York Receiving Ship.⁵⁷ During his visit to White Plains, a reporter from the *New York Evening Post* was able to interview Breault. The journalist's interview was summarized with the laconic headline 'Likes Life on Submarine'.⁵⁸ The interview appeared to have happened the day he was leaving for Panama and contains only one passage with a direct quote from Breault:

> 'Breault in an interview today made it plain that he plans to spend the remainder of his life on the job which made him one of the most famous young men in the country. He is twenty-three. His reply to the question as to whether he would stay in the service was, "I hope to tell you."'⁵⁹

There are some inconsistencies the reporter comments on, such as the home of the parents of Henry Breault being at a previously unknown address, 15 Harrison Boulevard, Silver Lake Park, Harrison, near White Plains.⁶⁰ The interview contains a description of Breault post-award:

> 'Breault is modest. He was not wearing the blue button which shows him to be one of the twenty-four men who have received the Congressional medal. He had both the medal and the button in his pocket.'⁶¹

Why did Breault elect not to wear his Medal of Honor? Perhaps he was grappling with his newfound fame, modestly accepting praise but not truly believing he was worth the accolades, inspiring the response the fictional McClenahan gave in the film several years later?⁶² The movie was based on the novel *The Goldfish Bowl* by author Mary C. McCall, who would have been an observer in New York at the time of Breault's visit. At least some contemporaries thought the movie represented Charles Lindbergh, but the fictional character was a submariner, not an aviator.⁶³ McCall, having been in New York, likely saw Breault's reaction and inserted him into the amalgam of characters that were represented by McClenahan.

Like all periods of leave, the time away would end, and Breault was shipped back to Panama to continue aiding efforts restoring the *O-5*. Despite the good publicity gained from the rescue of the two entombed sailors and his subsequent award, Breault did not receive similar attention in the future. One of the few pieces of evidence indicating anyone saw potential in his story is from 26 November 1924, when the officer in charge of the recruiting station in Brooklyn where Breault re-enlisted requested 'his picture and an account of his valor', for the expressed purpose of 'splendid publicity' in the local newspapers.[64] Two photographs from the award ceremony and General Order No. 125 were forwarded from the Bureau of Navigation to the recruiting station that December, but no newspapers from Brooklyn have been found that contained reports of this news.[65] Outside of the loss of the *O-5* and his Medal of Honor ceremony, Breault was not in the public eye frequently, which may have been of his own design if he was truly as uncomfortable with the newfound fame as is implied by his modesty. The desire to run from fame could also have inspired his request to serve in the Asiatic Fleet, which could be considered a distant outpost for US citizens.

Breault was now a formal hero and had the potential to make the most of his fifteen minutes of fame. New York was likely abuzz while he was freshly minted and looked forward to his return. His career did not end, however, and Breault still had at least sixteen years of service before he could retire with a pension.

Did his award change his prospects and how he interacted with American society? Overall, the answer appears to be 'no'. Breault went to great lengths to remain anonymous, and I believe that anonymity was, at least partially, of his own design. The numerous occasions Breault could have been in the newspapers and yet never appeared indicates either a forgotten hero or one who actively avoided any publicity, potentially even asking reporters to not comment upon his existence. I was surprised at how few times Breault appeared in newspapers, particularly when the presence of a Medal of Honor recipient could have potentially elevated a story's publicity. It appears that Breault, seemingly to his family's dismay, wanted to live the life of a sailor rather than that of a celebrity. The Medal of Honor was the highlight of his career from our perspective, but I don't know if that is how Breault would have felt. Exploring the rest of his career, the details of which have hitherto been unknown, is necessary to understand the rewarding vocation Breault sought to have.

# Chapter 5

# Post-Award Career (1924–41)

The submarine force had its first hero, but what would they do with him? One would expect the political and naval leaders to understand the potential of utilizing him as a symbol of the heroism of submarines. Despite this assumption, there is little evidence the USN actively sought to build up Breault's public reputation or make him a living legend in the Navy. Breault only re-enlisted after New York Congressman Benjamin Fairchild wrote a letter interceding on his behalf, requesting he be transferred to serve in the Asiatic Theatre.[1] Breault would receive further commendations, such as advancement to TM1, the Yangtze River Medal and a recommendation from his commanding officer to be advanced to Chief Petty Officer after serving as acting COB. His career wasn't only filled with accolades, however, Breault was sentenced in a Summary Court Martial, was denied shore duty and was medically disqualified from submarines. Sailors looking at Breault's career will recognize their own, ones beset by exuberant homecomings and the trough of naval life, and it is in this section that the OMPF is most valuable.

Breault would return to Panama and the *O-5* on 24 March 1924.[2] Efforts to restore the *O-5* had been ongoing since it had been raised, but the boat was considered an obsolete design, despite its relatively recent construction date. On 22 April 1924, an advert was published in the *Portsmouth Herald* stating the intention to sell the boat from Portsmouth Naval Shipyard.[3] This decision was likely motivated by cost; the USN, as it has always been, made decisions on a budget-conscious agenda. Instead of shifting resources to fixing an obsolete vessel, they would rather focus on constructing new S-Boats and experimental platforms that would eventually become Fleet submarines. Despite this decision, decommissioning the vessel required a crew and Breault remained on the *O-5* – or submarines in the division – until 11 August 1924, when he boarded the receiving ship in New York and was honourably discharged soon after on 23 August.[4] Breault was likely employed getting the boat ready for a move from the Panama Canal Zone to Portsmouth Naval Shipyard in Kittery, Maine, and he was considered essential enough to be kept beyond his enlistment period for 'convenience of the Government', for which he could expect to eventually be paid.[5]

## POST-AWARD CAREER (1924–41)

One activity Breault is known to have been assigned to do while still on the *O-5* is studying for the advancement exam that would allow him to move up to warrant officer rank. A document in Breault's OMPF indicates that his award entitled him to be advanced to Warrant-Officer Gunner, but in keeping with his modest inclination, he humbly acknowledged he did not feel he was ready:

> 'The above named man was presented with a Medal of Honor by the President of the United States on Saturday 8 March, 1924 for heroism and devotion to duty at the time of the sinking of the U.S.S. O-5 in collision with the S.S. ABANGAREZ, 28 October 1924.
>
> 'Due to the fact that he has not considered himself qualified to take examination for Warrant Officer (Gunner), the recommendation for such advancement ... has not been forwarded. His enlistment expires 17 July 1924. It is urgently recommended, in accordance with the above references, that upon reenlisting, or as soon thereafter as he feel himself qualified, he be given the privilege of taking this examination, as he had been studying faithfully to prepare himself for the same.'[6]

In response, Chief of the Bureau of Navigation W.R. Shoemaker acknowledged and ordered the recommendation be made when Breault was ready to take the examination, and then he would 'be given the privilege of taking this examination before a special board' on 28 August 1924.[7] In characteristic fashion, by the time the naval bureaucracy had gotten to this point, Breault had been discharged from the Navy.

Despite Breault's 'I hope to tell you' (a now defunct idiom that signified positive and emphatic affirmation) in his professed desire to spend the remainder of his life aboard submarines, as indicated in the newspapers, Breault did not immediately re-enlist.[8] He spent eighty-six days outside of the USN, once again divorced from a major portion of his identity. This is now largely a defunct practice, replaced by transfer leave, a voluntary period of time between contracts. No record exists as to what Breault did during his time in New York, but it was not due to external pressures such as manpower reduction or administrative discharge; this time off was clearly Breault's choice, to leave the service until 22 November 1924.[9] One possibility is he wanted to spend time with his family, even helping them move. If the Silver Lake address reported in the *Evening Post* was correct, the address at 47 Fulton Street, White Plains, may have been a house Breault helped them purchase. The VA Home Loan was not yet a programme (enacted in 1944), but it's likely that the Breaults had been trying to save for the ability to purchase a home one day after spending much of their time moving between Connecticut, New York and Canada.[10]

Another possibility was that Breault had played a role, said the things he was charged to say, but secretly wanted out. This is evaluated as unlikely, given his decision ultimately to re-enlist matched his previous poetic sentiments of a life at sea, as expressed to St Onge.[11] Another possibility was this time was spent pursuing a romantic interest in White Plains, potentially Catherine O'Rourke, who was in correspondence with Breault before 1927.[12] Disillusionment with romantic attachment may have even been a contributing reason to Breault's eventual re-enlistment, as it has been for so many young sailors. The contemporary film *Born to Dance* captures this type of disillusionment when one of the characters, 'Gunny' Saks, is received coldly by his wife, whom he had married before joining the service and not seen for four years. Due to a series of complications and misunderstandings that are unsurprising in a musical comedy, eventually he simply decides married life is not for him and re-enlists after having been discharged. As Saks states to the character Ted Barker, who had also been discharged and was also experiencing romantic issues: 'I don't know Ted, maybe I'm just a man's man. I'm getting disgusted with married life.'[13]

Saks' statement relates to the next question: why Breault decided to re-enlist in the end and maintain his identity as a 'man's man'? The most likely possibility is that he intended to re-enlist after an extended absence, once his purpose ashore was done; he was ready to go back to his 'real' life. The eighty-six-day period was just under the ninety-day limit given to sailors who wished to return to the service, and Breault had affairs to attend to and family ties to mend. Given his previously stated desire to remain in the service after a previous discharge, and his publicly stated wish to stay in submarines, it is no surprise he eventually did re-enlist.

When Breault re-enlisted, he made the request initially by writing to his Congressman, Benjamin Fairchild, a Republican who represented the 24th Congressional District, before 13 October 1924. While that letter is not in his OMPF, Fairchild likely summarizes it in his own request; with that understanding and used indirectly, it is an account of Breault's service as he remembered his tenure, as seen in previous chapters. The letter also details his request for submarine duty in the Philippines, in the Asiatic Theatre, specifically in time for the winter manoeuvres, which he believed would benefit his career. More likely, he thought of the potential Asiatic port calls. Breault intended to travel by rail to San Francisco, where arrangements could be made to go on to the Philippines.[14]

Fairchild/Breault's request was granted by Chief of the Bureau of Navigation W.R. Shoemaker on 16 October 1924, with a further authorization for a recruitment station to get transportation to reach the USS *Chaumont* for departure by 1 November 1924.[15] Issues or other affairs prevented Breault from reaching this deadline, requiring Commander J.M. Smeallie to write a memorandum addressed to Captain Fairfield on 22 October, stating he would be delayed until 1 December, when he would be transferred to the Asiatic station from San Francisco.[16] Breault still indicated he was re-enlisting in New York, which he did on 22 November 1924 at the US Navy Recruiting Station in Brooklyn.[17] He was put on leave until 3 December, when they found transportation aboard the USS *Black Hawk* and then the USS *Pillsbury* on 26 January 1925.[18] The *Pillsbury* was a new destroyer and perhaps Breault's first taste of life in the surface navy outside of the *Savannah*, the tender for the division of submarines the *O-5* was part of. Did Breault have any thoughts of how his career could have been different if he had been a TM aboard a 'tin can'? After a long voyage by sea, Breault reported to the submarine USS *S-38* on 8 February 1925.[19] As he promised, Breault was back on submarines in his desired duty station.

## *S-38*: 1925–28

The *S-38* was an S-class submarine, a next-generation submarine that was significantly larger than the *O-5* that Breault had previously served on. After several high-profile disasters, the S-boats were improved to become a serviceable vessel, but one that had an unfortunate tendency to ground due to the lack of a fathometer. They would last until the Second World War, when they were completely supplanted by new fleet boat designs. The *S-38* was far more comfortable than the *O-5:* the best picture of life for the crew on an S-boat is portrayed in Gugliotta's book *Pigboat 39*. Gugliotta paints a picture of hardship and sacrifice, but also close camaraderie:[20]

> 'S-boat personnel found out early that most fleet-boat sailors pitied them, but true Asiatic pigboat sailors had all the feisty pride of a cadre of hard-living, tough professionals who, by the very fact they'd been able to survive S-boat existence, considered themselves superior.'[21]

For Breault, the move to the Asiatic Fleet was likely a much-anticipated and hoped-for move. Time in the Asiatic Fleet was an experience he would have heard about from other sailors. Edward Beach remembers the perception of life in the Asiatic Fleet as a 'glamorous duty' prior to the Second World War.[22] Breault would not have to experience the cold winters of the North-east, and the American dollar went much further in Manila, Shanghai, Tsingtao and the other Asiatic locales than anywhere stateside.[23] This request indicated a desire for more of the warm weather he experienced in Panama, along with continued service in the submarine fleet. Breault's advancement towards the end of this period to TM1 likely helped him enjoy the locales too.

It has already been mentioned that despite Shoemaker's letter giving Breault permission to take the Gunner examination to become a warrant officer, he did not immediately attempt to take it. Like many, he likely dreaded the idea of taking an examination, as he appears to have been an unremarkable academic. He was literate and lists his highest education as grammar school, but his class rank at a rating school in 1937 lists him as fourth out of a class of four, suggesting academic achievement was a lifelong struggle.[24] Aware of this deficiency, when informed that his award granted him the ability to take the exam to become a warrant officer, he humbly acknowledged his perceived shortcoming, stating he did not believe he was qualified due to a lack of the prerequisite professional knowledge.[25] To their credit, the Bureau forwarded a syllabus with references to Breault to help ensure that he would be able to pass his examination.[26]

Advancing to officer was highly sought-after and a common trope employed in literature and film of the period. Edward Ellsberg's main character in *Pigboats*, Thomas Knowlton/Tom Knowles, begins the story commissioned as a lieutenant and spends much of the work attempting to return to his former status as an officer, though this time beginning as an enlisted QM. When he returns from two consecutive heroic actions, Knowlton/Knowles asks Admiral Sims to allow him the opportunity to command a submarine in a ploy to defeat the German U-boats.[27] The main character's path to revenge and a return to the status of commissioned officer serve as primary plot vehicles of the book, and the reaction of his love interest, Mary Martin, highlights the importance of the change in status:

> "'Cheerio! If the fairy queen hasn't been at it again!' Mary Martin stared at the new lieutenant's stripes on Tom's sleeves, then sank wearily into the chair alongside him ... "You were just a bit of all right, when you were a gob [seaman], Tom." She eyed him archly. "Now that you're a bally officer, like the rest of them, I suppose you'll think that every girl who smiles at you twice is just dying to sink into those gold-laced arms.'"[28]

She then notes Knowlton/Knowles had not answered as to how he had been advanced, comparing the advancement in the Royal Navy as being remarkably difficult and generally occurring as a battlefield commission.[29]

Similarly, the main character's path to love and commission were the primary plot points in the 1937 movie *Navy Blues*, with Russell 'Rusty' Gibbs being challenged by his shipmates to date a perceived undateable librarian named Doris Kimball.[30] To engage in conversation, Gibbs' ploy was to pretend he was studying for entrance examinations into the United States Naval Academy in Annapolis.

The subterfuge appeared to have been necessary to endear Gibbs to Doris and her family, particularly her mother, who greets the sailors who show up to her doorstep coldly. Considering Doris and her extended family were portrayed as academic and middle- or upper-class, the mother's disdain for the 'gob' at her doorstep indicates middle- and upper-class Americans were not as fond of sailors as they were officers. When Gibbs finally becomes an officer at the end of the movie, it was as a chief warrant officer, and he offers his commission as proof 'this time'.[31]

Another 1937 movie, *Sweetheart of the Navy*, also employs the main character's potential rise to the officer caste as a plot device. Yeoman Second Class Eddie Harris is a highly respected sailor and seeking a recommendation from his superior, Commander Lodge, to become an officer. In their interactions regarding Harris' participation in a championship boxing match, Lodge makes it clear that he regards boxing for exercise was acceptable, but that gambling and participating in fleet boxing matches were restricted to the enlisted men and unbecoming of an officer. Lodge finally states he would withdraw his recommendation for Harris to attend the USNA in Annapolis if he attends the bout: 'I'm thinking only of your future as an officer.' The movie ends with Harris heading to Annapolis and an engagement to marry his impoverished love interest, Joan Whitney, after he graduates, and an unofficial boxing bout with the middleweight boxing champ resolving her monetary crisis.[32]

Clearly, the opportunity to wear the rank of officer and join the officer caste was portrayed as highly sought-after by enlisted personnel, and still is seen as an advancement in social status by Americans inside and outside of the naval service. The Bureau of Navigation further helped Breault: when he took the test in 1927, he was not considered to be in competition with his peers, guaranteeing advancement so long as he passed the written examination. Despite this favourable boon, Breault failed the written examination and could not be considered for advancement.[33] On a mail routing slip, an anonymous author wrote a handwritten note stating 'if you want to advance Breault, it can be done. It would be against the policy + rules, because we have 75 in excess in that rating [*sic*].' After a break, the next note states 'authorize advancement to TM1c (Pa) by verbal order of Capt. Koch.'[34] A letter from Koch to the Bureau of Navigation led to an advancement authorization on 25 February 1928.[35] Breault's status was thus of enough gravity that his superiors were willing to look past his deficiencies. This advancement was similar to the Meritorious Advancement Programs (MAP), where E3–E5 sailors who were determined by their command to be worthy of advancement but were unable to do so based off their rating exams, were 'mapped' to the next rank.

Breault's inability to advance to warrant officer could reflect a lifelong academic struggle, but there is an alternative possibility stemming from the unique conditions of the period and his potential desire for remaining enlisted. Breault had already been exposed to the enlisted pride of hard work and making do with less for over ten years by this point. While officers were esteemed by American society, enlisted men had their own communities that respected one another for adherence to their own code of masculinity. Breault had been exposed to these ideas since he was a 16-year-old boy in the RNCVR. Breault met heroes during the Halifax Explosion whom we are only beginning to discover, such as Acting Boatswain Charles Mattison, Stoker Petty Officer Edmund Beard, Leading Seaman Charles McMillan, Ordinary Seaman Freeman Burnley Nickerson, Able Seaman Albert Saunders, Wireless Telegraph Operator George Veals and Stoker George Roley Yates.[36] The RN and the Dominions also admired the common sailor, in a fashion that American society never had, potentially influencing Breault's career choice.[37]

The emphasis on enlisted sailors was beginning to bleed in from other American military branches such as the US Marine Corps, embodied by two-time Medal of Honor recipient Sergeant Major Daniel Daly, who refused an officer's commission, allegedly stating 'Any officer [could] get by on his sergeants, but to be a sergeant, you have to know your stuff. I'd rather be an outstanding sergeant than just [another] officer.'[38] Daly's invocation and attitude could surely have been heard repeated within the submarine community, who depended upon their enlisted core, while junior officers under the rank of lieutenant were their primary COs and shifted to new experiences outside of the submarine force when their time was done. There was pride in being a submariner, one that Breault professed to buy into deeply, to the point he sought emphatically to devote himself to the profession, not as an officer, but as an enlisted sailor.

Breault was in no rush to take the officer examination, though what if the reason was that he simply didn't want to be an officer, like Daly? This would explain his inability to make chief; it was potentially an honour he did not desire. While I have conjectured Breault was an unremarkable academic, it would be an exaggeration to say that he had zero academic success, as he was advanced to TM2 on his own merit, without assistance. This opens the possibility that Breault simply sabotaged himself and failed the examination to avoid becoming an officer. While American society considered the rank and status of a sailor as lower than that of an officer, Breault's decision to remain a sailor indicates he bought into the community, donning the archetype as a central part of his identity and personality. Daly's explanation may not match Breault's actual motivations, but could explain why Breault remained a TM1 for the rest of his career: he'd rather be a good TM1 than just another officer or chief.

When viewed from this angle, Breault's career decisions could be viewed as deliberate efforts to maintain his current rank and status as a junior sailor, one who

## POST-AWARD CAREER (1924–41)

could ensure this status by attempting to remain banished to the Asiatic Fleet in the thick of action a war-weary and introspective America would prefer to forget. In the handwritten note on the routing slip, Breault's advancement to TM1 was the result of senior leadership's willingness to bend rules in his favour. The '75 in excess' was part of the overall planning of naval leadership to operate the USN with as little manpower as possible, a trend that only reversed after 1933.[39] The decrease of naval personnel was due to budgetary concerns that were out of Breault's control, but it was possible, given the manning concerns of the interwar period, that his service was more valuable as an enlisted sailor.

Breault's time on the *S-38* occurred during a time of increasing instability in China. The first leader of the Kuomintang (the Nationalist Party of China), Sun Yat-sen, would pass away on 12 March 1925, inviting a power struggle within the party that would eventually see Chiang Kai-shek become the leader of China. Regional warlords filled the void and were increasingly belligerent to foreign powers in the region, resulting in withdrawals to the coastline of China in strongholds such as Shanghai. American warships in the Asiatic Fleet such as the *S-38* were not mere poster boys showing the flag; they faced real, credible threats and acted as the primary enforcers of American will in the region. Breault was probably involved in the American response to occurrences in Shanghai and the Nanking Incident (the rescue of foreign residents after looting and attacks by Chinese Nationalists in March 1927) while aboard the *S-38*, and was awarded the Yangtze Service Medal for serving in a combat theatre.[40] Conflict did not diminish his desire to remain in the Asiatic Fleet, but he returned stateside to San Francisco at the end of his contract, with a recommendation that he be advanced to CTM, or Chief Torpedoman's Mate (TMC in the Navy today).[41]

## San Francisco, New York, Coco Solo, *V-2*, United States Naval Hospital Camapo, *S-41*: 7 January 1929 – 20 August 1930

Upon the end of his contract, Breault was returned to the receiving ship from San Francisco when discharged on 14 November 1928.[42] Details of Breault's time in San Francisco are unknown, but upon entering the port, Breault likely saw the same thing that the author of the 1920 *Guide to San Francisco* observed:

> 'SHIPS approaching the coast from the south cruise along the coast near Halfmoon Bay, and, if the day is clear, the crew catches a glimpse of the Montara Mountains raising their peaks above the foothills standing in close communion with the rugged shore. A spit of land, called Pilar Point, edges out from the mainland above

[Halfmoon] Bay and a few miles further on the ship passes Point Montara and Point San Pedro. After proceeding 10 miles or so along a coast, level in some places and rocky in others but always wave-beaten, the western water front of San Francisco comes into view. The ship cruises past the Life-saving Station, Seal Rocks ... and then rounds Point Lobos and enters the Golden Gate. Nearly every afternoon during the summer months, a cloud of fog is brought into San Francisco by the west winds sweeping in from the ocean and the fog horns are set roaring and steam whistles to shrieking – the ocean liner's deep-throated bellows being interspersed with the nervous scream of tugboats and other small craft.'[43]

Breault may have enjoyed a break from the tropical heat for the brief time he was in San Francisco, but it is likely the oppressive fog that he most remembered.

Breault's primary purpose to visit the city was his return from the Asiatic Fleet, a break between contracts. He only spent six days in San Francisco, then boarded a ship to the Receiving Ship in New York City. New York would not have changed in the short time he had been gone, but one could imagine the tanned Breault returning to his family in White Plains with souvenirs and stories from the Far East. His eldest sister, Diana, had been married to Everett Drennan, but Beatrice, Estelle, Joseph J. and Mary Breault remained at home. On 5 January 1929, Breault re-enlisted for four years in Brooklyn at the Navy Recruiting Ship.[44] Breault would return to the Navy on 2 February 1929, and on 21 February was transferred to the USS *V-2*, located at the Coco Solo Submarine Base.[45]

The *V-2* was truly impressive in size; it was double the submerged tonnage of the *S-38*, 100 feet longer at 342 feet and had more room for amenities. The size cannot be stressed enough; the *V-2* was only 20 feet shorter than the nuclear-powered Los Angeles-class submarine (though only a third of the tonnage). While they would ultimately prove to be unreliable, the V-boats were seen as the future of the USN's submarine force until an improved Fleet Boat design came out. For a 'lifer' like Breault, serving on a new boat with the newest technology and increased comfort should have been seen as an important milestone. Unfortunately for Breault, however, the larger space did not appear to correlate to a happy career. Breault would only spend a year on the *V-2* and would be sent to a Summary court-martial (SCM). On 3 August 1929, Breault was awarded half-months' pay for two months for being 'AOL for a period of twenty-three (23) hours and forty (40) minutes'.[46] The specificity of the time is likely the command electing to charge Breault with a lower punishable offence, or Breault reporting with just enough time to avoid a greater charge.

# POST-AWARD CAREER (1924–41)

It is difficult to imagine a Medal of Honor recipient today going to a disciplinary action of any sort. SCMs were not uncommon, as deck logs from the period recording daily activities frequently reported an SCM was held. Testament from *The Bluejackets' Manual* (May 1927, Seventh Edition) described unauthorized absence as 'the most frequent offense committed by an enlisted man'.[47] The same *Bluejackets' Manual* described the escalation of punishment available to the CO, in order of ascending severity: Captain's discretion (resembling modern-day NJP), the Deck Court, Summary court-martial and General court-martial. While a serious charge, the *Bluejacket's Manual* lays out the potential severity and the proceedings:

> '**Summary court-martial**. – This court consists of three officers as members and one officer as recorder. It is convened by the commanding officer for offenses which demand a punishment more severe than can be given by a deck court. A summary court-martial can assign any one of the following punishments:
>
> (1) Discharge from the service with bad-conduct discharge; but the sentence shall not be carried into effect in a foreign country.
> (2) Solitary confinement, not exceeding 30 days, on bread and water or on diminished rations.
> (3) Solitary confinement not exceeding 30 days.
> (4) Confinement not exceeding two months.
> (5) Reduction to next inferior rating.
> (6) Deprivation of liberty on shore on foreign station.
> (7) Extra police duties and loss of pay not to exceed three months may be added to any of the above punishments.'[48]

The only punishment that could not be meted out by an SCM would be the death penalty, which was reserved for the General court-martial. Breault could thus have been discharged more than halfway through his twenty-year tenure, threatening his potential pension and current livelihood.

Breault could have missed muster for a variety of reasons. The most likely, however, is that Breault simply missed a muster for a long period of time and decided to enjoy his day. He may have even elected to ignore an order to return to the boat, believing he had earned his liberty out in town. Breault might even have woken up late after a night out in town, then decided he was likely in trouble anyway, so he might as well enjoy the day. Sailors are trained on the consequences of their actions due to exposure in training and from reading *The Bluejackets' Manual*. Breault thus likely knew the exact guidelines; so long as he was back within a day, it was only absence outside of leave, not absence without leave, a much more severe article. It is a trope so common that Ellsberg's *Pigboats* opens with a scene where the main character wakes up after a rowdy night, contemplating the punishment he will receive for missing muster, though in the book's case it is implied that Knowlton was drugged.[49]

Breault was awarded what is commonly referred to as 'half-month's pay times-two'. Compared to other award ceremonies he had experienced, this post-SCM award ceremony must have left a poor taste in Breault's mouth. It appears that the big new boats, more regimental and navy-like in their traditions, weren't built for an Asiatic sailor like Breault, one of a brotherhood of sailors renowned for their ability to eschew naval decorum and regulations. It appears Breault was transferred off the *V-2* and was ordered to the receiving ship in San Francisco once more on 14 February 1930, likely due to issues with his kidneys.[50] While not recorded, Breault was sent back to the Asiatic Fleet per his request, where he was billeted for the USS *Henderson*, an FFT (training frigate), but on an unknown date was 'Not taken up on USS HENDERSON'.[51] He was transferred to the *S-41* on 30 April 1930, but his time aboard was interrupted due to hospitalization at the US Naval Hospital in Canacao, Philippines, on 4 June that year.[52] Breault's record indicates his injury was not the result of misconduct. He returned to the *S-41*, but was transferred again, this time to the *S-36*. As Breault would end up assuming a major leadership role, this transfer was likely to alleviate manning issues.

Breault's transfer indicates manning was a much less centralized effort than today. There were avenues for sailors to transfer to different vessels, such as for attending to major medical issues. If at a happy command, Breault likely would have ignored any medical issues, all but the most serious that prevented him from working. While a sailor was in hospital, a boat could get underway without him, likely making do without them or finding a replacement from the tender. The sailor, having had the medical issues he needed taken care of, would spend some time convalescing until a boat that needed more crew made a request. Alternatively, COs could simply transfer a troublesome sailor, offering them a fresh start in a different boat. Breault could even have initiated this transfer with a special request. Regardless of the vessel, the USN would ensure that it got the entirety of Breault's contract, on one boat or another.

## *S-36*: 1930–32

Breault was transferred to the *S-36* on 30 August 1930, where his career stabilized once more, and he stayed until 15 September 1932. The *S-36* would be part of a submarine division posted in Tsingtao to stabilize the region and would win

## POST-AWARD CAREER (1924–41)

the Battle E ('Efficiency') pennant for proficiency in torpedo firing. Outside of service on the *O-5* and receiving his Medal of Honor, these two years were likely the most professionally satisfying of Breault's career.[53] Breault's hard work as a TM1 would see him appointed to the position of COB, despite the lack of his prerequisite rank of chief, either due to the lack of qualified personnel aboard the *S-36* or the respect he commanded.

A document that is instructive to analyse is the letter of commendation that Lieutenant DuBois, CO of the *S-36*, wrote for Breault prior to his impending transfer, advising that he be advanced to the rank of chief petty officer. DuBois' recommendation reads:

'Subject: Letter of Commendation, in the case of, -
BREAULT, Henry 210-80-03, TM1c., USN.

1. Breault was acting "Chief of the Boat" of the U.S.S. S-36 during overhaul period as well as while this vessel was [operating] in full commission status. This responsibility covered a period of approximately five months, during which time he displayed qualities of natural leadership and initiative seldom found except in natural leaders and men of exception worth.
2. This man has a Congressional Medal of Honor for courage and the Navy E made by this vessel in this year's Torpedo practices is directly traceable to his untiring interest and leadership.
3. In the opinion of his Commanding Officer, Henry Breault is worthy and well qualified to be advanced to Chief Torpedoman.
4. A copy of this letter will be placed in this man's service record.

S.W. DUBOIS (unsigned)'[54]

DuBois clearly believed Breault's ability as a sailor was equal to his status as a Medal of Honor recipient. Further, this period of five months as acting COB may have been longer, as DuBois transferred shortly after writing the letter, a passenger list in the *Honolulu Star Bulletin* noting that he was returning from the Asiatic Theatre a month after writing the letter of commendation.[55] The letter may have been a final thank you to Breault acting as a member of the triad of his command, in the hope it would help his career. Breault's appointment as COB, despite lacking the requisite rank of chief petty officer, speaks volumes about the character of his service.

COB is an official, formal position today, acting as the senior enlisted advisor within the triad of command, one that has a qualification process, a billeted appointment and a bureaucracy in itself. A sailor who served as COB on three different submarines, Eric Antoine, gave his definition of what a COB represents in *American Submarine Review* magazine:

> 'The COB represents the institutional knowledge of the Navy and the Submarine Force ... He understands preparing for deployments and getting families ready to ensure what we now call individual readiness. Also consider that his shore tours have kept him close to the waterfront. He has, either as a technical expert or a leader stayed connected to the Submarine Force. Then, that institutional knowledge is leveraged to train and prepare Sailors to go to sea and operate in forward areas alone and unafraid. He uses that institutional knowledge and experience to improve the performance and capabilities of his Chiefs ... his institutional knowledge and his deployment experience is required to be used in the operational planning and execution of tasking of the ship by his crew. His experience is invaluable when training a crew and gives him the ability to provide sage counsel to the Commanding Officer. The training and proficiency of the Ship's Control Party, topside line handling and damage control, basic submarining and submarine qualifications fall under the responsibility of the COB. All of his experience as a Submariner up to point of him becoming a COB is brought to bear to ensure the success of his crew.'[56]

Today, the duty of COB is formally billeted to a senior chief petty officer or master chief petty officer (both established in 1958), though Antoine highlights that he believes this reflects the essential duty of COBs in the past. The formality of the position was not established within naval bureaucracy until well past the end of Breault's career, meaning much of the authority was informal and dictated by the buy-in of the crew.

Several Second World War memoirs describe the importance of the COB and how they were well respected. Robert Hunt was taken aback when his former CO called him in and asked him to be COB:

> 'He knew his former captain [Dick Kefauver] was going to ask him to volunteer for the *Springer*, and Bob already had the "no" half-formed in his throat. But Kefauver surprised him asking him to serve as chief of the boat. It was the most important post next to that of the captain [himself], and it was a great honor to be asked, especially by someone Bob respected so much.'[57]

That Hunt still considered joining Kefauver, despite his well-earned rest after twelve patrols on Tambor, is inicative of just how important the positon was, even this early in the submarine force. *Tambor*. COs reinforced the prestige whenever possible. Richard O'Kane mentioned his appreciation of having 'a real chief of boat' on numerous occasions, and Ignatius Galantin stated that the COB 'wields much unofficial but effective authority'.[58]

The most applicable work to describe Breault's selection to become COB is Gugliotta's *Pigboat 39*, which describes the prewar practices of the *S-39*. Gugliotta was the wife of one of the officers, Guy Gugliotta, who served aboard the ship. She compiled interviews, tape recordings, letters, conversations, remembrances and official correspondence to reconstruct the history of the *S-39* in the late interwar period and early Second World War.[59] The description of prewar Asiatic S-boats – the same class Breault was serving aboard and was acting COB of – describes the decision-making that occurred when selecting a COB. The first COB that is introduced is 'Pop' Bridges, 'an old-hand' who had served in the First World War aboard the *L-10* as a TM3.[60] Bridges' role included being a father to the crew, representing the crew, greeting, socializing, training and qualifying new submariners, and interfacing with the captain on a daily basis, all while performing an assortment of other duties.[61] An emotional scene saw the crew bid farewell to Bridges, who left just prior to war, and subsequent passages were devoted to selecting a new COB from the crew.[62] One can imagine a similar meeting occurring in the *S-36* wardroom, where the officers selected the COB from their crew, rather than having one appointed through formal channels.

The two candidates on the *S-39* were Chief Machinist's Mate Stanley Mandekic and Chief Torpedoman's Mate Earl Nave. The matter was not settled by simple seniority; other considerations included transfer dates, personality, temperament and respect, not only of the wardroom, but also that of the crew.[63] The CO made the decision, but allowed the wardroom to give their input and understand the process. The XO made the recommendation for Nave, whom he had previously advocated for. Guy Gugliotta, newly reported at the time, did not add commentary but contented himself with observing and making 'mental notes of the insights he'd obtained'.[64] This passage, like any that includes Gugliotta, is one that merits attention due to the close relation to the author. Even if the details were not remembered perfectly, the passage indicates that the selection of Breault as a COB, even only an acting one, was unconventional, but reflected the level of respect he commanded from the entire crew of the *S-36*, officers and enlisted men. He held a tremendous responsibility, well outside of his pay grade, and was rewarded with a recommendation to become a TMC.

## USS *Canopus*, USS *Holland* and USS *Narwhal*: 15 September 1932 – 13 May 1936

From the *S-36*, Breault was transferred to the tender *Canopus* and then the Receiving Station in Pearl Harbor, where he briefly interacted with a former submarine CO named C.W. (Chester) Nimitz, who would later become much more famous as an admiral.[65] Breault reenlisted for a third, four-year period on 19 December 1932 after a transfer and leave period to San Diego.[66] It is in this leave period that Breault would meet his soon-to–be-wife, Pearl Slaughter, as indicated by a letter written by her then-husband, William L. Slaughter.[67] While this was not the first time Breault had returned Stateside in the past decade, it was the first time he was back in the country for a prolonged period. Breault reported aboard USS *Holland* on 28 January 1933, the first prolonged period of time Breault had served on a ship that was not a submarine.[68] During this period, he likely serviced submarines attached to the tender and went underway as a surface sailor.

Something about surface ships continued to rub Breault the wrong way, as he was transferred to the USS *Narwhal* on 11 September 1933. The *Narwhal* was a V-type submarine attached to the *Holland* that had greater range than the S-boats. Breault had served aboard V-boats before, which were luxurious compared to the S-boats he had been on in the Asiatic Fleet. He would requalify for submarines on 1 December 1933.[69] The *Narwhal* spent a good portion of its time acting as the new 'show-me boat' in San Diego. Several newspapers detail the submarine's public events and contain pictures of life aboard the vessel.[70] Men gathered playing poker in the torpedo room while off duty, the cook working in the galley and the crew's mess, laundry hanging topside and the wardroom dining topside can all be seen in the *Honolulu Star Bulletin*.[71] The *Los Angeles Times* bragged about the 'world's largest submersible sinking craft', offering that 500 officers would get the chance to go underway over the next week.[72] The *Honolulu Star Bulletin* wrote that the submarines were always improving:

> 'Constantly these men and their craft exercise and maneuver in [Hawaiian] waters, improving their efficiency, which means their ability to destroy and defend. Through this unceasing work, life in submarines is improving. Until recently they were known as "[pigboats]," a description which [conveyed] some idea of the stuffy life aboard. But today Uncle Sam's latest underwater craft, the giant Argonaut, Narwhal and the other V-boats, seem to be the last word in grim efficiency and conditions for the crews … Ingenious ventilating systems, [using] fresh air when on the surface and oxygen from reserve stores when submerged, have banished

the old terrors or foul air. Vital equipment is considered first in V-boats ... Inventors of the earliest subs would be surprised if they inspected the Narwhal, surveyed its "modern conveniences." Cold storage, ice machines and chill rooms, [evaporators] and distillers for fresh water, enable the men to have regular landlubber meals.'[73]

It is surprising that Breault is not mentioned in any of these articles. One would think the gravity of the Medal of Honor recipient would add to the story, but he remains unmentioned, indicating it was possibly a request of his to be anonymous.

A major change in Breault's career occurred when he was transferred to the *Holland* again after his time on the *Narwhal* ended in 1936. Either Breault sincerely disliked V-boats, or his body began showing wear and tear, which is unsurprising considering the physical nature of work as a submariner. A stamp in his medical record dated 23 January 1936 indicates he was examined by CMDR G.B. McArthur, who found Breault was 'not physically qualified for duty aboard submarines' the change being noted due to 'defective vision'.[74] Breault's eyesight had previously been recorded as 20/20, and would be in the future too, but it is possible that Breault's eyesight had been declining. In a USN that was only beginning to expand, medical officers were likely more particular than they had been in the past when examining sailors.

While on the *Narwhal*, Breault married Pearl Slaughter and adopted Helen Slaughter as his daughter. While their marriage certificate hasn't been found, it is believed that Breault's enlistment paperwork covering 1932–36 offers the date the USN was informed of the union.[75] A red-ink change to the marital status and next of kin sections update both to 'married' and 'Pearl Breault', respectively replacing 'single' and 'Diana Breault Drennan'.[76] The date of the changes was recorded as 10 April 1935, indicating the marriage occurred shortly before then.[77] It wouldn't surprise me if Breault's expressed desire for shore duty was associated with Pearl and Helen, as sea duty is notoriously difficult on families.

Breault continued to serve aboard the *Holland*, *Decatur* and *Truxtun*, but never gave up on trying to rejoin the submarine fleet. On 23 February 1937, LTJG J.M. Jordan requalified him for submarine duty, a decision that was reaffirmed on 19 September 1940 by LCDR C.W. Schilling.[78] Breault's insistence on returning to the submarine fleet, despite a severe malady preventing him from being on them, indicates that he did not love duty on a destroyer as he had on submarines, a theme that defined much of his service. Sailors moving between the surface and submarine forces were not unusual, and likely shared similar atmospheres. It is even possible that Breault met sailors aboard the *Decatur* and *Truxtun* who had also been on submarines. Destroyer and tender duty continued to be essential but underappreciated duties performed in the USN, but they would both see increased roles during the Second World War in the Atlantic and Pacific respectively.

I will not delve into Breault's time as a surface sailor, though this is a potentially fruitful investigation for scholars of the subject of 'tin can' sailors. Despite the advantages afforded to surface sailors, Breault never appeared to forget his time on submarines as he kept trying to get medically requalified for submarine duty. As mentioned above, on 19 September 1940, Breault was examined by LCDR C.W. Schilling, who found him 'to be physically qualified for submarine duty'.[79] Schilling made this judgment after an examination under the guidelines established by 'ManMedDept.', which could be a possible insight into the physical demands of the submarine force. The willingness of Breault could be seen as a desire for a sailor to rejoin the force that made such an impact on his career. Whatever the reason, Breault was back in and was transferred to SUBASE NLON.

In an unfortunate stroke of bad luck, Breault's heart condition then flared up and he was taken from the SUBASE NLON barracks to the hospital dispensary on 24 November 1940:

> 'CC: Pain in chest. Shortness of breath. PI: Patient complains of above symptoms for past 2 days. Was getting worse just before admission. Was brought to dispensary from barracks in ambulance. Very uncooperative, moaning and groaning – refuses to sit still enough to exam. When MS gr1/4 was ordered he [immediately] got better and refused the medicine – only to start complaining in a few minutes. States he had these attacks several times previously and that they are aggravated by exertion. Physical exam essentially negative findings except for the way he was [carrying] on.[80]

Breault was treated 'conservatively', with rest and a light diet. After walking out of bed for a week, a Lieutenant Grugel decided he had no disease but suffered from Cardiac ischemia due to excessive smoking.[81] Grugel made this diagnosis with the aid of Breault's admission that he 'has been smoking 2 packages of cigarettes daily', and sent him back to duty on 9 December 1940.[82] Breault's lack of cooperation is unsurprising; he was likely trying to avoid a medical diagnosis that would prevent his time in the submarine service. After spending much of his time requalifying for submarine duty, he knew all too well that a diagnosis of poor health or a slow recovery would prevent him from serving aboard a boat. Breault appeared to recover well and was found physically qualified to reenlist on 29 April 1941.[83] Unfortunately, Breault would never make it to his

## POST-AWARD CAREER (1924–41)

scheduled duty, and he spent much of his remaining career at the submarine base performing unrecorded duties and at the United States Naval Hospital in Newport, Rhode Island.

Breault was transferred to Newport due to his increasingly severe attacks. From conversations with his doctors, we can discern Breault's condition during the last months of his life. During his time in New London, LTJG J.J. Donlon and LTJG S. Ullman recorded:

> '8-20-41: Condition about the same.
>
> 8-21-41: Complains of [moderate] dyspnoea [laboured breathing]. Temperature, pulse and respiration normal. Treatment continued.
>
> 8-26-41: Patient states dyspnoea receding. Orthopnea gone. Condition improved ...
>
> 8-30-41: Pulse 108, respiration 24. No complaints. No dyspnoea, palpitation. Occasional precordial sharp pain [intermittent] in character.
>
> 8-31-41: Condition about the same. Treatment continued.
>
> 9-1-41: Patient complains of slight precordial pain. Treatment continued.
>
> 9-4-41: Condition about the same. Transferred this date to the U.S. NAVAL HOSPITAL, Newport, Rhode Island for further treatment and disposition. [Handwritten note] Has been receiving [indecipherable] Digitalis daily.'[84]

Once transferred to Newport, CMDR F.P. Kearney gave an initial observation on Breault, who complained of chest pain, difficulty in breathing and 'precordial pain of varying severity' radiating down his left arm to his fingers. Breault had been dealing with these medical issues since 1937, though they had grown increasingly worse since November 1940. Kearney summarized his findings in the physical exam:

> 'A thin well-developed [extremely] nervous, 41 yr. old white male, exhibiting evidence of extertional dyspnea after walking down to [examining] room. No cyanosis or cough. Co-operative and rational. Moving about frequently during examination.'[85]

Breault's nervousness can be considered normal, considering his transfer to a hospital with symptoms of a heart attack and speaking to an officer of significantly higher rank than many of his COs had been. Breault's medical history continues with daily updates until his death on 5 December 1941:

> '9-4-41: X-ray of the chest; examination of the chest shows the heart to be within the upper limits of normal as to size. The lung fields are generally clear. There may be a slight increase in peribronchial marking in both upper lung fields.
>
> 9-6-41: No complaints. Feeling better. No dyspnea, less weakness. Kahn neg.
>
> 9-8-41: BMR 11% R&M normal.
>
> 9-12-41: ECG shows old healed coronary. ECG report; Rate 96. rhythm-Regular Sinus Rhythm ... Diagnosis: Old (healed) coronary occlusion, myocardial lesion (anterior wall).
>
> 9-15-41: No Complaints. Up and about. Examination today reveals moderate cardiac enlargement to the left. There is a systolic murmur at the apex. There is a definite gallup rhythm. Heart rate 11. Liver edge palapable 2 fingers [below] costal margin. Lung fields clear. No edema.
>
> 9-18-41: To be digitalized in view of mild [decompensation] mentioned above.
>
> 9-22-41: Pulse down to 70–80. Lung clear.
>
> 9-29-41: Digitalized. Today has coupled rhythm. Rate 76. Liver edge palpable. Lung fields clear.
>
> 10-4-41: Doing well. No evidence of congestive failure. Taking gr iss Of digitalis daily.
>
> 10-8-41: Pulse 80. Chest clear. Liver edge just palapable. No edema.
>
> 10-13-41: Pulse 92. No rales or edema. To take gr. Digitalis b.i.d. for a few days in attempt to keep pulse in 70s.
>
> 10-19-41: No dyspnea or distress. Walking about ward. Pulse 84.
>
> 102-6-41 [10-26-41]: No dyspnea or edema.
>
> 10-30-41: No change. Or gr. [digitalis] b.i.d.
>
> 11-7-41: Pulse 84. No dyspnea or edema.
>
> 11-14-41: No change.
>
> 11-21-41: no evidence of [congestive] failure. Is on maintenance dose of digitalis.

# POST-AWARD CAREER (1924–41)

11-28-41: No change.

12-4-41: Brought before a board of Med. Survey today. The board found Myocarditis, Chronic (cause Coronary sclerosis), duty, not misconduct and board recommended that he be retained for further treatment,

12-5-41: Patient apparently had a good night's sleep. He woke as well as usual this AM. He dressed, and was sweeping the floor in the ward when he suddenly collapsed and died before the O.O.D. could reach him. There was no apparent pain. He did not cry out. There was no cough or bloody sputum. Survey written yesterday not [forwarded].'[86]

Similar to the surface sailor section, the medical history section could be valuable to a medical history scholar. I simply do not have the training to make sense of all the notes, but I can use them for other sections, such as when Breault lied about the cause of his wife's death, for the next chapters. These logs indicate the extensive information available death on December 5, 1941, in the OMPF of prominent service members.

Breault was buried by his father in St Mary's Cemetery in Putnam, CT. Only two days after his the events at Pearl Harbor would lead to American submarines going to war in an identity-defining conflict, anchored by pre-war submariners like Breault himself. Breault, possibly sensing the potential conflict and the need

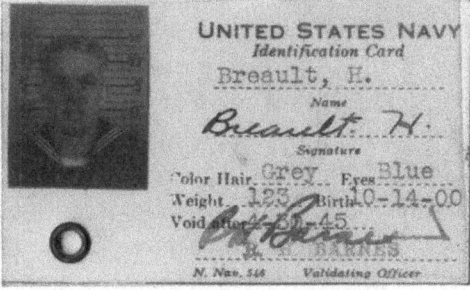
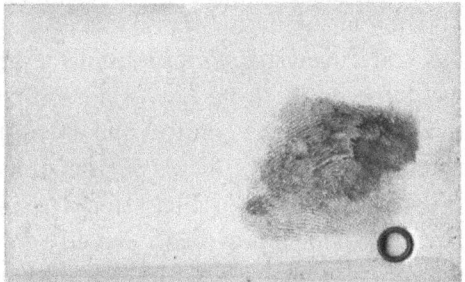

Portrait Shot of Henry Breault for Military Identification Card and Identification Card in Official Military Personnel File.

for sailors like himself, requested duty in Alaska, likely to be close to the brooding war in the Pacific. Breault's career was one any sailor could be proud of, though a comparison of his award photograph and a later photograph taken closer to his death reveal the toll a career of almost twenty years of sea service could have on an individual. Sailors like Breault were overworked and underpaid, but it was such individuals who took up the burden of manning senior positions and training the reservists in the Second World War.

## An Interwar Career

Henry Breault's career was forgotten by those who felt he served in a stable, non-threatening, peacetime environment, particularly when compared to sailors who served in the Second World War. Breault was a submariner serving on boats that were considered little better than coffins, the topic of DISSUBs being so recognizable it was used as a major plot point in contemporary films.[87] When the submarine was not trying to end his life, the areas Breault served in, particularly the Asiatic Fleet, were also detrimental to his health. Chinese and Japanese forces caused increasing conflict in the unstable region. Breault's career is an indication that the interwar period should be evaluated as an era with its own unique environment, rather than a break between the world wars.

Breault's career further indicates that naval service was respected well enough that at least one woman was willing to divorce her husband to marry him. Enlisted men had quite a heavy workload, but ample opportunities to request duties and ships they preferred. Breault himself was well-enough respected by his superiors that many of his special requests were granted, such as for duties in the Asiatic theatre, while his advancement to TM1 was the result of Captain Koch's willingness to eschew guidelines in his favour.[88] Despite this, the constant sea-duty took a toll on sailors in a way that would not be recognized until later; the improvement in sea/shore rotation in the present-day USN helps preserve sailors in a way that a manpower-strapped interwar USN could not afford.

Duty in submarine service faced evolution, becoming a distinct entity within the USN. Newspapers espoused the growing submarine fleet, predicting they would be on the front line of a Pacific war as early as 1935.[89] Recognition and the increasing size, comfort and amenities of the newer submarines ensured that career officers and enlisted personnel did not have to suffer the tropical heat that S-boat sailors had. As Fleet Boats became increasingly prominent, men such as Breault who had previously served on the older classes would anchor the service through the Second World War and provide the bedrock for an increasingly salient identity.

# Chapter 6

# 'A Pigboat Sailor's Lament': Danger and Discomfort

While Henry Breault did serve on other vessels, the majority of his seagoing career was spent aboard submarines or vessels attached to a submarine repair activity. His relationship to the technology that made him famous will be the primary subject of this chapter. How did Breault feel about the submarines he served on? Did the submarines define the sailors who served on them? The relationship between the technology, the people that utilized the technology and American culture's association of the two created new identities. This section will primarily focus on his experiences within the Navy as a submariner, looking at his time underway and in port during peacetime. There will be another chapter for his interactions within the area where he was serving, so this section will focus on characteristics unique to the life of a submariner, as Breault would have experienced them, looking at what his life looked like on a submarine.

## Submarine Recruitment

There were various reasons people were attracted to service aboard 'pigboats', as they were (sometimes) affectionately referred to. Breault was no stranger to submarines when he enlisted in the USN. An RNCVR submarine guarded the entrance into Halifax, and he likely spent much of his career preparing for a possible German submarine incursion into Halifax.[1] The extra pay was likely a factor in attracting personnel, submariners earning a dollar per dive, up to $20 per month.[2] Breault could have also been like Robert Hunt in 1940, who heard a submariner evangelize in Recruit Training Command about why the Submarine Service was the best duty in the Navy:

> 'When the workload was light, the chief would pull up a chair ... sit on it backward, and tell submarine stories. According to the chief, sub duty was the best in the Navy. You got the best food, extra pay, and as

long as you did your job nobody bothered you. No spit and polish and no saluting. You could even grow a beard if you wanted. The moral of each tale was the same, and invariably the chief ended his story with the line: "You boys should try to get yourself on a sub."'[3]

An experienced sailor who understood what 'spit and polish' truly meant, Breault would likely have listened to such stories with the same gusto as another sailor who volunteered for submarine service after serving aboard a surface ship, Joseph McGrievy:

'Whenever I worked [over the side] in undress blues I could see these submarines tied up alongside. The crew was sitting up topside in dungarees, having their ten o'clock soup and coffee. I told myself, "I think I'd like that."'[4]

Breault likely looked at the full package and assessed that the inconveniences, were well worth the incentives.

One consideration that may not have been explored is Breault's exposure to popular culture in the form of literature. There is no indication of whether or not Breault was an avid reader, but he was literate and at least one account indicates reading was a popular pastime underway.[5] The most famous submarine work was originally written in French, Jules Verne's *Twenty Thousand Leagues Under the Sea*, and Breault could have read it as a child in the original language.[6] Other contemporary authors such as Luis Serans and Victor Appleton also wrote young adult fiction about inventors who had numerous adventures that included submarines.[7] Victor G. Durham (a pseudonym) wrote the *Submarine Boys* juvenile fiction series, all focused on submarine antics, from 1909–20, marketed at young men corresponding to Breault's coming of age. Music of the period also portrayed submarines in the same whimsical light, with songs like 'Torpedo Jim' and 'In My Submarine'. The main figures of popular culture would portray submarines in a more peaceful, heroic setting than many post-Great War symbols would allow.[8] If this had been Breault's idea of a submarine before the Great War, his belief in a romantic version of life below the waves may have survived largely intact to see him volunteer when he got the chance.[9]

## The Pigboat

Submarines, before nuclear power, were dangerous, smelly and spartan. Breault served on three platforms – the O-Class, S-Class and V-Class submarines – all advancing in technical sophistication and increasing in size, though each had their own unique problems. Each experienced their particular teething problems with new technology and had their close calls with death. Submariners, though filled with pride in their vessels, were well aware of the danger. QM Francis J. Murphy, a submariner aboard the USS *Squalus* when it went on its fateful voyage that resulted in a DISSUB rescue, asked his mother: 'Pray for me, Ma.' Murphy was one of the survivors, and likely attributed his survival to his premonition and his parents' prayer.[10] Family members had to accept the risk as well, as Sherman L. Shirley's fiancée, Ruth Desantal, found out when her husband-to-be perished only three days before her scheduled marriage.[11] Similarly, Pearl Coffey, the wife of deceased sailor Robert Coffey, recalled she divorced her husband over his return to the submarine force, stating: 'I have always had a strange and terrible hunch that [something] like this would happen.'[12] The risks drove submariners to take pride in their ability to operate a vessel safely, and they trained rigorously to perfect the new art of submarining to avoid a tragic end.

By the end of his first enlistment, Breault knew first-hand about the danger, having experienced trouble on the *O-5* at least twice, culminating in his Medal of Honor action. Breault was rather laconic, stating: 'Some of the crew will never go in a submarine again. Fortunately it did not bother me at all.'[13] Despite knowing the danger, Breault emphatically desired to remain in the submarine force, as it constituted a significant portion of his identity.[14] A submariner was forced to adopt an existential attitude toward everyday life and to laugh at danger, as the *Squalus* survivors epitomized during their entombment. Allegedly, all survivors requested to continue serving in the submarine service despite their close calls with death. A newspaper clipping from the *LA Examiner* in the SFLM *Squalus* Archives contained a statement from the hero Lloyd B. Maness, who closed the watertight door to prevent flooding of the forward compartment:

> 'At such times as this, there is no time for sentiment. We are trained rigidly to act, so I gave no consideration of the fate of my [shipmates] any more than I would have expected similar [consideration] had I been in their place. It was not until the first impulsive action was over that I began to feel the awfulness of the men's situation in the after section. [Particularly] I thought of Sherman Shirley, my chum, whose best man I was to be next Sunday when he was to marry a Dover (N.H.) girl by the name of [Desantel] ... So when I had time to think I hoped Shirley was fortunate enough to be in a dry section, though hope was pretty remote. I don't know whether I mentioned anything about my thoughts. But I do remember

hearing Commander Naquin ordering no mention of the men in the flooded section ... I wish to make it clear that I acted according [to] the requirements of my duty in closing the bulkhead door. I have the utmost sorrow for my shipmates who died, but I would not hesitate to do the same thing if similar circumstances required and I want no credit for having carried out something that any other [member] of the crew would have done in my place.'[15]

Filipino submariner Mess Attendant Basilio Galvan confirmed: 'I was confident that everything was all right. That is kind of drilled into us, I guess.' Still, that likely made the decision no less easy for Maness.[16] The submarine forced friendship and intimacy, but could also rip those friends away in a cruel moment.

The USN submarine force saw numerous accidents and losses during Breault's tenure.[17] From Mary F. Romig's data, we can create a table to indicate how submarines were lost in non-combat circumstances. A total of 1,213 (the *H-1* was lost two months before Breault enlisted in 1920) submariners perished throughout Breault's career alone, from various nationalities. This number is likely underreported from outside the UK and US, as submarines from the USSR are not well represented, Germany conducted submarine experiments in secret, the only South American country represented is Brazil, and Japan has numerous gaps in existing information.

### Table 1: Submarine Disasters and Accidents During Henry Breault's Tenure in the USN (1920–1941)

| Date | Nationality | Submarine | Fatalities | Accident/Disaster |
|---|---|---|---|---|
| 12 Apr 1920 | USA | *H-1* | 4 | Grounding |
| 1 Jan 1921 | UK | *K-5* | 57 | Flooding |
| 26 Sep 1921 | USA | *R-6* | 2 | Flooding |
| 9 Nov 1921 | NL | *K-4* | 2 | Explosion |
| 23 Apr 1922 | UK | *H-42* | 28 | Collision |
| 1923? | JP | *No. 75* | 38 | Explosion |
| 21 Aug 1923 | JP | *No. 20* | 0 | Flooding |
| 29 Oct 1923 | USA | *O-5* | 3 | Collision |
| December 1923? | UK | *L-11* | 1 | Explosion |
| 10 Jan 1924 | UK | *L-24* | 41 | Collision |
| 19 Mar 1924 | JN | *RO-25* | 45 | Collision |

## 'A PIGBOAT SAILOR'S LAMENT'

| Date | Nationality | Submarine | Fatalities | Accident/Disaster |
|---|---|---|---|---|
| 1924? | JN | *No. 43* | 49 | Unknown |
| 8 Apr 1924 | JN | *RO-14* | 1 | Faulty Torpedo |
| 26 Aug 1925 | IT | *Sebastino Veniero* | 54 | Collision |
| 25 Sep 1925 | USA | *S-51* | 33 | Collision |
| 12 Nov 1925 | UK | *M-1* | 69 | Collision |
| 20 Apr 1926 | USA | *S-49* | 4 | Explosion |
| 9 Aug 1926 | UK | *H-29* | 40 | Collision |
| 17 Dec 1927 | USA | *S-49* | 40 | Collision |
| 6 May 1928 | IT | *F-14* | 31 | Collision |
| 12 Oct 1928 | FR | *Ondine* | 43 | Collision |
| 9 Jul 1929 | UK | *H-47* | 24 | Collision |
| 9 Jun 1931 | UK | *Poseidon* | 20 | Collision |
| 24 Oct 1931 | USSR | (Unidentified) | 50 | Unknown |
| 26 Jan 1932 | UK | *M-2* | 60 | Flooding |
| 25 Feb 1932 | UK | *H-42* | 26 | Unknown |
| 7 Jul 1932 | FR | *Prométhée* | 62 | Unknown |
| 25 Jul 1935 | USSR | *B-3* | 5 | Collision |
| 20 Nov 1936 | DE | *U-18* | 8 | Collision |
| 12 Dec 1936 | ES | (Unidentified) | 47 | Torpedo |
| 27 Jul 1938 | FR | *L'Espoire* | 1 | Explosion |
| 14 Nov 1938 | BR | *Tupy Ti* | 1 | Explosion |
| 12 Feb 1939 | JN | *I-63* | 81 | Collision |
| 23 May 1939 | USA | *Squalus* | 26 | Flooding |
| 1 Jun 1939 | UK | *Thetis* | 99 | Flooding |
| 15 Jun 1939 | FR | *Phenix* | 71 | Unknown |
| 6 Apr 1940 | NL | *O-11* | 3 | Collision |
| 20 Jun 1941 | USA | *O-9* | 33 | Flooding |
| 19 Jul 1941 | UK | *Umpire* | 15 | Collision |
| **Total** | | | **1,217** | |

An unquantifiable number of further close calls likely went unreported, even in UK and US sources, to avoid career turbulence for those involved. From this table, it becomes apparent that danger was always present, and a routine mission could quickly turn dangerous. The pressure of danger forced competency to become the ultimate goal of everyone aboard a submarine, represented by the submarine warfare insignia on their uniform which indicated they were qualified to perform anyone's watch station in an emergency. The ultimate goal of a submariner was to become qualified in submarines. As an aspiring submariner, a sailor was expected to become a living expert on the vessel they served on. They would then attend a board, which determined if the sailor had shown the requisite knowledge to be considered qualified in submarines and could wear the insignia associated with enlisted men or officers.

The qualification tradition was necessary; unlike on large surface ships that could have sailors do less work and afford more specialization, submarines had no room for waste. This included personnel, and aspiring submarines who couldn't cut it would be sent to a submarine tender. Ed Schab discussed how he dealt with the reality of submarines:

> 'When Schab actually came on board the *S-39*, he began to wonder why he'd requested sub duty. It was so small. It measured only 220 feet from stem to stern and carried just 42 men; machinery and torpedoes took up the most of the space. He pictured it all closed up and submerged, realizing that they'd be shoulder to shoulder, all breathing the same limited amount of stale air. He knew that the two things that got you off a submarine fastest were (a) to have an offensive body odor and (b) to request it; any man who asked to leave was released immediately, no questions asked, because he might endanger the rest of the personnel. But Ed was an old China hand now, and asking out would be called losing face. Was he scared? A little bit, but he hoped he wouldn't show it. It didn't occur to him that other people might feel the same way.'[18]

Schab's fears were well-founded, being reinforced by reality and popular culture. Submarine disasters happened frequently, even in peacetime; the *Squalus* disaster was recent news, and several films depicted a DISSUB as a primary plot point.[19] Smaller, though no less lethal to an individual, dangers permeated the submarine's atmosphere almost as poignantly as diesel fumes.

The reality of diving in a submarine became evident whenever a submarine went below the waves. Gaining a proficiency in diving a submarine was the most important daily duty for submariners in the interwar period, along with learning how to fight the ship. The way that Schab described his 'baptismal dive' confirms that all shared a similar level of trepidation, particularly on their first dive:

> 'The first thing he became aware of was that all the usual sounds – the snuffling, throat-clearing, slap-slap of sandals, occasional raucous laughter and four-letter words – had stopped completely. Quiet was necessary so that the diving officer's orders could be heard. Then a heavier vibration set in because the screws were turning at full speed, and Ed figured that his own quivers would be hidden by the quivering old pigboat. Captain Coe had come into the control room to stand by the periscope; the shoosh of air could be heard from the tanks being vented. Suddenly awash in perspiration, Ed felt a stream of it run down his forehead and land on his bare chest as they submerged, but to his astonishment his stomach stayed below his ribs. He had imagined it might be like the drop in a fast elevator, but in fact it was easy; he liked it, and he could feel the corners of his mouth turning up in a smile of relief.'[20]

Aside from the risk of flooding or collisions, there was always a distinct possibility of danger posed by a faulty torpedo, battery explosion, electrical shock or leak of chlorine gas – and other gases associated with stale air. All these and other potential dangers made submarines a unique challenge even during peacetime.

## Life Underway

If the submarine force deserved their reputation for lax regulations, it was only because the surface fleet was that draconian by comparison. The lack of room available on submarines to maintain decorum also contributed to the lax atmosphere. For those who have not read of the reputation of the USN surface fleet, James R. Reckner published the journal of Chief Water-Tender Frederick T. Wilson.[21] Wilson mused as his ship, the *New Orleans*, readied to pull into Manila in 1899:

> 'Had a most epicurean luncheon at noon ... The spuds were black as tar when broken open, and the coffee was no coffee at all as far as taste went. But the meat!! Salt horse of [Revolutionary] birth and the vintage of 1776 ... Every time I see this "Salt junk" I think of the sailors with plaited cues worked with tar and rope yard; sailors with a forelock to touch and pull for a "salaam" while they scraped with their bare feet upon the deck. Those "iron men and wooden ships" of the old navy, who knew not the meaning of fresh meat and "soft tack" aboard ship, who only received liberty at the end

of their cruise, and then got beastly drunk and remained so till they were shipped again. Yet we get their ration; the wooden walls are now steel walls; and [there] is required to man these steel walls 99% more brain than the old wooden ships required. Everything has changed, but the ration remains as it was in the last century.'[22]

Wilson served on a cruiser, one heavy in men with a distinct caste system that transcended rank at times, with engineering officers and sailors in engineering ratings being seen as lower than those employed in traditional ship positions.

Both in port and out to sea, a submariner followed an externally imposed routine. In port, the deck logs reported a morning muster when the crew members were not on leave, generally between 0700 and 0800 hours. Breault would likely be woken by a reveille call about two hours before, giving him time to eat breakfast and stow his belongings. They would then have a standard workday, which would end when the work was done, which could be well into the night. When he wasn't on duty, when Liberty was finally put down, Breault could take some time for himself, little though it may be. Breault probably lived, ate and stowed his belongings aboard the submarine tender due to the spartan conditions aboard the submarine, which did not have enough individual racks for each member of the crew.

Breault ultimately served on three classes of submarines, beginning with the *O-5*. All of the classes had their unique challenges, but the primary boats Breault served on were S-Boats, the main workhorse of the USN during his period of service in the submarine force. Two books, Stephen Jackson's *The Men* and Gugliotta's *Pigboat 39*, aptly describe what Breault faced.[23] S-Boats didn't have air conditioning or the ability to make fresh water while underway, leading to miserably humid and hot conditions which affected personnel and encouraged insects and rats to become 'stowaways'.[24] Fresh water, which was too precious and scarce to be wasted, would be strictly rationed, even for hygiene purposes. Sailors took infrequent showers with some of the fresh water or even torpedo fuel. Sailors would first show up and be assigned as mess cooks to assist the cook, learn the ship and meet the crew.[25]

Breault's quality of life underway was poor. He was likely stressed, had an irregular sleep schedule and depending on the sea state, may or may not have had a hot meal. Showers, when a boat even had them, were at a premium due to limited supplies of water. To clean themselves on the *O-5*, sailors used a bucket of seawater and a washcloth or some alcohol from the torpedo fuel. The S-Boats, designed for longer voyages, did have one salt-water shower located topside, aft of the sail. Bobette Gugliotta described how her husband, Guy, was taught to take showers and keep his clothes clean when laundry services from the submarine tender were unavailable:

> 'Larry Bernard cued newcomer Gugliotta into the routine. Handing him a bucket and saltwater soap, he said "Soak the clothes overnight in the bucket. In the morning I'll demonstrate the cleaning method." Came the dawn and Guy was ready for a shower on deck. Since fresh water could never be used causally on the primitive little submarine, except in port, where more was readily available, sea water was it. The only shower the boat boasted, on the after end of the superstructure, was used by both officers and men. But even the salty stuff that sprayed from it, and the saltwater soap that stripped off skin along with dirt, felt good after torrid temperatures. "Where's your bucket?" Bernard called. Guy held it up. "Okay, spread your gear out beneath the shower." Guy did. "Now turn on the shower, scrub yourself, and tramp hard on the clothes while you're doing it. Presto, clean clothes." It was a variation on the ancient method, still used in primitive spots around the globe, where women beat clothing on rocks.'[26]

A sailor underway was smelly, testy and suffered from deprivation that would only grow worse as the time at sea stretched longer. According to Gugliotta, the average weight loss of a sailor was 15lb per patrol due to the poor conditions.[27]

Between drilling, diving, watch duty, cleaning and numerous other maintenance tasks, there was not much free time. Still, for those rare moments when they had spare time between the activities, there were distractions for sailors while underway. Writing letters to family or sweethearts was a good usage of this time, though they couldn't send them back until they returned to port. Poker, cribbage and other card games were also popular, while chess was played by many too. At least some sailors did their best to continue a physical regime to maintain their strength. Some even attempted to fantasize they were doing something else other than the uncomfortable tedium they were currently experiencing. Submariners were allowed topside or onto the bridge when weather permitted during peacetime. Gugliotta wrote that reading was a particularly popular diversion. Unsurprisingly for submariners today, perhaps the most popular pastime was to mess around with other crewmates, generally through pranks or other sarcastic, mean-spirited exchanges. Deprived of many creature comforts, the best thing any submariner could do was to catch as much sleep as possible.[28]

An advertised benefit of submarine duty was the quality of food, though this did not always extend to the boats on which Breault served. The O-boat and

S-boats Breault served on had little space to prepare and cook food, and the crew would eat their subsistence meals from their racks or while standing.[29] As one S-boat responder to the *Submarine Cuisine* book noted:

> 'There was never enough fresh water on the S boats for normal usage. The crew's use of fresh water was limited to drinking-water and food preparation. The only exception to the rule was that the ship's cook was allowed to "wash up" before going to work in the galley. For this purpose he was rationed seven cups of water in a bucket. The wash-up consisted of washing the face, neck, arms and hands using socks or skivvies as a rag. Next, the same water was used for the trunk, legs, and feet. Last came the privates, then the socks and skivvies themselves were washed. It is said that some cooks then added the used water to the coffee urn after the sock and skivvies had been squeezed into the bucket.'[30]

The less than desirable addition to the coffee urn aside, the cook was likely the cleanest person aboard. When seas were too rough, which was likely often, cooks would serve simple meals such as hot dogs, beans, cold cuts, chilli, soups in a cup and saltines (cracker biscuits).[31]

Gugliotta recorded the cook aboard the *S-39*, Walter L. 'Rocky' Schoenrock, was a master chef while in port. He kept soup ready for the crew at all times in case they grew hungry.[32] Schoenrock had the tendency to be temperamental and sentimental, but he took great pride in his culinary creations, genuinely caring for the crew of the *S-39*, knowing their preferences on menu items.[33] One of the individuals interviewed by Jackson, Robert Burr, was also a cook on an S-boat. While Jackson was surprisingly mute on the subject of food, he did recall that powdered sugar was the most important ingredient to the crew and that there was limited space to store food:

> 'Well you didn't have no place to put anything. On them old boats, all we had at that time was a commercial refrigerator. We barely could carry; when the 24 boat went back to the States, we barely could have enough fresh stuff to get to Panama from San Diego.'[34]

A sample of life on the *V-2*, where more space was available, can be observed in the deck logs. On 16 July 1929, the ship took stock of its received victuals:

- 150lb of bread
- 8 gallons of milk

## 'A PIGBOAT SAILOR'S LAMENT'

- 53lb of calves' liver
- 58lb of celery
- 83lb of lettuce
- 66lb of tomatoes
- 164lb of watermelon
- 106lb of onion[35]

LCDR L.D. McCormick must have had a standing order to record all of the food stores that were received, as none of the other boats Breault served on seem to have had this requirement. McCormick was also the CO who would send Breault to a SCM, so it was possible he was particularly fastidious in his observation of naval regulations. Another list can be found for 7 August 1929, when the *V-2* received thee following:

- 64lb of bread
- 480lb of potatoes
- 83lb of lettuce
- 70lb of cabbage
- 45lb of Squash
- 54lb of tomatoes
- 150lb of oranges
- 140lb of watermelon
- 20lb of apples[36]

An emphasis on fresh fruit delivery indicates how quickly food needed to be replenished while underway. Overall, a well-balanced meal could be provided on the *V-2*, a submarine that finally had enough space to take care of its own crew. The V-boats and successive improvements in space came at a cost, for as the space grew, the boundaries of rank began to creep into the everyday life of the submarine force. Fleet boats designs, while still famous for lax regulations, would see increasing space allowed for 'officer country'.

Despite Breault's fondness for the service, his time was filled with hardship and deprivation, that fact ensured pride in the status of being a submariner. Only the toughest sailors could be submariners, and their technical experience in an increasingly technical Navy afforded them a degree of respect. As officers rarely remained in the submarine force until V- and Fleet-boats were a larger portion of the submarine force, the service depended heavily upon its enlisted core to ensure safe operations aboard a submarine. A career submariner who hadn't been overworked or forced to transfer for medical reasons was one of the most valuable people aboard a submarine, attaining a status unachievable in the surface fleet. They could even politely contradict an officer, should they feel it necessary to prevent a life-threatening situation. A junior officer, even one not qualified in submarines, could rely on the enlisted cadre to perform the most dangerous of evolutions, such as getting the ship underway before a typhoon or mooring unassisted, two of the examples highlighted in Gugliotta's *Pigboat 39*.[37]

Despite the prospect of respect and informality, many in the USN shook their heads in amazement that submariners like Breault would be willing to go underway on a ship so spartan as an S-boat. As Gugliotta described it, even the crews of more advanced submarines pitied them:

> 'S-boat personnel found out early that most fleet-boat sailors pitied them, but true Asiatic pigboat sailors had all the feisty pride of a cadre of hard-living, tough professionals who, by the very fact that they'd been able to survive the S-boat existence, considered themselves superior.'[38]

There is no doubt in my mind that Breault was incredibly proud of his time on submarines, particularly as a pigboat sailor in the Asiatic Theatre, and that pride sustained him even as his body began to fail him.

## The Submarine Tender

While in port, Breault would likely get the opportunity for a fresh water shower, fresh food and fresh air. He also probably had a barracks room or a spot in berthing onboard the submarine tender the ship was moored to, where he could get more room and a longer shower than any submariner on patrol could hope for. The submarine tender was designed as a mothership concept, which was not popular with naval bureaucracy, but until they devoted enough time for infrastructure to support the submariners in far-off bases, they were forced to stomach the high expenses associated with the mobile shipyards. One of the tenders, the USS *Canopus*, is described in detail in *Pigboat 39*:

> 'Acquired by the U.S. Navy in 1921, *Canopus* had originally been a merchant ship of the Grace line named *Santa Leonora*. She had machine shops and forges, carried enlisted men's uniforms and small stores of all kinds, and boasted messes for officers and men, movie facilities, barbers, medical treatment, and postal services. *Canopus* had real showers, unlimited ice cream, and cold drinking

water. She was a floating town. After a long stretch on an old S-boat … to go aboard *Canopus* could be heaven. To serve aboard her, whatever work you did, had its compensations, since she hardly ever got underway – everyone joked about having to dredge out the coffee grounds under her keel in order to move her. What's more, it was possible to get liberty almost every night, which ensured longevity with a Manila girlfriend if you had energy and money enough to afford one.'[39]

Primarily drawn from the surface fleet and former submariners, the rotation of personnel to tenders could be considered a sort of early sea-shore rotation. In the interwar Navy – where manpower was always lacking – they did not have the ability to send sailors for a proper shore rotation. For submariners, tenders were often easier duty, but they carried within their hulls the trappings of the surface Navy. One of the *S-39* sailors, Tom Parks, was transferred to the *Pigeon* once he recovered from a hand injury sustained in a fight. However, he found there was a difference between a tender and a sub when he went AWOL to spend the weekend with his brother:

'Sunday night, as soon as he set foot on the *Canopus*, a heavy hand was placed on his shoulder by the master-at-arms. He was under arrest, spent the rest of the night in the brig, and after quarters in the morning was led out on deck for a captain's mast. The informality and homey touches of an S-boat were lacking here – no sloppy shorts, bare chests, and sandals. The drizzly, gray light of the rainy season showed a grim-faced Commander Earl Sackett, his leading petty officer, a division officer, and the master-at-arms who had put Tom in the brig. With all speed Tom was set for a summary court martial. He began to realize that his impulsive act could have serious results.'[40]

Parks was absolved due to timely circumstances, but disciplinary infractions that would have been settled quietly on the boat were no longer dealt with so leniently on a tender. This helps explain why Breault left after short periods of time when he was rotated to the *Holland* and the *Canopus*. Despite working closely with the submarine force, the submarine tender was a surface ship, a repair activity that looked suspiciously like the real Navy, one that bothered itself too much in regulation and polish. For submariners who revelled in the lax Asiatic submarine force, they would not find similar attitudes elsewhere. When space returned and danger receded, it did not matter the excellence of the enlisted submariner: he was still an enlisted man when the ship moored to the pier. Life on a tender was an attempt by the USN to give submariners a break, but it only served to remind many that the submarine force, as difficult as it could be, was still better than the alternative. While a submarine was, to some extent, an experiment in naval democracy, the tender was a return to the old status quo seen by Wilson in his tours. Tenders had a poor reputation overall, but the rotation was a sincere attempt by the USN to recycle its sailors to allow for breaks after experiencing the hardship of time underway on an early pigboat.

The tenders also offered a recruitment avenue for sailors to learn about submarines. Young sailors dissatisfied with their current place could volunteer for submarine duty and be given a quick out. They could join the submarine force, be given more responsibility and immediately contribute to a warship. Those sailors who went would replace the veteran submariners who needed a break. When they had their fill of surface navy 'rubbish', they would ask to be transferred back to submarines. The method of transferring labour was a feedback loop, one that guaranteed a steady pool of new recruits and submariners who could provide the expertise to fix the boats while they recuperated.

## Bubblehead Brotherhood

A submariner, particularly one serving in the Asiatic fleet, would have ample opportunity to mingle with submarines from other nations' navies. Many who did so found kindred spirits, such as Tom Parks did in Sorebaja on Java. Parks described the Dutch sailors as warm and friendly, which confirmed to him that 'special bonds exist between all seafaring men of all nationalities, especially submariners'.[41] In much grimmer circumstances, on 23 June 1931, the crew of the *S-40* presented to the British Consul $350 in gold for the widows and relatives of HMS *Poseidon*, lost near Weihaiwei while on patrol in the China Station.[42] The crew also sent a letter explaining that the gift was 'an expression of [kinship] for those who gave all in the submarine service, with the wish that it may help you to carry on'.[43]

It is unsurprising that submariners who routinely faced danger would find comfort in fellow submariners of other nationalities. They would share a bond that could transcend the bonds of nationality shared by men in the same force, should the correct circumstances be present. It also explains why sailors from other navies, such as Breault and Stanley Mandekic, were able to assimilate rapidly into American submarine culture: because their ethnicity didn't matter. I don't wish to exaggerate this sentiment, as African-American and Filipino sailors were not always treated so graciously, but the general focus was on competence rather than race.[44] So long as they were competent submariners, they were deserving of their spots on a submarine. The *esprit de corps* speaks volumes as to how a ship or technology could become more than a simple tool for projecting seapower; it also created new subcultures that had profound identity implications for those involved. Likely, it was this distinction of danger that attracted aspiring submariners and kept them long after a healthy dose of reality set in.

Breault was both a sailor and a submariner, and his actions indicate that even when he was disqualified from submarines, he still yearned for his younger days as a member of the submarine force. When a submarine disaster occurred, it was (and still is) felt by the submarine community, a reminder that they continued to operate in danger. No matter how long a submariner remained away, they would always find a willing friend in a fellow submariner.

# Chapter 7

# Family, Friends and Forced Alienation

This chapter will attempt to explore the relationship Breault had with his father, mother, stepmother, sisters and potential friends. There are scarce mentions of Breault's relationship to friends and family in his OMPF, but there are several hints that his connection with his family was potentially tumultuous. Unfortunately, there were even fewer instances suggesting that he had any friendships. It is likely Breault's later teenage years and early twenties were spent estranged from his family, for unknown reasons; those reasons could have ranged from abuse to a simple lack of interest in keeping in touch with his family. The letters Breault's family wrote to the Bureau of Navigation asked for a mailing address, implying it was a frequent occurrence for him to neglect to mention his whereabouts to his family, meaning the disinterested Breault thesis was probably closer to what occurred.

There are hardly any indications that Breault made any friends, with no one mentioned, but one newspaper recorded that Lawrence Brown's praise of Breault was echoed by the crew of the *O-5*.[1] The life of a sailor was filled with fast friendships, most of which persevered, but others melted away once the common association of life underway ended. There is circumstantial evidence that Breault was at least a respected sailor aboard the vessels on which he served, such as his temporary appointment as acting COB of the *S-36*, but there are no known instances in his OMPF of a sailor writing to inquire how to reach Breault.[2] Either old shipmates did not need to write to get in contact, never lost Breault's contact information or simply preferred not to keep up with him. This may not be entirely due to the interactions between Breault and his friends, but to the taxing nature of years of service at sea.

It can be assumed that Breault was well-liked in his first enlistment, and likely in successive enlistments, as he surely would not have been as enthusiastic to return to sea if he hadn't been. Being an unpopular member aboard any ship is an unpleasant experience, as displayed in the reaction of the *S-39* crew to Les Dean, a former Fleet Boat sailor who was forced to take refuge aboard the *S-39* after the bombing of Manila but was treated badly by his new shipmates.[3]

## FAMILY, FRIENDS AND FORCED ALIENATION

Despite the lack of information, attempting to examine Breault's relationship to those important to him could reveal insight into the level of potential alienation an American sailor could have experienced. Unfortunately, there are few letters included in his OMPF, most written to the Bureau of Navigation after communication dropped off. The most frequent inquirers were members of his family, particularly his father. The estrangement thesis comes to mind, but why would this have been so? Did Breault not keep his family informed due to a lack of time? Or did Breault intentionally ignore his family due to lack of interest in maintaining a relationship, for reasons unknown? The insight that can be gained could also be compared to local historians who have personal documents on sailors' relationship to their families, but will be limited in analysis.

Similarly, Breault's lack of known friendships does not indicate he had few friends, rather that his friends knew how to keep in contact with him and did not need to reach out to the Bureau if they needed to reconnect. The submarine force on the West Coast was small, and when sailors transferred off the pigboats, it was often to the tender that headed the submarine squadron. It was much easier for 'lifers' like Breault to keep in contact with other 'lifers', but there is no evidence that he sought to remain in contact with sailors who were discharged from the service and returned to their hometowns. Was this also self-imposed? The insular nature of sailors meant those who were outside of the circle, even those who had previously served, can be reasonably excluded from the active-duty circle. But what insight can be gained from Breault's relationship with his family and friends?

## Family

A shift in Breault's relationship to his family can be traced to his service in the RNCVR. When he enlisted, the address he gave was his father's, but when he was discharged, he elected to be sent to Putnam rather than return to his immediate family's household.[4] After tasting independence, he likely wished to retain it, but this does not fully explain the estrangement. This estrangement continued until 1923, as indicated by his enlistment paperwork listing L.R.B. Hale as his next of kin rather than one of his family members.[5] The Bureau of Navigation had the duty to inform family members during the *O-5* disaster of the status of personnel involved, and sent out reports for newspapers to reprint the names and addresses of those involved. In the immediate aftermath of the *O-5* collision, letters were also sent to Hale updating her on Breault's status (missing, then safe, hospitalized and returned to duty), issued shortly after the Bureau received the update themselves.[6]

Due to the extensive coverage in the newspapers, letters from his father and sisters trickled in, inquiring about his status, but so too did those from other persons who believed Breault was a lost relative. Josephine Breault of Detroit, Michigan, sent a telegram to the Bureau of Navigation asking if it was possible the Henry Breault rescued from the *O-5* was her son, Leo Breault, who had left home five years ago.[7] A.M. Brady of Belle Harbor, New York, sent a telegram requesting information about Breault, believing Breault was potentially a relative.[8] An A.A. Brault sent a handwritten letter asking if he was her husband, who had enlisted out of Providence, Rhode Island.[9] The Bureau of Navigation replied to all the letters and telegrams, including to two other requests that were not put in his file, from Marie E. Nathan of Providence, RI, and Louis A. Breault of Los Angles, California.[10] These latter requests highlight that the USN was perceived as a place of possible refuge for estranged family members, which supports the estrangement thesis.

Henry's father, Joseph J. Breault, identified as J.J. Breault of White Plains, NY, sent a telegram at 1007 (likely Eastern Standard Time) on 1 November 1923 to the Secretary of the Navy, which was then forwarded to the Bureau of Navigation. It read succinctly: 'Newspaper reports so conflicting please wire whether Henry Breault on Submarine O 5 reported sunk canal zone is safe and if injured what extent[?]'[11] The Bureau of Navigation received the message at 1022 the same day and sent a follow-up telegram at 1612 to the anxious Joseph, informing him that Henry Breault was among the three sailors rescued and that there was 'No report of any injury sustained by him in accident.'[12] Rapid updates did not quite match the speed of a cellular phone, but it was still a remarkable turnaround time, considering the distance from all three points of contact. The Bureau would have to be informed by authorities in Panama, then relay that information to White Plains shortly after. Within a span of six hours, a relative like J.J. Breault would have been able to make an enquiry and have a response in an emergency situation. This led to his reunion with his family shortly after receiving his award, between 13 and 15 March, as reported by the *New York Evening Post*.[13]

Within the *Daily Argus*, a sentiment of J.J. Breault can be found describing his son:

> 'The elder Breault said today his son felt the call of the sea when sixteen years old and shipped on a sailing vessel. He has been [seafaring] ever since. A year ago the O-5, according to Breault, was in difficulty off St. Thomas, Virgin Islands, and Henry then proved himself a hero by saving several shipmates.'[14]

Considering the possible lack of correspondence, how would J.J. Breault have known about this circumstance? It is here that I must introduce a difficult possibility, that the reason Breault moved away and at times avoided his family was that they were seeking to profit from his newfound fame. If Breault did not want to be the hero, but his family wanted him to be the hero and increase their lot by association, then Breault likely rebelled against that by avoiding them.

Analyzing the information his father provided to the newspaper raises several questions, such as how would J.J. have known about the *O-5* when he probably hadn't been in correspondence with his son? This indicates potential aggrandizement on his part to elevate the image of Breault as more than a one-time hero. Further, we know Breault reported to the *Niobe* when he was 16, not some sailing vessel, assuming he meant that literally as there were still sailing vessels underway in the period. There are grains of truth to make the statement more than likely true, but there is enough circumstantial evidence to force me to question whether their relationship was more tumultuous than previously considered.

Even after Breault's reunion with his family, they had difficulty staying in contact with him shortly afterwards, as indicated by Mary Breault's letter to the Bureau of Navigation on 25 September 1924.[15] Instead of immediately setting out to go back home, he indicated that he was visiting L.R.B. Hale, despite having previously stated that he was returning to White Plains. Regardless of his activities away from his family, his relationship appeared to be reconciled after his award: he updated his next of kin to be his father during his 22 November 1924 reenlistment, and all subsequent enlistment paperwork when he was not married would have his father or sisters as next of kin.[16] Breault's retention of them in this crucial field supports the disinterested Breault thesis; that Breault simply neglected to update his family when a duty station changed and there was no longer any level of estrangement. Considering Breault's father was likely a major inspiration for Breault's service, the frequent requests for his address could have been due to a simple combination of losing his address and him forgetting to keep them updated.

Assuming the letters indicate those that cared most, it can be discerned that Breault appeared to have been closest to his sister, Diana Breault.[17] Beatrice Breault also wrote, towards the end of his career, while Estelle did not appear to write at all.[18] Alternatively, it could indicate that Joseph and Mary never lost his letters or his mailing address, as they did not appear to write after Breault's second enlistment. As Beatrice and Estelle did not leave the Breault household until after Henry's death on 5 December 1941, they likely had access to his address and didn't need to write to the Bureau, while Diana's multiple moves could explain the requests for an address: as she moved, she may have lost his correspondence address. The most important evidence is Diana's marriage to Everett, as she likely met her husband, who was a submariner stationed in the China Station at the same time as Breault, through her older brother, therefore it is unlikely they would have met without correspondence and sporadic reunions.

Breault did have extended family: at least one branch is known through remembrances of Fred St Onge in the *Putnam Observer*.[19] St Onge had fond memories, which were shared at a remembrance in Breault's honor. Most remember the deceased fondly and the event was in Breault's honor, so the likelihood of these sentiments being accurate but skewed positively should be considered. The St Onge family welcomed him back from the RNCVR, an arrangement that had probably been coordinated prior to his discharge. None of these members of extended family needed to contact the Bureau of Navigation for his whereabouts, implying they kept the address up to date or simply had no need to contact him. This is not a detriment to their character, for they were likely depending upon Joseph and Mary to keep them informed, rather than taking the primary duty themselves.

It is assessed that Breault was probably closer to his family than official correspondence has portrayed, but it proves difficult to find evidence in the surviving documentation in his OMPF. Breault would not always be able to keep up with his family, particularly after his time in the Asiatic Theatre, but this seemed to have been as much a self-inflicted isolation as much as a geographically enforced one. Breault's relationship with his family is not covered well by surviving documentation, though the correspondence between father and son could be a potential treasure trove of information if the two spoke freely to one another. At any rate, Breault had the convenient excuse of naval duty to hide behind when avoiding his family, and some of the alienation was self-imposed as he simultaneously actively sought duties that were away from his family, like the Asiatic Fleet submarines. This may indicate an adventurous sailor or one weary of familial bonds; the circumstances are elusive, but sailors from all walks of life have experienced similar distance from their loved ones.

## Friends

There are even fewer indications that Breault had friends aboard the ships he served on, but there are some hints. A submarine has a small crew that implicitly depends upon one another in the most dangerous maritime working environment, so they are bound to be close-knit. This section will seek to uncover Breault's male friends within the USN, as there is little evidence he had friends outside of the USN. The lack of official correspondence that mentions Breault's friendship explicitly is not a unique problem when studying sailors through a corpus of official documentation. Breault's time in the USN was spent in submarines, submarine tenders or destroyers; submarines in particular were noted for a casual, friendly atmosphere. There are only a few instances that suggest Breault was well liked and accepted. There is little evidence to suggest he had many friends outside of his family from his life prior to the service, with L.R.B. Hale and Catherine O'Rourke evaluated primarily in the next chapter. This section will focus on his potential friendships aboard the ships on which he served and will emphasize newspaper and circumstantial evidence, rather than his OMPF.

Sailors are known to be social creatures, highly valuing amicable friendships with their shipmates. While Breault professed to be teetotal, it is certainly possible that he lied or drank in purely social settings, especially if he sought to join his shipmates during their time in port. At the time, popular culture in the United States highly valued friendships and the virtue of having a friend who was near and dear. Movies such as *Navy Blues*, *Born to Dance* and *Submarine D-1* displayed both officers and enlisted sailors sharing the bond of friendship through trials of shipboard life persevering ashore. In *Men Without Women*, drunken sailors carouse in Shanghai with fellow seamen, being most truthful in the level of debauchery, though exaggerating the alcoholic consumption of one character in the process.[20] *Born to Dance* has a scene that takes place in the Lonely Hearts Club, with a milkshake bar standing in for a nightclub or bar and the sailor Tracy sucking down six ice-cream drinks in a display that shocks his shipmates. The theme is clear throughout, sailors were seen first as part of the Liberty party, then as individuals wearing uniforms ashore.

Despite their portrayal, the romanticized, long-term, lifelong friendships that persist after a change in duty station, seen in films like *Submarine D-1* and books such as Ellsberg's *Pigboats*, were becoming increasingly rare in the USN. Shipmates were always welcome if reunited, but it was simply more difficult to keep up with old shipmates as duty stations changed homeports or those who were discharged headed back to their home states, their duty to the nation fulfilled. Always a transient profession, naval sailors were recruited from a far wider net that was no longer confined to coastal communities. Considering how frequently Breault's family lost contact with him, I have no doubt that old shipmates likely had similar issues, if they even had time to write a letter to keep up. Sadly, the more accurate depiction would be that of *The Last Detail*, which ends with all three sailors going their separate ways once their common association ended.[21] There are no shared goodbyes, each ending their journey as lonely as when they began. While immensely beneficial to the Navy, communities that once hosted sailor-towns became far more transient as the sailors no longer needed to stay for employment. Although immensely beneficial to recruitment, it broke the traditional methods of recruiting near coastal towns and the considerable influence coastal communities once had on naval affairs. It was no longer unusual to see sailors in the USN from states with no connection to the oceans, such as Ohio or Illinois, represented by Everett Drennan and Thomas Metzler seen in the following sample.

## The Crew of the *O-5*

The crew of the *O-5* was likely close to Breault; close enough that he was willing to risk his life to rescue anyone trapped below decks, unaware of the severity of the collision. Considering it was a split-second decision, Breault likely would have performed his act of heroism for any shipmate. Yet if we evaluate the potential that one of the other four sailors who were initially missing was good friends with him, what does that tell us about Breault? Assuming he knew his other friends would be rescued by the tugboat and that he potentially did a mental count of who was missing, then the conclusion that one of his friends was missing could have spurred him to action. This is a stretch, but it acknowledges the possibility they were friends and addresses the fact they certainly knew each other, serving aboard such a small vessel.

EMC Lawrence Brown, stuck with him on the ocean floor, could not have been more effusive in his praise of Breault. Brown was a Chief with First World War experience; a kinship of Great War service could have underpinned the pair's friendship. Brown was from Tyngsboro, Massachusetts, a short distance from Breault's hometown of Putnam, Connecticut.[22] As a fellow New Englander, it is likely they bonded over shared memories of an infamous climate. During my experience in the USN, there was a strong divide between chief petty officers (E7 and above) and the junior sailors (E6 and below), but in the interwar period, the divide did not appear to be as impenetrable. Examples in *Men Without Women*, *Born to Dance* and *Submarine D-1* portray chief petty officers who party with junior sailors, with at least *Born to Dance* having a naval attaché who exercised considerable influence over the film's accuracy.[23] From an officer's perspective, it was not unusual to see chiefs and junior enlisted men acting in a friendly manner, particularly submariners. It is surprising that Breault did not appear to keep in close contact with Brown, though according to Julius Grigore, the two presented Sheppard Shreaves' Gold Lifesaving Medal and a gold Waltham watch.[24]

## FAMILY, FRIENDS AND FORCED ALIENATION

Another chief who was initially missing was Charles R. Butler, from New Haven, Connecticut. Butler, who was originally trapped for eight minutes, shot up to the surface in an air bubble, so it is certainly possible that Breault noticed Butler was not topside and that this played into his decision-making.[25] This almost unbelievable story foreshadows potential methods to surface from a disabled submarine, but it was observed by sailors watching from the *Abangarez*.[26] As a fellow Nutmegger,[27] Butler was most likely friendly to Breault for the same reasons Brown would have been. However, Breault and Butler do not appear to have kept in touch or served together again.

Thomas Theodore Metzler was a First Class Fireman from Philadelphia, Pennsylvania. He was born on 28 July 1900, meaning he was 23 at the time of the collision, which was misreported by local newspapers. Metzler was also a veteran of the Great War, but not as a sailor; he served in the 26th Division of the US Army, but was likely demobilized, like much of the Army, in 1919.[28] Metzler was married and had a young son, named George, and had been a mechanic before being laid off from his previous work. One could imagine a conversation between Metzler and Breault about their attempts at reintegrating after their service. Breault and Metzler likely didn't associate due to a shared background, as while Breault did spend time in urban areas, he seems to have preferred smaller towns like Putnam and Marysville. Metzler died, leaving his wife and child in Philadelphia, but a photograph shows several sailors allegedly from the *O-5* in a burial detail for either Metzler or Fred Collins Smith.[29] The shortest sailor with his back turned to the camera could have been Breault, remembering these two shipmates.

Two sailors about whom we have much less information are Clyde Edward Hughes and Fred Collins Smith. Hughes was an MM1 from Manito, Illinois, and Smith a Mess Attendant, first class, from Barbados, who resided primarily in Cristobal in the Panama Canal Zone. Hughes likely got along well with Breault as a career sailor, but even Illinois newspapers only had the barest of information, indicating he had few connections ashore. Smith may have presented a unique experience for Breault during his time in the USN: service in an integrated command. Black or African-American sailors were commonly seen as Mess Attendants or cooks in the USN, along with Filipino or Polynesian sailors.[30] According to the website Eternal Patrol, Smith was born in 1886, making him one of the elder statesmen aboard, a potential mentor for the younger sailors.[31] I will withhold praise for Breault for a potential friendship with Smith, but exploring the nature of integration within the submarine fleet could illuminate how sailors reacted to non-white shipmates in a segregated society.

Harrison Avery's relationship to Breault was likely amicable before the award, and paternal afterwards. It may have crossed into friendship at times, but the barrier between officer and enlisted man was arguably stronger in the interwar period, particularly as it was reinforced by film and literature. A major theme in Ellsberg's *Pigboats* is the main character's quest to return to an officer's rank, and the drive of the male protagonists to become an officer are major plot points in *Navy Blues* and *Sweetheart of the Navy*. Avery advocated for Breault's opportunity to take the examination for chief warrant officer, even when he was no longer under his command.[32] Perhaps they had conversations about his future that resembled those between Eddie Harris and Commander Lodge in *Sweetheart of the Navy*.[33] Avery likely saw himself as a mentor to Breault, seeking to have him join the ranks of the officers for his meritorious service.

While the crew of the *O-5* offer the best record we have of Breault's interactions with his shipmates, the evidence is still scarce, with suppositions our primary method of looking at the interactions of sailors and their shipmates. Examples in film indicate Breault was likely part of circles, particularly as a member of the 'torpedo gang' represented in Ellsberg's *Pigboats*.[34] Breault professed to be teetotal, but he also enlisted during Prohibition, where an admission of drinking alcohol was an admission to committing a crime. Regardless, there were circles for drinking and nondrinking sailors, neither possibility of which precluded him from access to friends within the crew.

## Everett Dewey Drennan

Previously unknown, Everett Dewey Drennan offers another example of heroism in Breault's life. Drennan was a QM from Ohio who had served previously during the First World War, being recalled to active duty where he finished out his contract.[35] He served four years in China, then spent time in San Diego and three years in Honolulu, Hawaii.[36] Drennan died on 22 October 1932 from burns he received while attempting to rescue his neighbour's two-year-old daughter, 'Little Joy Poole', from a burning building.[37] He was reported by *The Portsmouth Times* of Scioto, Ohio, to have been 38 at the time of his death, but the 1930 Census records that he was born the same year as Breault, making him 32. Drennan is only known due to his marriage to Diana Breault, which occurred in 1925, when he was 25 and she was 22.[38] Due to the timing and lack of likely naval contacts Diana had, it is assumed that Drennan was potentially a shipmate of Breault's, close enough that he was willing to introduce him to his family in White Plains. Drennan and Breault may have met during Breault's first enlistment, suggesting he was like part of the submarine squadron in some capacity or even a shipmate aboard the USS *O-5*. When he died, he was part of the crew of the USS *Argonaut*, a V-Class submarine, whose crew later buried him at sea in accordance with his final wishes.[39]

## FAMILY, FRIENDS AND FORCED ALIENATION

The marriage of a seaman's sister to a shipmate was not unusual, considering the insular circle of a sailor. Sailors had little professional contact with women, being transients in many of the communities they visited, meaning any contact was treated with suspicion or ended when the sailors went back underway. Sailors were not always welcomed with open arms, particularly by middle-class women, as portrayed in *Navy Blues*, thereby limiting their chances to single women who frequented known sailor watering holes and gathering points within sailor-towns. When they did meet women, some were open to a relationship, but Dorothy Reynolds – the eventual wife of Ed Schab from *Pigboat 39* – explains that she and her friends were partial to flirting with sailors in 1939 because they didn't have cars; dating could thus move in a more organic fashion, without any pressure that an invitation to a boy's car could entail.[40] Cars were pivotal to dating, as they offered privacy, which explains why the first activity of the group of sailors in *Navy Blues* was to rent a car.[41] It is possible that through his friendship with Breault, Drennan met the Breault family; an initial attraction was sparked between Diana and Drennan that became marriage, allowing him to circumvent the public courtship ritual through personal connection.

What kind of friendship did Breault and Drennan have? They were close enough that Breault likely introduced his family while in New York. Drennan and Breault may have resembled most friendships Breault had, one that was characterized by their shared hardships as submariners. They likely remained close friends due to familial bonds, though they still may have had issues communicating between Hawaii and the Asiatic Theatre. Unfortunately, the actual connection between Breault and Drennan is ultimately unknown, due to a lack of personal documents, and these points are pure speculation.

A comparison of Drennan and Breault's stories of heroism allow for some stark contrasts. Drennan tried save an innocent child from a burning house, succumbing to his wounds later after the failed attempt. Drennan fits the mould of a tragic hero, one whose death enhances the associated tragedy at great cost to the Navy. His story ended but provided great honour to his shipmates and family, both of whom could look back on him as a good man. While they missed him, Diana and their son, Robert, could always look to him as a shining example of selflessness that could enhance their familial line. The death of the hero enhances the story, but the lack of success does prevent it from being as prestigious.

Breault, meanwhile, rescued a fellow shipmate and survived. Like Drennan, his act of heroism was selfless and left him vulnerable, but Breault recovered from his injuries. His memorial in this case was decided by an outside circle, one from which his friends and family were kept at a distance due to Breault's decision to remain a sailor, eschew promotion and perform duty on the West

Coast and with the Asiatic Fleet. Breault's survival does not necessarily detract from the award, but it was not the culmination of his life. His continued service provided increasing distance from a historic past. It is not only through the Medal of Honor that we are exploring Breault's life, but Drennan's life is only known to us due to his association with Breault. Drennan and Breault were kindred spirits in their desire to help others, but one died in trying to do so, while the other wasted away in a naval hospital to end his life.

Drennan's death completes his story, similar to Solon's story of Cleobis and Biton to Tellus the Athenian, the brothers Cleobis and Biton died happy men at the peak of their heroism, honoured by their family and community.[42] Drennan was honoured similarly (sans the statue), and his actions would continue to be a shining example of heroism to his community, friends and family. Breault had to continue to live, past the peak of his heroism, where it was difficult to look past the failings of the person as the temporal distance increased each year. Breault likely contributed to his increasing anonymity with his decisions, and his survival from his act of bravery removes a certain literary ending. But did Breault and Drennan remain in contact prior to Drennan's passing? Like all of Breault's potential friendships, there is no known information, yet Drennan is the most likely candidate for an enduring friend whom Breault had during his tenure.

## Cultural or Self-imposed Alienation?

The lack of information provided in Breault's OMPF suggests that he died alone in the Newport Naval Hospital, self-estranged from his family, with no known friends, a wife who died (likely after an act of infidelity) and away from his daughter Helen (of whom he did not even know her whereabouts after Pearl's death). It is hard to reconcile the positive Breault remembered by Fred St Onge with the lonely man who died in the hospital, completely isolated from anything he loved in life – family, friends or the shipboard atmosphere.

While there are several hints that Breault had friends, there is little to suggest he was close to anyone for an extended period of time. While he may have been alienated from the communities he was a part of, we must credit him for making these circumstances possible. The numerous letters from his relatives suggest Breault had as much a role in his own isolation as did cultural and communal pressures. Breault's family found it increasingly difficult to keep in contact with him, he had fewer friends from virtue of his rank and age in a youth-dominated crew, Pearl had died in 1939 and Helen appears to have wanted nothing to do with him. Breault thus died in a naval hospital with no family and few if any friends surrounding him.

## FAMILY, FRIENDS AND FORCED ALIENATION

Breault requested duty in Alaska, likely sensing the impending conflict with Japan. The unfortunate fact is that Breault's service that would have mattered to authorities, his experience in the Great War, took place in the RNCVR rather than the USN. He furthered this alienation through his own desire to serve in the Asiatic Fleet whenever possible. There is simply not enough evidence to be certain of much in this section, but it does suggest that sailors from an industrial age, divorced from coastal communities that housed permanent sailor-towns, was not a positive change for the individual sailor, though it certainly created a larger pool from which the USN could draw for the labour-intensive sea duties of the fleet. Sailors who returned to their home states were pillars of their communities and remembered for their duty to the nation, but how much did they miss the happy times they spent in the service? The memories of the sailors as they transitioned out of the service are well worth a deep dive into in future research.

## Chapter 8

# 'Falls in love with Kate and Jane, then he's out to sea again'

Breault's relationship to the women in his life is a major gap in our understanding of his character. Within official correspondence, there are only the briefest of glimpses into his relationships. Outside of family, the four primary female figures directly correlating to Breault are L.R.B. Hale, Catherine O'Rourke, Pearl Breault and Helen Breault. They were identified, respectively, as friend, friend, spouse and daughter in relation to Breault, and their impact on his life and his relationship to them reflects the best knowledge we have on his connection with the women in his life. These have been somewhat filled out with census records and newspapers, but each individual presents problems with documentation.

## Masculinity and Sexuality in America

What did it mean to be a 'man's man', as identified by Gunny Saks in *Born to Dance*?[1] Masculinity was far from a concrete concept throughout Breault's life, even though he likely had martial influences throughout his life. Breault probably felt that a life in service and in danger, and as a provider, made him a man's man. Joseph Breault was a soldier in the Spanish-American War, and the First World War erupted as Breault was a teenager, indicating his formative years were filled with war stories. Joseph was also a carpenter, which biblically held conceptions of masculinity that matched his name. With a military background and a blue-collar job that emphasized hard work and manual labour, Joseph Breault undoubtedly served as Henry's first role model for manliness, and could have driven Breault junior to attempt a similar – though sufficiently differentiated as naval – martial career. Fatherhood was a major part of American conceptions of masculinity, primarily as a provider. As the First World War came to a close, involvement in the war, particularly in the trenches, would define masculinity for the countries that had been involved as combatants.[2]

Where did Breault fit in with this conception, having survived the horrors of the Halifax Explosion? If Breault felt anything like Ernest Vincent Wright, he believed the activities of sailors were underappreciated. Wright wrote about his frustration in a self-published book of poetry:

> '"Boys in the trenches!" Tell me, please.
> How they got "over there!"
> They couldn't march; they didn't swim;
> Well, well, now, I declare!
> It must have been the Navy lads!
> Yes! Sure! That's how it came.
> That half a million khaki lads
> Got there to play the game!'[3]

Breault never claimed that was how he felt, but a photo printed in Putnam's *Observer* newspaper, which displayed a smiling Breault in his USN or RNCVR dress blue uniform, suggests he was proud of his service and openly displayed it.[4] Further, his gregarious claims of only feeling well out to sea indicates that Breault felt a sailor's profession was his path to manhood, as part of a larger coming-of-age story influenced by society and the challenges of the period. Breault was a man in uniform on the victor's side in an era that was fond of uniforms.

A much more difficult subject, one that has received greater interest, is the sexuality of men in the period. Based on surviving evidence, Breault likely identified as what we would now call a heterosexual man, but the distinction was not as clear as it is in the present day. As George Chauncey has noted, sexuality had not evolved to the modern pillar of identity:

> 'Within and sustained by this community, a complex system of personal identities and structured relationships took shape, in which homosexual behavior per se did not play a determining part. Relatively few of the men who engaged in homosexual activity, whether as casual participants in anonymous encounters or as partners in ongoing relationships, identified themselves or were labeled by others as sexually different from other men on that basis alone. Most observers recognized that many "straight" sailors (their term) had sex with members of the gang, but, as I will explain below, few believed that this alone meant such sailors were homosexual. The determining criterion in labelling a man as "straight" or "queer"

was not the extent of his homosexual activity, but the gender role he assumed.'[5]

Other scholars who have also observed this trend, such as Cynthia Barounis, noted that transient lower-class individuals in masculine professions, particularly sailors, were not damaged, but enhanced by other-than-female interactions prior to the First World War, so long as they played the masculine or 'active' role in the exchange.[6] This understanding should not be recognized as open acceptance of such activity; during Breault's tenure in Newport, a now infamous sting operation targeting homosexual and transsexual sailors was initiated and conducted from 1919–21.[7] Breault was likely not a part of this operation, but if he had been aware of it, what would he have thought? And does this match the popular portrayal of submariners in film?

As late as 1936, jokes were employed in film that hinted at sailors being known for homosexual behaviour. In the film *Born to Dance*, several such cases, all involving sailors, are commented on in song and scene. In the first scene of the film, 'Mush' Tracy is polishing the most forward part of the torpedo, singing about the fair lady he missed an opportunity to court because his chief ordered him to 'polish' his pet torpedo.[8] The scene featuring the tall character lazily doing circles on the long, cylindrical, phallic-shaped torpedo and the chief's obsession with it indicate a potential joke that long-time sailors are obsessed with a male polishing his own torpedo. This could also be a masturbation joke, but the fact that Tracy's chief even has a pet torpedo implies a tendency towards the act being menial to Tracy, but potentially homoerotic for the chief. There are other instances of sailors utilizing phallic instruments (only one has the long flute, the others having submarine-shaped instruments) in the Lonely Hearts Club, and Tracy lays on top of the deck gun during field day, but none match the phallic implication as far as the early scene involving the torpedo polishing.

The next joke intimating homosexual tendencies of sailors is reserved for Chief Ted Barker. After his public date with the famous and beautiful Lucy James, Barker meets her publicist, Mr McKay, and exclaims that he is not as fond of her as she is of him. Barker, who already is dating the protagonist of the show, Nora Paige, only went on the date because his CO ordered him to do so. McKay brushes his concern aside, chiding: 'Barker you've been in the Navy too long, she'll grow on you.'[9] Without understanding Barker's dating predicament, McKay made an assumption that as a sailor, Barker had tendencies to look towards same-sex relationships. This seems to confirm Barounis' thesis that sailors had a reputation for seeking homosexual acts. Furthermore, McKay's nonchalant comment indicates that he found no issue if Barker was so inclined, so long as it was kept private and the matters were dropped ashore, indicating the powerful pull of compliance to fit within standards of masculinity.[10] While open homosexuality was not condoned, the trend was that society simply looked the other way, preferring to pretend it did not exist and redirecting the conversation politely away from the topic.

The final joke in the film is perhaps the most ambitious, as it attacks the person of highest authority. A subplot engages Tracy and Gunny Saks in finding the Brooklyn Navy Yard to deliver a letter to RADM Stubbins. When the letter is finally read, it is an invitation from the CO to the RADM to 'park his battleship in the harbor' and join him to attend the Lucy James show.[11] The implication of the two naval officers on a date has layers that only a person aware of the context understands. The specific mention of parking is an allusion to a car parked in an inconspicuous spot. In this era, inviting a woman you were dating to your car was a serious step. One of the major reasons Dorothy Reynolds says that she enjoys dancing with sailors is their inability to own a car, thus avoiding the implications of going to a parked car.[12] Parking the battleship invokes the idea of proceeding to a parked car, implying the sailors could proceed privately. Further, a subtle bit of revenge may have been in play. A previous scene, with Tracy reporting to the CO while engaged in fishing that he couldn't find the Brooklyn Navy Yard, had to be rewritten to no longer include RADM Stubbins. According to the Picayune-based *Times*, the scene sparked a Navy Department objection stating it was 'ridiculous, impossible and a lot of other things'.[13] The short article states that the scene was modified without complaint, with the CO standing in for the RADM and Tracy reporting he had failed to locate the RADM. The letter may have never been read in the original screenplay, but the screenwriters may have included the implication as an insult to naval authority, which the CO represents in the film as the only officer. In this case, the suggestion is intended to insult the two members of authority in the film by suggesting that they, too, partake in the activities commonly associated with lower-class naval personnel, degrading them to the same status as enlisted sailors.

The tone of the jokes was mostly light-hearted and knowing, acknowledging the existence but also politely looking away, which matches the idea espoused by Barounis and Chauncey that homosexuality was not considered a dominant trait in a sailor's personality.[14] The only joke that likely had a mean-spirited implication was that regarding parking the battleship in the harbour, which was probably intended to have a bit of sting from resentment towards outside direction. There is no indication that Breault was anything other than a heterosexual male. However, should he have met homosexual males during his time in the service, he may not have viewed them as anything out of the ordinary, possibly even seeing them through a cultural lens that condoned alternative forms of sexuality that deviated from the American cultural norm.

## Easy to Love: Courting Ashore

There is no evidence that suggests Breault was anything but a heterosexual man, with the goal of marriage, fatherhood and assuming the role of provider for a family. In *Born to Dance*, there are numerous examples of men courting women, being the primary plot for two of the male characters and three of the female characters. Due to its status as a film, the relationships should be seen as idealized, as should the interactions between the sailors and their love interests as models for how such liaisons should occur. One commonality is the frequency of sailors being engaged in social activities where women were often involved.

Despite *Born to Dance* following the adventures of both the sailors and the women fairly evenly, the film's main protagonist is Eleanor Powell's character, Nora Paige, with James Stewart's Ted Barker playing a complementary role. In movie posters and advertisements, Powell's figure is seen mid-dance, with Stewart assuming a supporting role despite his stature in the film industry. In one such advert contained within Seattle's *Daily Times*, headshots of Barker looking at a smiling Paige can be seen under the dancing figure.[15] Enlisted sailors served a supporting role; had Barker been an officer and not an enlisted chief, the emphasis in the movie would have been on the officer. Perhaps the most important reason the script included enlisted sailors was for marketing, as the advertisement also contains a friendly reminder to also catch Paramount's *Popeye the Sailor Man*, 'Beyond a Doubt the Greatest Cartoon Sensation Since "The Three Little Pigs".'[16] The film was designed to appeal to the fans of the cartoon and by extension the common sailor, who was a vogue symbol in the period.

The inclusion of enlisted sailors is therefore a marketing device, one in which the USN took an interest, assigning a technical director who went so far as to have the actors report to him for inspection of their uniforms.[17] The screenwriters were aware of the marketing potential, to the point it become a plot device used within the film. The shrewd McKay recognizes the potential immediately of using Barker as a prop after he saves Lucy James' Pekinese dog from the water; while looking at the picture, James laments that Barker is not an officer, to which McKay offers assurance that 'it's better this way falling for an ordinary gob'.[18] Once explained, James also recognizes the appeal, calling it a 'Cinderella angle', appealing to the forgotten caste of enlisted sailors who are ultimately ordinary, like their audience.[19] While an individual sailor did not have the appeal of an officer, as a collective they had a charm that is displayed the fun-loving antics of Tracy, Saks and Barker.

The movie's first scene portrays the resentment of the three sailors that their profession frequently interferes with their attempts at courtship. The first song, with lyrics from supporting members of the crew, establishes that the men are hungry for any female attention:

> 'Rollin' home/ Across the bounding blue/ So, Boys, give her class/ And start rubbing the brass/ We're roll-rolling home/ Come on, you lazy crew/ Our holds are so set/ To race over the wet/ We're roll-rolling home/ Oh, Can't you see the light in your mother's eye/ When a son-of-a-gun her roving son/ Attacks a piece of pie/ And can't you taste/ The lips of a certain miss/ When her pride and her joy, her sailor boy/ Smacks her with a kiss? ... Our tours are nearly through/ So step lively, pals/ You'll soon be with the gals/ We're roll-rolling home.'[20]

The first sailor is Gunny Saks, who recalls the poor food and hard conditions, saying his reward will be 'from now on it's duck soup and a pure platinum blonde', a reference to the picture of his wife which he carried with him through his tour.[21] Sailors were not oblivious to the idea that monogamy was very much at risk when separated by a tour on a boat. Breault likely would have commented as Barker and Tracy did in the film when Saks stated his wife had also stayed faithful waiting for him: the pair simultaneously stating bluntly, 'you hope'.[22]

The introductory scene moves on, Tracy polishing his chief's pet torpedo and saying he 'still could swear, when I think of the fair Venetian maid I met 'neath stars above she taught me to love, at least to love spaghetti/ But when I tried to return to her side and visit her on the Lido, the chief said no and sent me below to polish his pet torpedo.'[23] This scene has been evaluated in the previous section, but it must be noted that it ends with Tracy getting ready to strike the torpedo with a hammer, much to the dismay of his shipmates.[24] The act of threatening to strike the warhead imitates a threatening position towards the genitalia of the chief, rather than an irrational anger towards an inanimate object. Further, it indicates that more-senior sailors appear to have gone out of their way at times to punish junior enlisted men who sought female companionship.

Barker's scene also discusses the resentment of being separated from female companionship:

> 'I hate romance when I think of the chance I missed at Honolula/ I scanned the beach and there was a peach enjoying the hula-hula/ I could plainly see she was flirting with me and my heart was filled with hope/ But how can I show I'm a Romeo through a rusty periscope?'[25]

The resentment is most clearly commented on by Barker, who argues he could see the beautiful women of the world but hates that he couldn't partake in any sort of romance. He represents himself as the 'rusty periscope', a symbol of a male visitor who could not be seen as a person, but as an extension of the boat on which he served. This portrayal in the movie could potentially represent how the American public saw sailors as worldly and firmly planted in their identity, though at the great cost of profound alienation.

The next noteworthy scene is after the introduction of Paige and Gunny Saks' wife, Jenny, at the soon to be identified Lonely Hearts Club, which Jenny appears to own and operate. Saks entreats Barker and Tracy to join him and meet his wife. Upon hearing her husband is at the counter, she excitedly runs out, past Gunny, and embraces Barker! The long period of time causes Jenny to forget what her husband looked like, to the point she embraces another man in a uniform.[26] The misidentification of enlisted sailors is a running gag, where the sailors are consistently mistaken for others, particularly by the CO. While Saks tries to win his wife over once again, Barker and Tracy are talking to Paige and a waitress respectively.[27] To indicate Barker's lack of experience with courtship rituals associated with dating, the film has Barker asking a fellow patron: 'Look, uh, when a guy's lonely around here and he sees somebody he'd like to meet, what's he do about it?'[28] He is informed that he simply goes up and talks to her, which is how his running comedic conversation with Paige begins. Tracy is much more confident, but his advances towards the waitress are initially rebuffed, though he has spent significantly less time at sea than Barker, who has two stripes that indicate at least eight years of service.[29]

In the song 'Hey Babe', all three characters attempt to invoke masculinity in various forms to attract their respective targets. Barker invokes worldliness and experience, particularly with women, chiming in with a nautical metaphor that he thought Paige looked 'sort of shipshape' to him.[30] The linking of the profession to the diction used during the group song indicates sailors tended to portray themselves as such on shore, though it would be hard not to in an era where they were required to wear dress uniforms ashore. Saks similarly invokes a sailor archetype by getting on one knee and beseeching Jenny to become part of his 'crew', particularly as a 'lookout, to find some shady nook out', presumably where the pair could spend some time together.[31] Saks' position on a knee indicates his status as the only married man, somewhat recalling the engagement process. Tracy appeals to a feeling of loneliness, stating that he hasn't 'a darn thing to do' as he downs six ice-cream soda drinks simultaneously through a multi-straw device.[32] Tracy is the only one who drops all nautical vernacular and seems to be looking for a quick fling, rather than full courtship. Tracy's ultimate pitch is his drinking and musical ability, which he displays by briefly turning the multi-straw device into a harmonica. The drinks are not too dark onscreen, almost clear, indicating they were likely a stand-in for drinking beers or another mixed drink. Sailors and alcohol have a reputation, but Tracy's feat impresses his woodwind sailor friends who are supporting him in his song, sharing knowing glances, and the tallest one continues to shake his head in amazement.[33]

The Lonely Hearts Club does not seem representative of any actual club, but reflects how sailors would have sought to portray themselves when meeting women. This is frequently played for comedic effect, with the expectation that the audience would understand the references. One could almost imagine Breault in his dress blues at a cafe, freshly tanned and returned from the Asiatic Theatre, attempting to woo Pearl through his profession and other traditional sailor symbols. The attraction to a uniform, paired with Breault's accolades, would certainly attract any woman seeking independence, like the character Jenny. The scenes seen within the club can be contrasted with *Sweetheart of the Navy*, where the Snug Harbor is more of a show venue, rather than a true nightclub, and the opportunities to meet the women much fewer.

*Born to Dance* and other contemporary films display an idealized form of dating that is recognizable to a contemporary audience as desirable. This may not be the best method to display the norms and mores of dating, as it is a sanitized version. The sailors are displayed as alternately shy, polite, devoted and socially awkward ashore. The film touches on undesirable parts of relationships that resolve around naval career, but does not dwell upon them, such as long periods away from spouses. There are no scenes of the drunken debauchery for which sailors are infamous (though the club has ice-cream sodas as a stand-in), no prostitutes and no scenes that even contain a curse or swear word. The closest the film goes to the gutter are the few jokes on homosexuality and the mostly off-screen scuffle between McKay and Barker. *Men Without Women* does have such scenes, but the movie takes place in Shanghai, where it is much safer to show the truth of sailors ashore as it did not damage any particular American community. Unfortunately for Breault, even if he had a whirlwind romance ashore, the twin rigours of duty and distance quickly injected a dose of realism into his life.

The three sailors in *Born to Dance* represent aspects of the sailor archetype, but each reflects phases of life a sailor moved through as they grew older. The young, fun-loving, individualistic, drunken, carousing Tracy represents sailors seeking adventure and companionship in their youth. The experienced, world-weary Barker depicts a sailor seeking companionship and a new identity outside of the Navy. Finally, Saks portrays the lonely married man, one who cannot enjoy the freewheeling antics but looks forward to the day he can be reunited with his family. In his life, Breault experienced life as sailor in all three dimensions, but how did that manifest itself? Did he meet Hale and O'Rourke in his freewheeling days, but hope to settle down with Pearl, as Saks and Barker sought to do with their female counterparts?

## L.R.B. Hale: Friend

We have already touched on L.R.B Hale's identification as next of kin on Breault's enlistment form. Next of kin is meant literally, as seen in the correspondence after the *O-5* collision, the USN depending on this address to keep family members informed. This is one of two major supporting pieces of evidence that suggest Breault was estranged from his family after his service in the RNCVR. The other piece, Breault's time in Putnam upon discharge, indicates he did not wish to see his family, for reasons unknown. A potential clue lies in St Onge's remembrance, incorrectly recalled in his interview, that Breault was born in Grand Isle, Vermont, and not Putnam.[34] While this may not be important, the context of Grand Isle as his residence prior to enlistment indicates Breault did mention it at some point in their interactions. Was it always Breault's plan to head to Vermont? Did Breault quit his job and return to Putnam briefly, sharing the plan to make his way to Grand Isle? This seems to be the most likely reason he would have mentioned Grand Isle, but that still does not answer how he knew Hale.

One major question is that regarding what form of transportation was provided to Breault upon discharge? If it had been rail, it may be possible that Grand Isle was a stopping point along the way to Putnam. This remains speculation; as a sailor, it is evaluated that transportation by ship was more likely for Breault. It is therefore unlikely that Hale and Breault met during his service or discharge. Three possibilities will be evaluated: extended familial relationship, employment or a friendship (either platonic or romantic). Each of these will be assessed, along with the possibility that two of them may have been true.

It is possible that Hale had an extended family link with Breault, though there is nothing beyond the circumstantial evidence of her knowing him prior to his enlistment. As Breault had stayed with extended family before in Putnam, it is certainly possible that Hale was on his list of contacts to stay with prior to enlistment. This also may explain the work he conducted for only a few weeks.[35] The major knock against this theory is from the *Boston Globe*, which attempted to contact residents who reported that Breault was not known to them.[36] Later reports substantiated that Breault had only been in Grand Isle for a few weeks, but in this era, it was not uncommon to report visitors, especially family, to small towns. These small reports in the newspaper described the relationship and the person's name. But how was Breault an unknown figure within the town if he was there visiting a familial relationship?

Exploring what we know about L.R.B. Hale's story offers insight, but no conclusive evidence. Hale was born on 9 February 1888, which made her 32 at the time of her interactions with Breault, who was then 19.[37] She had been abandoned by her husband, Edward Chaloner Hale, since 1 August 1914, and eventually was divorced from him on 8 February 1923. In the divorce, she noted that Edward Hale had abandoned her for a period greater than three consecutive years, committed adultery with unknown persons and treated her with intolerable severity.[38] Hale had ties in Montreal, where she was a member of Christ Cathedral's congregation, and it is possible that the two had met while in attendance at mass, though there is no evidence that Breault was a member of the congregation himself.[39] Hale ultimately died of a lingering illness on 24 May 1940, at the age of 52.[40]

Hale's divorce was part of a growing trend in American society. Though significantly smaller by present-day standards, the number of divorces steadily grew through the twentieth century due to wars and increasing economic and political freedom for women.[41] This should not be seen as a norm that society particularly wanted to embrace, as seen in the statutes that Hale had been required to bring forth against her husband. In movies, divorcees were not generally represented; in *Born to Dance*, a scene that indicated Paige was potentially married caused Barker to halt his pursuit.[42] This suggests that Breault, staying with a woman who was still technically married but in the process of a divorce due to absence, could have been part of a scandal if his presence had been known and they took steps to hide it.

Due to the significant age gap, restrictions of contemporary society and lack of evidence to suggest otherwise, it is evaluated that a mother-son relationship, rather than a romantic liaison, was what characterized the Hale-Breault friendship. While it may be tempting to wonder if Breault adjudged his relationship with Hale romantically, there simply is no evidence that any such liaison occurred. Barring an unforeseen breakthrough, this must then be evaluated as a friendship, and nothing more, one that helped Breault deal with his estrangement from close family.

## (Miss) Catherine O'Rourke: Friend

A principal of White Plains Public Schools, (Miss) Catherine O'Rourke was in correspondence with Breault prior to 1928, a fact that is known due to her request for an update of his address after losing his last letter.[43] On 28 January 1928, a letter was issued stating that Breault was currently serving on the *S-38*, which O'Rourke received by 31 January, when she issued a polite thank-you letter in response.[44] It appeared to be a fairly straightforward process to request the address of a sailor, so long as his name was known. Breault's OMPF has numerous requests from relatives, friends, businesses and – in the wake of the publicity following the *O-5* collision – people looking for their lost spouses or relatives. Nevertheless, O'Rourke's letter merits attention, for various reasons. Her letter addressed to the CO of the Brooklyn Navy reads as follows:

> 'Can you tell me the address of Henry Breault? He is in the submarine service and the last that I heard was from the fleet, in duty off the coast of China, in December, 1927. I would appreciate receiving his address as I regret having lost the card. Thanking you very much for your [cooperation]; I am,
>
> Very truly yours,
> (Miss) Catherine O'Rourke, prin.[45]

The document is written on paper from the desk of the principal of White Plains School District, and O'Rourke identifies as the principal in her signature. Given Breault's ties to White Plains, it is evaluated as highly probable that they had met in person, most likely during his break in service in 1924, and had decided to continue communicating via letter. O'Rourke's explicit identification that she is '(Miss)' O'Rourke indicates she was unmarried and had never been married. This was likely to preserve her dignity, writing to an organization where the letter would be seen by many male hands. Despite her status as single, O'Rourke had her own career, one that she could not just put on pause for a sailor boyfriend, but the romantic idea of writing to a sailor in an exotic locale like the Philippines or China likely seemed appealing for the independent young woman.

The assumption that O'Rourke was a young woman of similar age to Breault is unfounded, however. After careful examination and the discovery of a 1930 census record, it has been determined that O'Rourke was eighteen years his senior at 48, and a widower.[46] If it was previously evaluated as unlikely that Hale had a romantic relationship with Breault due to a twelve-year age gap, I must, by the same logic, conclude here that an 18-year age gap made a liaison equally unlikely. But is that assumption also unfounded?

It is possible that in his younger days, Breault had a 'type', that is, older women who were divorcing. Though tastes change, this is still evaluated as unlikely due to the fact that the only woman we know Breault had a romantic relationship with, Pearl, was two years his junior. To make assumptions on taste based on scant information contained within official documentation would be too hasty. Since there is no further evidence that the two dated, an alternative must be considered, namely that they were just friends. Perhaps O'Rourke and the Breault family were in the same congregation, and she acted as a family-friend correspondent, providing another 'mother' Breault could depend upon should estrangement settle between he and his family. Maybe O'Rourke had been a former teacher or mentor of his, and they kept in contact due to sentimental reasons. Another possibility was O'Rourke's desire to communicate to the schoolchildren in her care the cards and letters Breault wrote, talking about the exciting life of a sailor in the far-away lands of the Asiatic Theatre. That may even explain why a letter was lost; a particularly maritime-inclined child could have acquired the letter for safekeeping, to read over in private and dream about being a sailor. While O'Rourke may have played a large part in Breault's life, barring any new evidence, her role is evaluated to have not been romantic or sexual in nature.

## Pearl Breault: Spouse

In a letter dated 24 December 1933, William L. Slaughter of San Diego accused a H. Breault, stationed aboard the USS *Narwhal*, of attempting to break up his marriage and requested Breault be transferred from his current duty station.[47] Slaughter indicated he had previously served in the USN for three years and six months, and that the situation was detrimental to the health of his 10-year-old daughter, who was already unwell. The letter reads:

> 'Dear Sir
> 'I was in the navy for 3 yrs + 6 mo, but since that time I have been married for twelve years, and have a daughter ten yrs old and we have been happy until now, but there is a sailor H. Breault aboard the USS narwhal who is trying to break up our home and something must be done at once as it means so much for my daughter because she is not well.

'Would it be asking too much for you to transfer this man out of the San Diego district? I could go but our home is here and so is my employment

'If you would do this real soon I surely would appreciate it. But if you do or dont please dont mention this to him as he would tell my wife and it would only make things worse.

'Thanking you in advance
'I remain
'William L. Slaughter (signed)'[48]

While the matter was eventually dropped, the USN treated it seriously, indicating the institution valued its relationship with local communities. The 'Secretary of the Office' received the letter on 26 December 1933, stamped it, then forwarded it to higher authorities. Once the matter was reviewed, a letter was sent to William Slaughter asking for specific details, and it is here the trail initially ran cold in Breault's OMPF.[49]

I was eventually able to discern that Pearl Slaughter was the same person as Pearl Breault. While there was initially little evidence of this in Breault's OMPF, there was enough in Slaughter's letter to suggest that it was a possibility. The first indication was that the age of the Slaughters' daughter, who was 10 at the time the letter was written, was close to the age of Helen Breault, who had been born on 19 January 1924.[50] One can imagine a concerned, tired and anxious William Slaughter writing on the night of Christmas Eve in a year of economic turmoil. He couldn't, nor did he particularly desire to, move in an era when California was one of the few areas that employment could be maintained throughout the Depression. Adding to this was his concern over the effect of his potentially failing marriage on his sick daughter.

It is tempting to read this evidence and ask whether Breault was a home-wrecker, as Slaughter claimed. Or was Pearl, stuck in the patriarchal framework of Depression-era America, looking for freedom and stability? Frankly, I don't have evidence to support any assertion, but I argue that these would be the wrong questions for historical analysis. These are moral questions, answers to which reflect more on your own morals. What insight can we gain from their relationship that may not have been clear?

Census records in 1930 provided the answer that Pearl and Helen Breault were previously Pearl and Helen Slaughter. William Slaughter, along with his wife, Pearl, and their daughter, Helen, lived together as a family in San Diego.[51] It appears that Mr Slaughter's urgent tone was merited, for at some point between 1933 and 1935 Pearl left him for Breault. William worked in a garage

*Above left*: Unknown Photographer, Henry Breault, March 8, 1924, Library of Congress Photograph, https://www.loc.gov/item/2016836978/.

*Above right*: Unknown Photographer, Henry Breault, March 8, 1924, Library of Congress Photograph, https://www.loc.gov/item/2016836979/.

Unknown Photographer, Henry Breault, March 8, 1924, Library of Congress Photograph, https://www.loc.gov/item/2016836982/.

*Above left*: Unknown Photographer, Henry Breault, March 8, 1924, Library of Congress Photograph, https://www.loc.gov/item/2016836981/.

*Above right*: "Henry Breault, Portrait Photograph," from The National Archives (US), St. Louis, Persons of Exceptional Prominence, *Series: Record Group 24 Records of the Bureau of Naval Personnel 1798 – 2007 Official Military Personnel Files, 1885 – 1998*, Official Military Personnel File for Henry Breault 145766579.

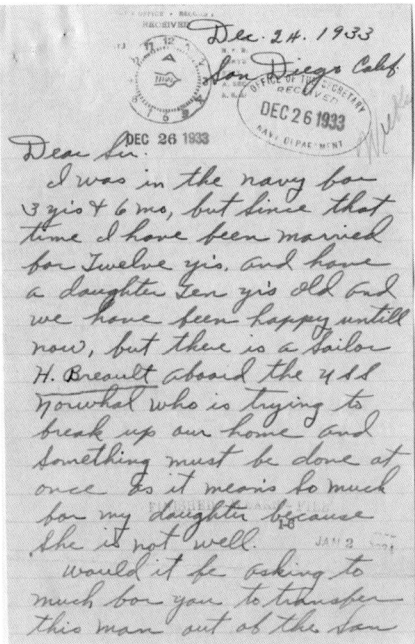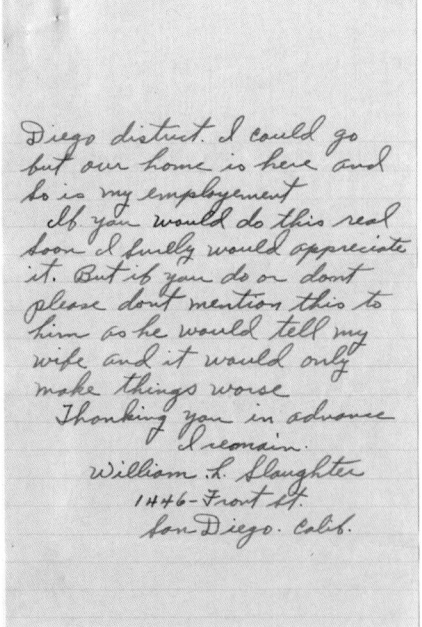

"William Slaughter's Letter to the Bureau of Navigation," from The National Archives (US), St. Louis, Persons of Exceptional Prominence, *Series: Record Group 24 Records of the Bureau of Naval Personnel 1798 – 2007 Official Military Personnel Files, 1885 – 1998*, Official Military Personnel File for Henry Breault 145766579.

"Catherine O'Rourke's Letter to the Bureau of Navigation," from The National Archives (US), St. Louis, Persons of Exceptional Prominence, *Series: Record Group 24 Records of the Bureau of Naval Personnel 1798 – 2007 Official Military Personnel Files, 1885 – 1998, Official Military Personnel File for Henry Breault 145766579.*

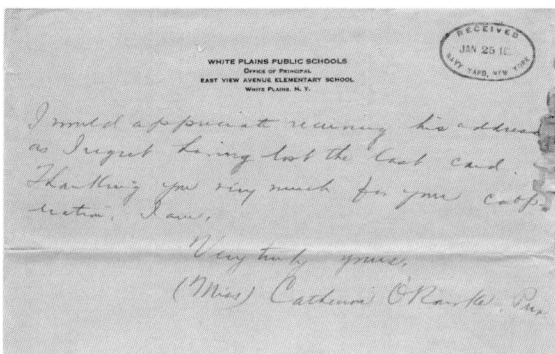

"Congressman Benjamin L. Fairchild's Letter to the Bureau of Navigation," from The National Archives (US), St. Louis, Persons of Exceptional Prominence, *Series: Record Group 24 Records of the Bureau of Naval Personnel 1798 – 2007 Official Military Personnel Files, 1885 – 1998, Official Military Personnel File for Henry Breault 145766579.*

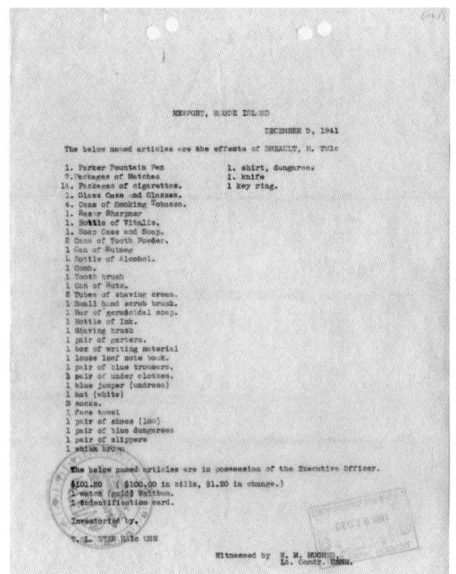
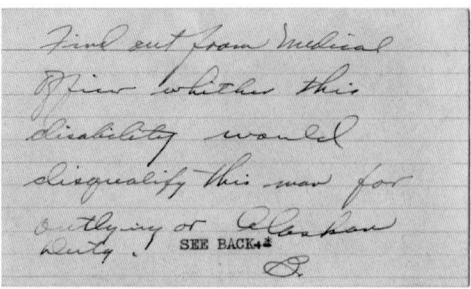
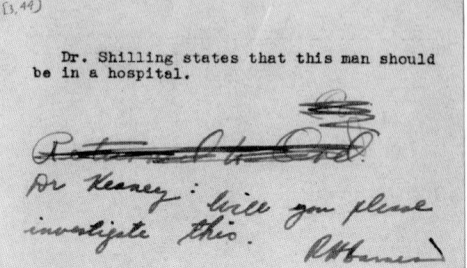

*Above left*: "Henry Breault's Postmortem List of Possessions," from The National Archives (US), St. Louis, Persons of Exceptional Prominence, *Series: Record Group 24 Records of the Bureau of Naval Personnel 1798 – 2007 Official Military Personnel Files, 1885 – 1998, Official Military Personnel File for Henry Breault 145766579.*

*Above right*: "Notes Regarding Breault's Medical Condition," from The National Archives (US), St. Louis, Persons of Exceptional Prominence, *Series: Record Group 24 Records of the Bureau of Naval Personnel 1798 – 2007 Official Military Personnel Files, 1885 – 1998, Official Military Personnel File for Henry Breault 145766579.*

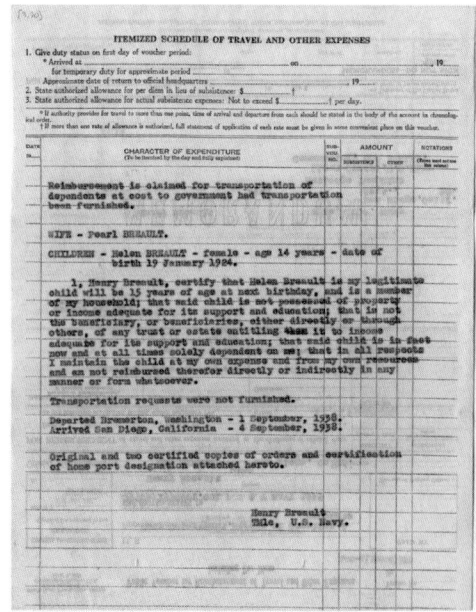

Itemized Schedule of Travel And Other Expenses," from The National Archives (US), St. Louis, Persons of Exceptional Prominence, *Series: Record Group 24 Records of the Bureau of Naval Personnel 1798 – 2007 Official Military Personnel Files, 1885 – 1998, Official Military Personnel File for Henry Breault 145766579.*

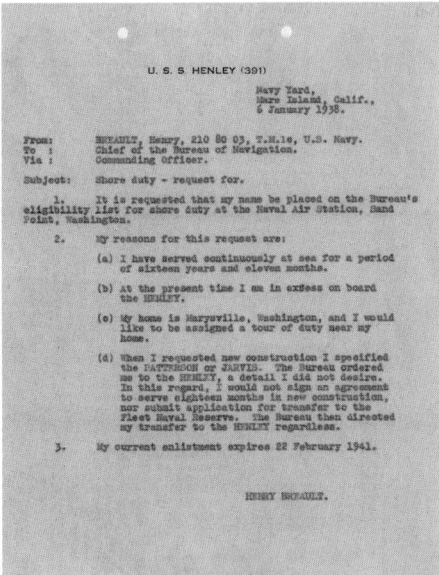

*Above left*: "Henry Breault's Request for Shore Duty," from The National Archives (US), St. Louis, Persons of Exceptional Prominence, *Series: Record Group 24 Records of the Bureau of Naval Personnel 1798 – 2007 Official Military Personnel Files, 1885 – 1998, Official Military Personnel File for Henry Breault 145766579.*

*Above right*: "Henry Breault's Request for Asiatic Fleet Duty," from The National Archives (US), St. Louis, Persons of Exceptional Prominence, *Series: Record Group 24 Records of the Bureau of Naval Personnel 1798 – 2007 Official Military Personnel Files, 1885 – 1998, Official Military Personnel File for Henry Breault 145766579.*

*Right*: "Henry Breault's Identification Card With Fingerprint," from The National Archives (US), St. Louis, Persons of Exceptional Prominence, *Series: Record Group 24 Records of the Bureau of Naval Personnel 1798 – 2007 Official Military Personnel Files, 1885 – 1998, Official Military Personnel File for Henry Breault 145766579.*

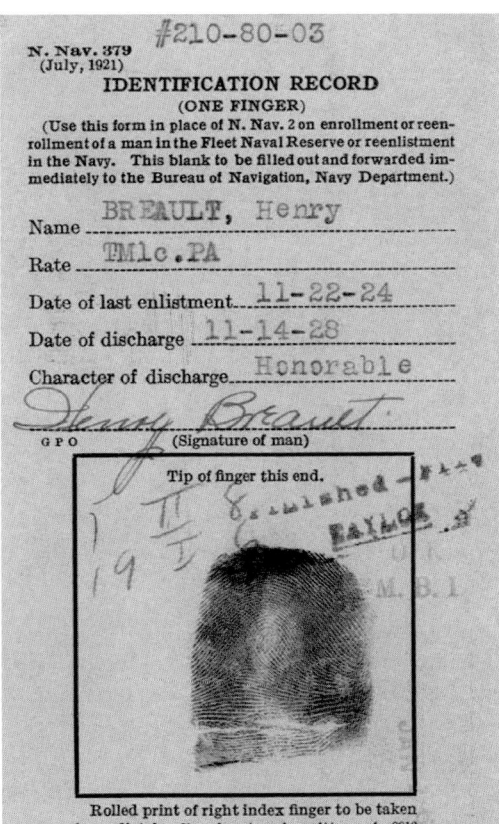

"Henry Breault's December 29, 1932, Enlistment," from The National Archives (US), St. Louis, Persons of Exceptional Prominence, *Series: Record Group 24 Records of the Bureau of Naval Personnel 1798 – 2007 Official Military Personnel Files, 1885 – 1998, Official Military Personnel File for Henry Breault 145766579.*

"Letter of Commendation," from The National Archives (US), St. Louis, Persons of Exceptional Prominence, *Series: Record Group 24 Records of the Bureau of Naval Personnel 1798 – 2007 Official Military Personnel Files, 1885 – 1998, Official Military Personnel File for Henry Breault 145766579.*

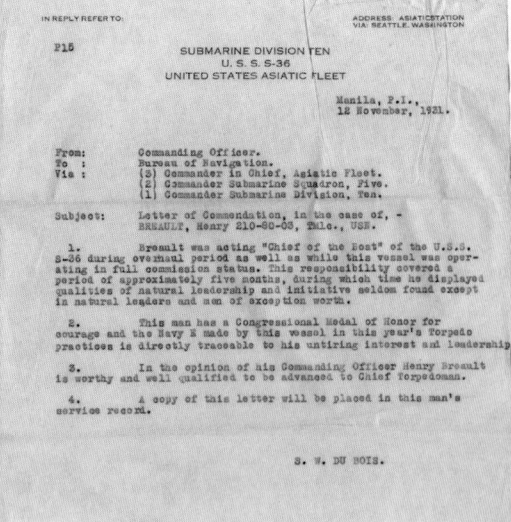

*Above left*: Mario DeMarco, US Navy Photo. "NH 86982 Torpedoman Second Class Henry Breault, USN." Naval History and Heritage Command, Digitzed Picture of Navy Times, https://www.history.navy.mil/our-collections/photography/numerical-list-of-images/nhhc-series/nh-series/NH-86000/NH-86982.html

(Diclaimer: Use of released U.S. Navy imagery does not constitute product or organizational endorsement of any kind by the U.S. Navy)

*Above right*: Ryan C Walker, (photographer), Submarine Force Library & Museum, Henry Breault: Torpedoman 2nd Class, U.S. Navy, U.S.S. O-5, Museum Exhibit, Medal of Honor Section.

*Right*: Ryan C Walker (photographer), St. Mary's Cemetery, Henry Breault Original Headstone, March, 3, 2022.

Ryan C Walker (photographer), St. Mary's Cemetery, Henry Breault Headstone and Medal of Honor Marker, March, 3, 2022.

*Left*: Unknown Photographer, *Submarine O-5, 1923,* Library of Congress Photograph, https://www.loc.gov/item/2016848189/.

*Below*: Pennell, Joseph, Artist. *Submarines in Drydock*. Pennsylvania United States Philadelphia, 1917. Library of Congress Photograph. https://www.loc.gov/item/2007666691/.

and was likely the primary provider, but it was not enough for the family. Pearl also had to work, as a waitress in an unknown cafe.[52] This may have even been where Breault and Pearl met, while Pearl was at work and Breault was a fresh arrival from the *S-36* in the Asiatic Station. Breault would have been in his naval uniform, freshly tanned and flush with cash from his long voyage back to the United States. Perhaps Pearl even recognized him from the newspapers almost a decade ago, the sailor who defied death and was awarded the Medal of Honor. There are alternative explanations, but sailors meeting women, particularly married women, has been under-examined. One film, *Submarine*, suggests it occurred in the same locations where a sailor could reasonably expect a single woman to be.[53]

While this is a love story, it was not Romeo and Juliet; much closer to a commoner's Horatio Nelson and Emma Hamilton story, with an unwilling third party in the place of Sir William Hamilton. There were contemporary observations on the issue of marital infidelity. In *Born to Dance*, both the female and male sides of the story are addressed, with an attempt to show the proper principles as seen in the characters Jenny and Gunny Saks. Jenny remained faithfully ashore, waiting for four years. Despite her cool greeting, reintegrating returning sailors into a household was a recognized issue, one that perseveres to this day. Jenny's coolness was not a defect of her character, but her reconciling her appreciation for independence and desire for a husband. Elsewhere in the film, Barker, after assuming Paige was married, immediately drops his pursuit until he is informed that she was indeed single.

Jenny and Barker represent the ideal, not necessarily the realistic response of individuals who found themselves in these situations in the contemporary period, indicating adultery was considered an issue in American society. Pearl and Breault's relationship highlights that Barker's respect for a potential relationship was not the response that always occurred, but would have been considered by their peers to be the correct response. Perhaps even more surprising, the woman having a child was not a 'deal-breaker'. Helen's inclusion in the deal indicates Breault was willing to adopt a child, reflecting the tendencies of sailors to be more open to a non-conventional marriage, though this shouldn't be exaggerated. *Son of the Navy* also portrays adoption as a noble goal, and the film was almost blatant advertising for US Navy recruiting, not reflective of cultural norms.

It is not known for certain when Breault married Pearl, as no marriage license is known of, but he did claim Pearl and Helen Breault as his spouse and daughter in 1935; the most likely approximate date for the marriage is 10 April 1935.[54] At the time of a dependent's move in 1938, Helen was said to be aged 14, having been born on 19 January 1924, which matches details provided by William Slaughter, thereby further confirming her identity.[55]

The lack of a traceable marriage certificate raised questions during the research for this book. The waters are muddied further by the suggestion that Pearl appeared to be in the process of leaving Breault before her death. On 11 February 1939, she was found dead with travelling salesman Alfred Hatfield in a motel.[56] Both deaths were ruled as accidental carbon monoxide poisoning. The particulars indicate that Pearl was not monogamous to either Breault or Slaughter during their marriages.[57] Again, it is difficult to avoid criticizing one party or another. Breault's significant time away at sea likely made this an inevitability, as he relocated Pearl to towns with no ties, as frequently happens when young sailors bring their newlywed high-school sweetheart to their new duty station, away from their family or a social support network. While rare, it is certainly possible that this situation appealed to the lifestyle Pearl wanted to live as an independent woman, with an absentee husband allowing her significant latitude to do as she pleased without a patriarch. This would also explain why Helen did not want to be a part of Breault's funeral and remained on the West Coast after Pearl's death, as she likely felt no bonds to her stepfather.[58]

But how did Breault feel about Pearl's death? He must have been torn between grief and anger. In one of the movies that seriously treats infidelity, *Submarine*, sailor Chief Jack Dorgan meets his beloved wife, Bessie. When Dorgan goes out to sea for one week, his best friend, Chief Bob Mason, meets Dorgan's wife in a social setting. They spend a week of romance, until Dorgan is set to return home. Mason meets Dorgan on the pier, and Dorgan decides to bring him home to meet Bessie. The surprise on Bessie and Mason's face goes unnoticed. In this case, Bessie is treated by the film as the devious character, understanding her timeframe to commit marital infidelity.[59] The only problem she runs into is the insular community of sailors; most sailors, especially submariners, knew each other. Pearl's choice of a travelling salesman indicates she was aware of this potential issue, and sought other transient people who were not necessarily of that community.

Through exposure to popular culture, Breault likely felt that pursuing a woman and becoming a father were pillars of identity as a sailor and a man. Coming back from the Asiatic Theatre after several tours, Breault probably had his fill of quick relationships, as Ed Schab remembered fondly in *Pigboat 39*.[60] The next step for Breault to become a man was no longer through sexual conquests, but a steady relationship that resulted in marriage and fatherhood, as Barker and Gunny Saks pursued in *Born to Dance*. Breault, at the age of 32, was still appealing: he was employed in a steady profession with a masculine identity, prospects of advancement and potential independence, which a woman could not always achieve on her own in a conventional relationship.

Stevie Moore in *Son of the Navy* and Jenny Saks in *Born to Dance* are potentially representative of the independence required of a sailor's wife. Both of their primary conflicts involve the surrender of some of their independence. Wives of submariners have been enshrined as independent since at least 1917 in songs such as 'Torpedo Jim'. In the latter, despite Torpedo Jim's bravery out at sea, the song ends with him hiding in a lion's cage from his wife, who was enraged that she hadn't been informed that he was going underway, matching the personalities of Jenny Saks and Stevie Moore.[61] All of these female characters have attributes of fierce independence that clash with our conceptions of demure wives who only act as supportive creatures that rear children.

Based on her somewhat unconventional actions, Pearl probably had a streak of independence and a self-sufficient personality. While married to Slaughter, she worked as a waitress at a cafe. She dated Breault while married, potentially off and on for approximately two years before their eventual marriage, and then dated at least one other man while married to Breault. All of this while being a mother to her daughter from her previous marriage to Slaughter. She likely would have found that opportunity of independence in a marriage with Breault appealing. The reality of time away quickly added a sobering dimension to their relationship. Being the wife of a sailor included periods of loneliness and anxiety, while supporting a man who worked long hours for a ship that never seemed to be fully operational. The romance of a sailor returning as a conquering hero was a brief, fleeting triumph; the reality of long days away, short stays at home and other burdens of duty have fractured relationships to this day, and were likely worse in Breault's manpower-starved interwar Navy.

How did Breault feel about Pearl's death? The event was likely a heartbreaking, disillusioning and embarrassing one for Breault. Infidelity, for both parties, was not unusual; it has likely occurred throughout history, in every culture, as men went to war or to sea in service of the nation.[62] There is a negative stigma associated with the action of infidelity, for both the perceived victim and perpetrator. Breault carried a bit of this shame with him: when he was asked by a medical CMDR how his wife died, he lied, stating she passed away due to 'heart disease'.[63] The lie indicates the hurt was still with him shortly before his death, that he had not forgiven Pearl and likely had a difficult time reconciling how the relationship ended through the actions of his wife. Alternatively, this could have been Breault trying to save face for both of them. Their romance was, as so many military relationships become, a tragedy filled with struggle and infidelity, where the needs of at least one party were ultimately unmet.

## 'All the Nice Girls Love a Sailor

Some hints of deeper relationships bleed through official documents, but they are not enough to paint a conclusive picture. Overall, Breault was likely a heterosexual male who sought female companionship and was even willing to create a blended family with a woman who already had a child. It is safe to assume that Pearl found his status and allure attractive enough to end her marriage, a risky proposition in most eras prior to the late twentieth century. From this, it can be extrapolated that Breault was a sought-after commodity, though whether this was due to his status as an enlisted sailor or Medal of Honor recipient requires further research. What is clear is that if he did have other female connections, the twin rigours of distance and duty made relationships difficult to maintain. As the lyrics of the song 'Ship Ahoy! (All the Nice Girls Love a Sailor)' state, the sailor falls in love with multiple women in port, then is out to sea again, preventing the possibility of any relationship beyond a fond memory.

On the other hand, a life of service with a guaranteed job was not only honourable, but also provided a stable income. Sailors sought to be good husbands by playing the role of provider, though they were gone more frequently than the average husband in the US. Breault would have had opportunities to mingle with women, both at home and abroad, and a life that was filled with adventure.

# Chapter 9

# Permanent Change of Home Station

**Oh, The Places You'll Go!**

Breault's life was remarkably mobile, reflecting the experience of the lower classes of a population that industrialization had uprooted. Based on surviving census records, Breault was born in Putnam, and likely lived there until he was aged 8 or 9, when his family moved to White Plains, New York. Even this has been discerned circumstantially and is dependent upon honest answers having been given to the census recorder; only Beatrice, then just one year old, had been born in New York, while Diana was also from Connecticut.[1] As seen in previous chapters and in Table 2, Henry Breault moved frequently, his career allowing him to travel to exotic locations that would not have been possible for someone from his socio-economic circle without naval service.

    This chapter will explore the places Breault lived or visited in his time ashore and in the USN, attempting to reconstruct them through his experience. While there are few mentions of such places by Breault himself, there are opportunities to investigate them from local historians, contemporary travel guides, Sanford Maps and contemporary photographs from the Library of Congress. This will not seek to be an exhaustive search on the contemporary experience within the named places, but will instead attempt to see them as Breault could have seen them. Various assumptions have had to be made, as there is sparse contemporary evidence for some of the locations that he visited or resided in. Even his childhood could potentially have been split between several known towns. As a sailor, he was alienated from the communities he identified as home, but the areas he likely considered to be home will be given precedence.

## Table 2: Henry Breault's USN Duty Stations, 1920–41

| Duty Stations of Henry Breault | Date Attached | Date Detached |
|---|---|---|
| Manchester Recruiting Station | 7/14/1920 | 7/14/1920 |
| US Naval Torpedo Station, Newport RI | 11/1/1920 | 6/3/1921 |
| USS *Eagle* #33 | 6/3/1921 | 6/10/1921 |
| USS *O-5* | 6/10/1921 | 2/25/1924 |
| USS *Capella* | 2/25/1924 | 3/4/1924 |
| Washington D.C. | 3/5/1924 | 3/13/1924 |
| New York | 3/13/1924 | 3/15/1924 |
| Panama Canal Railroad Line | 3/16/1924 | 3/23/1924 |
| USS *O-5* | 3/24/1924 | 8/11/1924 |
| Receiving Barracks Hampton Roads | 8/22/1924 | 8/23/1924 |
| New York | 8/23/1924 | 11/22/1924 |
| Receiving Ship New York | 12/1/1924 | 12/12/1924 |
| Receiving Ship San Francisco | 12/22/1924 | 12/30/1924 |
| USS *Pillsbury* (DD 227) | 1/26/1925 | 2/8/1925 |
| USS *S-38* | 2/8/1925 | 8/25/1928 |
| Transport to San Francisco | 8/26/1928 | 11/7/1928 |
| Receiving Ship San Francisco | 11/8/1928 | 11/14/1928 |
| Transport | 11/15/1928 | 1/6/1929 |
| Receiving Ship New York | 1/7/1929 | 1/10/1929 |
| USS Camden Transport | 1/30/1929 | 2/4/1929 |
| Submarine Base Coco Solo | 2/4/1929 | 2/21/1929 |
| USS *V-2* | 2/21/1929 | 2/7/1930 |
| Transport | 2/8/1930 | 2/17/1930 |
| Receiving Ship San Francisco | 2/18/1930 | 3/24/1930 |
| San Francisco and Transport | 3/25/1930 | 4/25/1930 |
| Cavite Submarine Base | 4/26/1930 | 6/4/1930 |
| USNH Camapo PI | 6/4/1930 | 6/18/1930 |
| USS *S-41* | 6/18/1930 | 8/30/1930 |
| USS *S-39* | 8/30/1930 | 8/30/1930 |
| USS *S-36* | 8/30/1930 | 9/15/1932 |
| USS *Canopus* | 9/15/1932 | 9/25/1932 |
| Receiving Station Pearl Harbor | 9/25/1932 | 11/22/1932 |
| USS Pai | 11/24/1932 | 12/4/1932 |

## PERMANENT CHANGE OF HOME STATION

| Duty Stations of Henry Breault | Date Attached | Date Detached |
|---|---|---|
| Leave in San Diego | 12/5/1932 | 12/28/1932 |
| USS Rigel | 12/29/1932 | 12/29/1932 |
| USS Holland | 1/30/1933 | 9/11/1933 |
| USS Narwhal | 9/11/1933 | 10/21/1935 |
| USS Holland | 10/21/1935 | 5/13/1936 |
| USS Decatur (DD 341) | 5/13/1936 | 12/26/1936 |
| Unknown, (likely in Marysville WA) | 12/27/1936 | 2/22/1937 |
| Receiving Station PSNY WN | 2/23/1937 | 3/4/1937 |
| Naval Air Station San Diego | 3/30/1937 | 4/27/1937 |
| USS Chaumont | 4/27/1937 | 8/14/1937 |
| NY | 6/9/1937 | 8/14/1937 |
| USS Henley | 8/14/1937 | 10/16/1939 |
| USS Truxtun | 10/12/1939 | 9/4/1940 |
| Transport | 9/5/1940 | 9/12/1940 |
| Submarine Base New London | 9/13/1940 | 9/4/1941 |
| Naval Hospital Newport RI | 9/4/1941 | 12/5/1941 |

## Putnam, CT

Much of Breault's early childhood was spent in the small town of Putnam, located in Windham County in the north-east corner of the state of Connecticut. In 1900, the population of the town was recorded as 7,348 persons.[2] The Sanborn Insurance Fire Maps for 1903 and 1910 show a small mill town, closely centred along the Quinebaug River.[3] Both the 1903 and 1910 map comment on the impressive firefighting facilities, indicating the town had a significant revenue to afford such services, while the streets were still unpaved.[4] Two of the places that Breault likely knew best in the town in his childhood were St Mary's Cathedral and the Israel Putnam Grammar School. Completed in 1870 and still stands today. St Mary's was probably a major part of the Breault family's life, where they likely attended Mass every Sunday. Breault in all likelihood attended the Israel Putnam Grammar School, which had been opened in 1902. Several pictures exist of the school from 1933, when it had fallen into disrepair.[5]

While there are no records from Breault that prove these formative years had an impact on the direction of his life, there are several indications that Breault remembered Putnam fondly, including his return there after the First World War. One can imagine the young Breault learning to walk with his mother and father on the unpaved roads, then walking with his parents to church and school. Did

Breault learn to fish along the river, becoming fascinated with the water? Did Joseph Breault have his friends from Company G over frequently, reminiscing on the good days spent travelling at sea to new locations in defence of the East Coast against possible Spanish excursions? After a disillusioning discharge from the service, experience in the Halifax Explosion and potential estrangement from his immediate family, Henry Breault likely sought a familiar place. If viewed in that light, Breault finally returned home when he was buried in St Mary's Cemetery on 10 December 1941.[6]

## White Plains, NY

White Plains would continue to be a part of Breault's life from his move there around 1908–09 onward. Breault spent time there from 1909–14, then again after the *O-5* in 1924 for two separate periods consisting of less than ninety days. He retained ties throughout the rest of his life, with his immediate family and with Catherine O'Rourke. The village was rapidly growing due to its close connection to New York City, its population increasing from 7,899 in 1900 to 15,949 in 1910.[7] Breault was a part not only of this trend, but of the intensifying shift of the United States from a sedentary, agrarian population to a mobile, urban population that moved with employment. While White Plains itself was not urban, it was close to major urban populations in New York City, Yonkers, Brooklyn and other places. This must have been a shock to the young Breault, as the urban area around New York was much more cosmopolitan than Putnam.

Breault's move here may have had a major impact on his future, as it could have inspired an early interest in the rapidly developing submarine technology located in nearby Elizabeth, NJ, and Bridgeport, CT.[8] Another major ongoing event locally in White Plains was the trial of Henry Thaw, who had murdered Stanford White in 1906.[9] At the centre of this trial was Evelyn Nesbit Thaw, who was married to Henry Thaw but had been introduced as a muse for the art world by architect Stanford White's studio.[10] In some respects, Nesbit's fame and notoriety makes her one of the first American celebrities; people famous for their antics, beauty and the fame already afforded to them. Was Breault one of the witnesses to the solemn sojourn of Henry Thaw and Evelyn Nesbit walking to the White Plains Courthouse?[11] Would he have looked like the young boy in the far right of a picture showing Evelyn Nesbit walking to her trial, in the corner, staring at the beautiful woman from afar?[12] One could almost imagine Breault attempting to sneak glances from the same position the boy occupied, hearing the commotion of the men and understanding the importance of the woman due to the photographers' presence.

White Plains marketed itself in newspaper advertisements as a 'desirable place of residence'.[13] The following pitch from an advertisement in New York's *The Sun* newspaper indicates the town was seeking the rich of New York City, likely businessmen and other captains of industry:

> 'The White Plains Board of Trade desires to call attention of homeseekers to the many attractions of White Plains and its many advantages as a desirable place of residence. It has the best of railroad facilities, cheap commutation, miles of improved and well shaded streets, excellent public and private schools, churches of all denominations, good elevation, pure water, good sanitary conditions, and all city improvements amid rural surroundings which are the most beautiful within the same distance of New York.'[14]

The above statement could sound familiar for many pitches heard for growing cities today. The mention of sanitation and pure water indicates such matters were a problem in other large cities such as New York, while luxuries such as roads were now necessary to attract people to leave the city. A more verbose statement from the *New York Tribune* offered similar sentiments:

> 'White Plains is neither white nor is it a plain. It is a delightful stretch of undulating country, consisting of hill and woodland, fertile slopes, rich valleys and green fields ... The distinguishing characteristic of White Plains is the number of drives and walks to every direction. These are almost endless in the variety of scenery, of woodland and lake, hill and dale, and they offer opportunity to those desiring to make short trips of anywhere between five and twenty-five miles ... New York is not so far off, either. The commutation is but $6.95 a month, and the train service is unsurpassed at this date, and it is to be still further improved in the near future by the electrification of the road.'[15]

The development of White Plains indicates the beginning of the sleep-in community, one that has little employment but offers the commuter an ability to work in a nearby employment centre in a city, while returning to the suburbs for their residence. Thus, the luxuries of free mail, parks such as the local Broadway, excellent infrastructure, low taxes, excellent schools and the surrounding countryside were the focal points of emphasis for advertisements.

It is unlikely that the Breault family was able to enjoy the best houses White Plains had to offer, though the boom in new home construction probably allowed Joseph Breault opportunity as a carpenter. Employment rather than these benefits likely drew the family to the area. The Breaults would leave in 1914, in all likelihood to work in Canada for the booming war industries, but they would return to the area once again before 1923. When Breault was to be sent back to the *O-5* after his award ceremony, he was first sent to the receiving ship in New York, where he was granted a period of leave on 13 March 1924. It is assessed that in this two-day period he returned to the Breault home at 15 Harrison Boulevard, just outside of White Plains in Silver Lake.[16] After he returned, Breault moved his family to a home they now owned at 47 Fulton Street in White Plains, NY.[17] It is thought that Breault helped his parents to move, perhaps offering money to combine with the family's savings to afford a down payment on the home, as they indicated in the New York census in 1925 that they owned the property. They would continue to own their successive properties, all in White Plains.[18]

Henry Breault would remain connected to White Plains through familial connections for the rest of his life. However, he was still a stranger and did not appear to enjoy the northern climate of New York. White Plains likely played as much a role as Putnam, CT, as a home for the young Breault. Knowing he had a home, one in which his family resided, also likely motivated some of his periods of leave.

## Halifax, NS

While Breault spent time in Montreal, the city in Canada that influenced Breault the most was Halifax. After Breault enlisted in the RNCVR in 1917, he was shipped to Halifax, Novia Scotia, to serve aboard HMCS *Niobe*. This time has already been addressed in Chapter 3, but a continued look at his life outside of career-related events will be pursued. The 1920 *Seaman's Guide to Ports* outlines key points of interest within the city of Halifax. After covering the essentials, it says lodging was provided at The Sailor's Home, YMCA and Salvation Army Home, while the three laundry places listed were the Globe Laundry, Halifax Steam Laundry and Angars Laundry. For Breault, these spots would have been useful, particularly the lodgings for nights he could go on leave, but he would mainly have been living aboard the *Niobe*. What would sailors do for fun in Halifax? Alice Howard recorded that many of the sailors enjoyed theatres and movies. Further points of interest were the Citadel that looked over the city, the Public Gardens, Memorial Tower, Point Pleasant Park, the Provincial Parliament Buildings and the Royal Navy Yard. This is a sanitized list for a visiting sailor, and Breault would have had a more realistic appreciation of Halifax's attractions as part of a depot ship attached to the city.[19]

Breault's relationship with the city would have been somewhat different. The sailors were allowed to go out and explore the city, and they did so in pairs and groups. A visitor prior to the Halifax Explosion, Nye, reflected:

> 'In walking about the town the number of men in khaki attracts the attention; almost every other man is a soldier. Now and then a group salute another figure in brown, an officer on his way to some one of the numerous military offices that are scattered about the city. The sailors usually travel in pairs or groups of three or four.'[20]

The observation of Nye indicates that sailors were social creatures. To be on the outside of a crew was an intensively negative experience; one sailor from the *Niobe* attempted to kill himself by slashing his throat with a butter knife when a razor was not available. The reason he gave speaks volumes as to how important it was to be liked:

> 'The ugly wound was sewed up and the unhappy man given every care, the police authorities in Halifax being [notified] meantime. Sadly enough the seaman does not want to recover, but begged that something be [administered] to "put him to sleep" forever. As a reason for his attempt at his life, he gave the fact that his companions on shipboard did not like him and in his own words, "made it hot" for him.'[21]

The happy experience Breault recounts indicates he was liked well enough. Was he among the groups of sailors that could be observed shopping, visiting theatres or other points of interest?

One thing Breault showed up in time for was the Halifax Exhibit on 17 October 1917. The event was held in the Armouries, a building the Halifax *Evening Mail* proclaimed was large enough to accommodate at least 8,000 sailors on the main floor alone. The primary feature was intended to be the war trophies brought from overseas, captured by regiments from Nova Scotia, which allegedly numbered in the hundreds. A tearoom was available for people who needed a break, along with an ice-cream booth and a tobacco booth so that men would not have to forgo their smoke. For the evening entertainment, there was amateur opera, theatre performances and a band of sailors from the *Niobe* playing the

Hornpipe, while an orchestra noted for its dance music would play for an open dance floor. Furthermore, field hospital equipment and a collection of historical Halifax photos were to be displayed for those interested in academic exhibits.[22]

The Halifax Explosion destroyed much of the city, after which Breault would have been unable to do much besides helping fix the damage and continue his duties. This was recognized by the naval authorities, so athletic leagues were organized. Football, baseball and basketball leagues were set up, with the *Niobe* football team being lauded as excellent. Sports provided an effective distraction for sailors and civilians who were dealing with the aftermath of the disaster. There is no record of Breault's participation in any of these events, but it is possible he supported the team effort by being in the crowd or standing by for the sailors who took part.

After Breault was discharged on 31 December 1918, it is unknown if he stayed in Halifax for any prolonged period. Perhaps he initially sought employment in Halifax, not finding any opportunity as the labour market was saturated by returning servicemen. Breault's experiences in Halifax would have been remembered fondly by Breault for the rest of his days, both for the fun times and the difficulty of dealing with the Halifax Explosion. He was likely preoccupied with dealing with the influenza epidemic referred to as the Spanish Flu, but there are no records that Breault had any issue with sickness.[23] Breault returned to Putnam as a war hero, no doubt relieved to be away from the stress of rebuilding Halifax.

## Newport, RI

Upon enlisting in Manchester, Breault was sent to Newport, Rhode Island, for his training. Newport was in a period of transition due to the presence of the Naval Torpedo Station and Naval Training facilities for officers and enlisted men.[24] Breault's time in RTC was spent socializing himself in USN traditions, naval lifestyle, and other norms and mores associated with naval life. Breault likely excelled in marlinspike Marlinspike is a USN term used to describe traditional seamanship practices in RTC damage control and other shipboard practices he had been exposed to in the RNCVR. His engagement with the town of Newport would have been minimal until his graduation on 27 October 1920, when he transferred to the Naval Torpedo Station to continue his training and become a rated gunner's mate/torpedoman's mate.

From 27 October 1920 until approximately 1 June 1921, Breault's primary responsibility would be to participate in work in the Torpedo Station and learn about his new role. When he was not engaged in his duties, he would have had time to explore the local town, allowing him access to the cliff walks, the old stone mill and numerous other landmarks that can still be visited today. Sailors were a large part of the population and often had their own societies that intermingled with the insular community. Shutterstock footage of Newport shows a chief petty officer talking to a civilian by the old Stone Mill, indicating they were a part of the town's identity by Breault's time in Newport.[25] Many of these landmarks can still be seen today.

As evidenced by advertisements in the *Newport Mercury*, jazz was a popular form of music and a likely feature in the nightlife of the community, which featured its fair share of speakeasies and distilleries.[26] 'Coke', likely the soda product we know today, was sold at the Newport Gas Light Company.[27] Assuming this wasn't referring to the drug cocaine or acting as a codeword for illegal spirits (this being the era of Prohibition), Coca-Cola probably acted as a substitute at social gatherings that once would have included alcohol. The *Newport Mercury* had a surprisingly slim amount of local events, festivals or parades; it may not have been a season to explore Newport as an outsider, or perhaps the *Mercury* was not the type of paper to concern itself with local events. If Breault got tired of Newport, there were options to visit New York by steamship or Providence by rail.[28]

## Eastern Connecticut

Breault arrived in New London, Connecticut, in June 1921, reporting to the USS *Eagle* for further duty. New London is a historic port, one with brick streets that contained one of the centres of industry in eastern Connecticut, alongside Norwich. Breault spent a few days at the *Eagle*, but shortly afterwards transferred to the *O-5*. The *O-5* was part of a submarine division centred around a tender, likely stationed initially at SUBASE NLON, located in Groton, CT. Benjamin T. Marshall described the situation around the same time that Breault arrived:

> 'With the development of the submarine and its utility for harbor [defense], a new use was found for the Thames Naval Station. It was [discovered] to be a specially good place for the maintenance of undersea craft. However, not much progress was made in the way of needed improvements until the World War, and then the Submarine Base took on a pronounced boom. An appropriation of several millions was spent in developing it. Officers' quarters, barracks, wharves, storehouses, etc., were erected, until [it] has grown to be a city by itself. At one time during the war, nearly ten thousand men were stationed or in training there. Since the close of the Great War, the force of men has been much diminished, but the work of developing is still going on.'[29]

It is possible that Breault visited New London, Norwich and Groton, prior to his service, as a Connecticut native it would not have been a long journey. David J. Bishop and *The Day* would outline the development of New London Submarine Base using images in two works. An undated old postcard labelled 'New London Conn. Old Navy Yard. General View' displays the first three buildings and a dock with a few ships.[30] This would transform into the photograph taken on 14 April 1918, where multiple buildings can be seen obstructing the view of the docks, which now hummed with activity from the submairners and support crew, who included some of the Navy's first female sailors, rated 'Yeomanettes'.[31] Bishop and Marshall estimate that 10,000 sailors trained at the newly established training facilities, and at least twenty submarines were permanently stationed at the base itself in this development period.[32]

Breault likely spent most of his time working on the base, but he would have had the chance to explore Norwich and New London. The *Norwich Bulletin* has numerous instances of sailors who visited the town to marry local women, host or participate in sporting events, commit crime or take part in numerous other interactions with the citizens of the prosperous town.[33] The interconnection between submariners and the communities of eastern Connecticut were well documented, and could serve as future avenues for research.[34]

## US Virgin Islands Territory

Breault mentioned that he visited the Virgin Islands, which had been acquired by the US from Denmark in 1917. While Breault claimed to be teetot on his enlistment paperwork, he may have had the chance to drink in the Virgin Islands. As reported in *The Bridgeport Times and Evening Farmer*, Prohibition was not in full effect here until 30 August 1922, and even then there were no funds allocated to enforce the law, which would have made this territory a popular port of call for sailors.[35] The climate was espoused by visitors like T.R. Owen of Charlotte, North Carolina, who proclaimed:

> 'While there is the delightful [tropical] climate on the islands ... there is no malaria or [prevalent] sickness of any kind. There are no poisonous animals and no venous [insects] and reptiles usually found in the tropics. The temperature seldom rises above 91 degrees and rarely drops as low as 67 degrees. The average [temperature] is 84 degrees, and it is [delightful] there at all times. For a lover of the outdoors, it is the garden sport of the world. The death rate is [remarkably] low, the inhabitants seeming to die from old age only.

The sanitary conditions are extremely satisfactory. Living is cheap, wages are low and help is plentiful and of a good class. Vegetables of all kinds are in [abundance] and fish are easy to catch. Fish of every color known can be seen in the Caribbean waters, and, as they flash to and fro under the surface they are beautiful beyond description.'[36]

There are few records in newspapers of sailors doing much with their free time ashore. The islands may, however, have witnessed the birth of a trope that populated romantic fiction in the future when a sailor on the USS *Dolphin*, C.R. Streeter, found a letter in a bottle while on liberty in the Virgin Islands. He wrote to the originator, the then 18-year-old Myrtle Brown of Louisville, who had thrown a bottle into a nearby creek with nothing more than her name and address when she was 12. Streeter found the letter contained within the bottle, shared it with his shipmates and resolved to write to her. Once received, she responded to the letter.[37] Unfortunately, however, the trail ends here, as any romance or heartbreak that occurred appears to have been a private matter.

While a cute story, it potentially indicates that sailors did not have much to do with their free time in the Virgin Islands, seeking amusement through other means such as writing to a woman who threw a bottle. Breault only appears to have mentioned his time in the islands in his letter to Congressman Fairchild, and didn't indicate much other than that he had been there.[38] The temperature may have appealed to him, as it was likely the first taste of a tropical climate on the way to Panama. He would confirm this bias in Panama; seeking a more tropical climate could have been one of the reasons he later requested service in the Asiatic Fleet.

## Panama Canal Zone

Coco Solo became home for Breault for many years during various enlistmnets, beginning when the *O-5* took station in the Coco Solo Submarine Base. As an economic and military chokepoint, it was recognized that the area needed defending. Submarines were envisioned as coastal defence platforms by naval authorities, and this was a realistic employment for O-class subs. A. Hyatt Verrill noted:

'We are accustomed to think of Panama, when we give it a thought at all, as a tiny, worthless country of utterly no interest and no possibilities and it comes as a distinct surprise to find that Panama has an area of over 32,000 square miles or, in other words, is four times as large as Belgium or twice as large as Vermont and New Hampshire combined. And when we learn that some of its mountains rise for nearly two miles above the sea; that some of its rivers are navigable for one [hundred] miles inland; that one may ride for days across open, level prairie land; that much of its territory has never been explored or penetrated by civilized man and that within 150 miles from the busy, up-to-date port of Colon dwell primitive, savage Indians who permit no [strangers] within their borders, we begin to realize that there is something of interest in Panama from being the worthless bit of country many assume.'[39]

Verrill's commentary on contemporary American opinion likely reflects the most Breault had ever thought about Panama, but it also tells of the average American's interest in Panama today.

Verrill, who claimed to have lived in Panama since the failed French attempt to build a canal, described Colon, the city on the Atlantic near the Coco Solo Submarine Base where Breault was stationed, only a year before he arrived. He wrote that Colon was built on a 'swampy islet', one that only a 'crazy Yankee' – as Panamanians liked to refer to Americans – would choose. Verrill observed that the town had changed from a Wild West boomtown, filled with bad characters and rough neighbourhoods, to a sanitized modern town, patrolled by local authorities, the military and naval police. The streets were paved, municipal buildings were surrounded by flimsy wooden tenements, and there was Silfer Park, two motion picture theatres, cabarets, 'a superabundance of saloons, and shops innumerable'. Panamanian hats appeared to have been of high quality, sold by Asian storekeepers, but the most exciting locale for Breault was likely 'Bottle Alley', a narrow street with cheap cafes, cabarets and saloons.[40]

If Breault had time, he may have visited Cristobal, an older, quieter city that had more amenities. As a USN sailor, he had access to the Canal Zone Clubhouse, the restaurants and amenities of the Canal Zone, the Army and Navy 'Y' (a YMCA associated with the US Army and Navy) and excellent quarters. Sailors likely did not stay frequently, particularly a future Asiatic serviceman such as Breault, who would have found Colon more appealing than Cristobal. Verrill labeled the Canal Zone government as a 'beneficent despotism', in which the individual was sacrificed for the good of the 20,000 employees. While Breault observed the benefits of living in the Canal Zone and was probably recruited while stationed there, he would have found the authority unappealing. He may have had the chance to visit Porto Bello and Balboa, which were also well known.[41]

## PERMANENT CHANGE OF HOME STATION

While a US Navy Department publication of the time was written for officers who had just received orders to deploy to the Canal Zone, Breault too could have indulged in some of the local delights the pamphlet listed: swimming activities, tennis courts, golf, sailing, fishing, sightseeing, a trap-shooting range, the YMCA's ice-cream machine, basketball, baseball, an amusement hall and many more activities were recommended. The only things that would have been prohibited were boxing and the officers-only clubs. Breault could have listened to the Balboa radio station while lying on the beach with a few friends, or attended a musical or other diversions. Panama likely had no end of fun for a determined sailor, which gave Breault his first taste of an Asiatic mentality.[42]

It was during Breault's time in Panama that he performed the action that saw him receive the Medal of Honor. The rescue of Breault and Brown was celebrated by the Canal Zone employees. It was probably once he had returned to full health that Breault received the same celebration that greeted diver Sheppard Shreaves.[43] When Breault returned from DC, was he met with fanfare? Breault's story seemed to survive in the Canal Zone, but either he did not enjoy his second spell in Panama or he hated the USS *V-2* in 1930, as he took the first chance he could get to transfer back to the Asiatic Fleet. Panama changed Breault's life, though in ways we could only guess at, but it did not have the same effect on him as would his time in the Asiatic Fleet.

### Asiatic Fleet Duty (Philippines, China, Japan, Hawaii)

When Breault reenlisted on 22 November 1924, he did so with special orders that guaranteed him a billet on a submarine with the Asiatic Fleet, writing to Congressman Benjamin Fairchild to ensure he would be able to do so.[44] Why did Breault desire to join the Asiatic Fleet? The reason he gave to Fairchild, for advancing his career, was likely accurate, but there was an intangible desire associated to the request. Clues as to why Breault desired such a posting are revealed by Edward Beach, who wrote in his book *Salt and Steel*:

> 'In the prewar Navy, tours in the Asiatic Fleet had been glamorous duty, individuals rotating back full of exotic stories and eagerly volunteering for repeat tours. It was also known for being "non reg" (regulation). Most of the *U.S. Naval Regulations* seemed to have been left somewhere east of the date line ... To the junior officers and enlisted men of the Asiatic Fleet, unconcerned with matters of state or higher [strategy], duty in that section of the world, so different from our own, presented many opportunities for

"the good life", whatever one might individually consider that to be. The situation even entered our naval vernacular: to be "Asiatic" meant to behave somewhat unusually, to follow one's own ideas and inclinations, to have greater than ordinary fondness for wine, women, and song, and somewhat less respect for the law (foreign or U.S.) ... Concubinage was not unknown if discreetly done, and the rules were even more lax for the sailors and younger officers, who were expected to sow wild oats. So long as one was on board ship when expected and able to do his duty, few questions were apt to be asked.'[45]

This is substantiated by the pre-war sections of Gugliotta's *Pigboat 39*, where submarine sailors were properly Asiatic. One of the sailors Gugliotta wrote about, Edmund Schab, recalled why he enjoyed the Philippines:

'[Schab] had several girlfriends; scotch was 75 cents a bottle; you could get along anywhere in the English Language; and in the dancehalls the Filipino bands played the kind of swing music that a sailor could jitterbug and shag [a popular dance of the time] to. Besides, the local girls were small and slender, had rhythm, and could follow the intricate dance steps that sometimes became gymnastics ... he was a 20-year-old who knew how to have a good time. He also knew how to stir up excitement when things got dull but was expert, most of the time, at staying out of trouble.'[46]

There was an appeal to being Asiatic, one that Breault had likely been exposed to during his service, so he made sure that there was some authority behind his request.

Breault would be one of those repeat sailors that Beach commented upon, serving two tours on S-Class pigboats from January 1925 to September 1932, probably connected to the overall downsizing of the Asiatic Fleet. Breault appears to have enjoyed his tenure, as he requested on 29 June 1933, after nine months on the USS *Holland*, to be transferred back to the Asiatic Fleet.[47] Breault's request was denied due to a lack of available billets for a TM1. Nevertheless, it indicates that Breault desired a return to the station that forged him into an Asiatic sailor and the benefits that came with duty in Manila, where an ordinary sailor could live like a rich party boy, the working-class version of Henry Thaw, Ernest Hemingway or F. Scott Fitzgerald.[48]

## PERMANENT CHANGE OF HOME STATION

One of these benefits was the annual Pacific tour the fleet would embark on, voyaging to China, Japan and briefly back to the United States. Breault would have had the chance to visit exotic cities like Shanghai, Tsingtao (Qingdao) and Yokosuka, though the homeports of Olongapo and Manila were frequently as exotic.

Paul C. Hutchinson, a contemporary expert and former editor for a newspaper in Shanghai, wrote an article describing the cosmopolitan Chinese city:

> 'For here is one of the magic cities of history, into which there has poured wealth [almost] beyond computation. While all the rest of China has been racked with civil war, with famine, with the looting and plundering of lawless armies, Shanghai has gone on piling up its wealth ... It is hard for the average American to realize that Shanghai is as much of an upstart among the world's great cities as Chicago or Detroit ... What sort of place is it? A combination of almost all the kinds of places found on earth. The famous bund – an avenue with [landing] stages on the river side and skyscrapers on the landward side. Lively parks, residential districts that remind one of American cities. Then the narrow, ill lighted streets, lined with low, wooden shops and dwellings in the teeming Chinese city, a place purely oriental. There is a general tradition that Shanghai is a pretty wild town ... Men who sail the seven seas will testify that Yalu Road is just as bad as they come. Shanghai is a great town for sailors – [the] fifth port in the world.[49]

Where did Breault go within the bounds of the city? He likely stayed within the International Settlement, an area granted to the European powers in the region. Within the Settlement, there were known spots where sailors congregated: cafes, bars and luxury shopping even the enlisted men could afford. Most of them were concentrated in the aptly named Blood Alley, where sailors would frequently get into scuffles over national rivalries.[50] Or perhaps he found himself in a rickshaw similar to the one Steve Rivnack was pictured occupying in 1929 while posing for a picture for the *Los Angeles Evening Citizen News*.[51] If any city knew how to cater to sailors, it was Shanghai. Indeed, Gugliotta noted:

> 'There were many reasons for the men to enjoy China. Upon arrival the 39 would have open gangway in Shanghai for several weeks. This meant, "Come back only when you have the duty." Also the

exchange rate had jumped to 19 Chinese dollars to one U.S. dollar, so that an enlisted men could make a good liberty on $3 or so. There was another advantage: at certain bars you could sign chits when you ran out of money, then square away the bill on payday. And then there were the girls. Most of the cabarets in Blood Alley had orchestras for dancing, with Chinese hostesses lined up on one side of the room and White Russians on the other.'[52]

While the exchange rate was not as favourable during Breault's service, Shanghai was still a common conversation point for sailors returning to the United States. In 1932, the *Spokesman-Review* – based in Spokane, Washington State – contained an advertisement for a new ladies' hat with a veil over the eyes made by The Vogue; it was called the 'Shanghai Sailor'.[53] It is unknown whether it was inspired by sailors who brought gifts back to the US, but its mere name indicates that Asiatic sailors played a major role in contemporary culture.

The next stopping point for Breault and the fleet would probably have been Tsingtao (now Qingdao), further north. Like Shanghai, Tsingtao was the scene of intermittent fighting in 1928. Gugliotta described Tsingtao from the perspective of a submarine officer's wife as 'the Riviera of China'.[54] German influences could be seen in the street signs, *biergartens* and plentiful beer from the eponymous Tsingtao Brewery. Breault would have also had the opportunity to indulge in peaches, pears or strawberries; as Dottie Lautrab recalled in *Pigboat 39*, she felt like she was 'at home in Connecticut'.[55] Unfortunately for Breault, his months in Tsingtao occurred as Chinese warlords fought for supremacy; the city was reported to be quiet but filled with foreign soldiers, including Japanese and Americans.[56] As a sailor aboard the *S-38*, he was likely on one of the ships moored alongside the *Beaver* in a picture that was reprinted in numerous newspapers to advertise the USN presence and salve the concerns of citizens.[57] One of the final events of the Asiatic Fleet manoeuvres was a gala for the boat's crew, with the enlisted sailors telling their stories, drinking and at times fighting with one another.[58] This would have also been Breault's farewell from the *S-38*, as he was thereafter transferred to San Francisco.

Other ports Breault for which there is only circumstantial evidence to suggest that he visited included Amoy and Hong Kong in China, Yokohoma or Yokosuka in Japan, and even Surabaja in the Dutch East Indies. The Asiatic theatre was filled with Chinese and Japanese fighting, and tragedy for British ships, with several submarines lost in the period. Breault spent time as acting COB aboard the *S-36*. His service in the Asiatic theatre likely gave him purpose, and he actively sought opportunities to return. For a single sailor with an Asiatic mindset, it was the perfect place, and it offers an understudied opportunity for understanding the motivations of sailors in the Far East.

## San Diego, California

The West Coast of the United States defined the second half of Breault's career, particularly California, as he visited San Francisco, San Diego and Los Angeles. San Diego was likely the spot that made the greatest impression on him as it had the reputation for taking care of sailors and for being the place he met his future wife. California, partially in response to the naval activities in San Diego, San Francisco, Los Angeles and other military bases, saw a period of economic prosperity due to the increased investment in the region. By 1934, San Diego maritime industry workers were confident enough to hold massive strikes and protests, indicating the health of the sector.[59]

The migration of labour to California is a major theme in John Steinbeck's contemporary novel *The Grapes of Wrath*.[60] While other states struggled, particularly those in the Midwest and the South, California gained its identity as the land of plenty and beauty. In *Grapes of Wrath*, Ma Joad questioned the stories of the opportunities in California but hoped they were true:

> '[Tom] turned and looked at her. "What makes you think they ain't?" he asked. "Well – nothing. Seems too nice, kinda. I seen the han'bills fellas pass out, an' how much work they is, an' high wages an' all; an' I seen in the paper how they want folks to come an' pick grapes an' oranges an' peaches. That'd be nice work, Tom, pickin' peaches. Even if they wouldn't let you eat none, you could maybe snitch a little ratty one sometimes. An' it'd be nice under the trees, workin' in the shade. I'm scared of stuff so nice. I ain't got faith. I'm scared somepin ain't so nice about it ... But I like to think how nice it's gonna be, maybe, in California. Never cold. An' fruit ever'place, an' people just bein' in the nicest places, little white houses in among the orange trees. I wonder – that is, if we all get jobs an' all work – maybe we can get one of them little white houses. An' the little fellas go out an' pick oranges right off the tree."'[61]

Breault was thus going to a place where the lowliest farmer could hope for small blessings like working in the shade, sneaking an occasional ripe peach, cool weather, and with enough hard work, the opportunity to own a nice house.

California, though far from perfect, offered a secure employment opportunity, and San Diego needed the labour.

Breault was not one of the migrant workers, though he probably saw the 'Okies' – as they were called – congregating to seek employment during his tenure in California. How did he feel towards them? After a childhood of moving for employment and a career in a service that required constant movement, was he filled with empathy or pity? San Diego defined its prosperity in relationship to the USN, developing the city around the investment in naval infrastructure during the 1920s.[62] Despite some detractors, the relationship with the USN paid dividends during the Great Depression as naval spending accelerated.

The Federal Writers of the Workers Progress Administration (WPA) wrote a guidebook on San Diego in the 1930s, the introduction of which stated:

> 'San Diego (0–500 alt., 170,000 pop.) is a loosely knit community of residential districts, business centers, and suburban towns covering 96 square miles of seashore, canyons, and mesas. Climate is its main product; tourists are its principal customers … At first glance seems to belie the figure of its population. There is little of the hurly-burly, the noise, and the mad scramble of traffic – automobile, streetcar, and pedestrian alike – that characterizes the usual city of this size … These traffic habits, combined with the unusually short blocks – particularly in the downtown area – all add to the characteristically leisurely atmosphere.'[63]

The climate of San Diego is well-known, and the WPA guide for the city notes that summer clothing is appropriate year-round, the only recommendation being to wear a light raincoat during the rainy season from December–March.[64] Breault would have found the California climate offered the best of the tropics, without the rain, humidity and Olongapo mosquitoes.

Several attractions awaited Breault upon his arrival. A postcard of the time displayed Balboa Park and its Botanical Gardens.[65] The WPA list of things to do boasts of music venues, sports, hiking, theatres and notable annual events.[66] Of particular interest to Breault would have been the Navy Day celebration. Navy Day was a celebration similar to Fleet Week, held annually on 27 October and featuring parades, visits to naval and marine bases and tours of ships.[67] Local newspaper *The Chula Vista Star* described the planned events in 1933:

> 'Residents of San Diego and Imperial counties are especially invited to inspect the 40 warships that will be [anchored] in the bay,

the 250 airplanes at the Naval Air Station, and the various shore establishments. An outstanding feature of the Navy Day program at San Diego will be the appearance of Secretary of the Navy Claude A. Swanson. He will arrive on the 10,000-ton cruiser Indianapolis October 26, and will inspect the shore units on the afternoon of October 26 and 27. The Indianapolis will be berthed at the mole pier and will be open to visitors ... Plans are being perfected to bring the 42,000 ton aircraft carrier into the harbor on Navy Day, enabling visitors to inspect virtually every type of watercraft from the giant fleet submarines to cruises, destroyers and carriers.'[68]

While the *Indianapolis* was the star of the occasion for this specific Navy Day, Breault was serving aboard the *Narwhal*, the show-me boat that was likely included in the festivities. Once that was done, Breault could have gone out on the town to continue the celebrations.

It was in San Diego that Breault sought to own a vehicle. It was possible to enjoy San Diego without an automobile, but the WPA noted:

'[Motoring] is particularly popular locally because of the smooth highways and excellent natural setting. The ratio of cars to population is quite high, there being 99,000 motor vehicles registered in San Diego County. Mountains, seashore, and city recreational areas are all within easy reach of the pleasure seeker.'[69]

A strong appeal to be an automotive enthusiast in a city that seemed to be designed with them in mind potentially inspired Breault to purchase a vehicle. He may have also needed it to visit sister Diana and her husband, old shipmate Everett Drennan, who also resided in San Diego briefly. California was a growing state during Breault's tenure and contained exciting new possibilities, among them owning an automobile.

## Marysville, Washington State

In a special request chit from 6 January 1938, Breault requested duty at Naval Air Station, Sand Point, WA. The reasons he offered were as follows:

'(a) I have served continuously at sea for a period of sixteen years and eleven months.
'(b) At the present time I am in excess on board the HUNLEY.

'(c) My home is Marysville, Washington, and I would like to be assigned a tour of duty near my home.

'(d) When I requested new construction, I specified the PATTERSON or JARVIS. The Bureau ordered me to the HENLEY, a detail I did not desire. In this regard, I would not sign an agreement to serve eighteen months in new construction, nor submit application for transfer to the Fleet Naval Reserve. The bureau then directed my transfer to the HENLEY regardless.'[70]

Breault's time in Marysville was profound enough that he considered it 'home', something he rarely referred to in his special request chits. He had not previously expressed sentimental attachment to his family or any geographic location, yet Marysville was special enough for Breault to call Marysville his home.

Marysville was a small town, smaller than Putnam, with a population of 1,354 and 1,748 persons in 1930 and 1940.[71] According to Phil Dougherty, there were numerous venues of entertainment that developed prior to Breault's arrival in 1935, with radio shows, movies, dances, the 'Stuck Up' Club, various social clubs and a bandstand in City Park for concerts. The town also held the Strawberry Festival from 1932 onward, to celebrate the abundant strawberry production on surrounding farmsteads. Dougherty notes:

'Marysville enjoyed a small economic growth spurt during the late 1920s, and was not as severely impacted by the Great Depression of the 1930s as some communities, despite government reports listing Snohomish County as one of the state's neediest counties ... Businesses in Marysville during the thirties included grain mills, a fertilizer plant, a boat works, a tannery, a berry packing plant, and a vibrant farming community, known for producing berries, hay, and oats.'[72]

After time spent in California and the bustling cities of Asia, Breault would have found his time in Marysville quiet and peaceful.

One of the possibilities as to why Breault enjoyed his time in Marysville was his brief period of marital bliss. Pearl and Henry were married before April 1935, and she and daughter Helen resided with him in Marysville, as indicated by the dependents transfer from Bremerton to Los Angeles in September 1938.[73] Perhaps Pearl and Helen were initially against the move, but came to love the rural, strawberry-covered fields of Marysville. Perhaps Helen learned more about her father, and Pearl gathered a large group of friends who supported her as a new navy wife. They remained longer than Breault in Marysville, only leaving several months after Breault's special request for duty in Washington was denied. While more independent, the Breault family learned the lesson all navy families do when the honeymoon period ends; once you are finally acclimatized, it's time to move once more, 'PCSing' (i.e. transferring) to a new home.

## Join the Navy and See the World!

For Breault, the recruiting slogan 'Join the Navy and See the World' was an accurate one.[74] He had the chance to travel to domestic and international locales that may have been restricted to him without the USN, due to his socio-economic background. The price to pay for this was the lack of personal ties or roots in the communities where he resided, a struggle that sailors were increasingly facing as recruiting was moved from traditional sailor-towns that had served as stable residences.

The struggle of being divorced from one's community was a new problem that is increasingly the norm in the present day. The modern world may be increasingly connected, yet frequently we remain strangers within our own local community. The freedom and willingness to move were bought at the price of a stable identity associated with roots in a community. Many more people now see the world, but we are often not able to appreciate our local part of it, acting as visitors in our own hometowns or adoptive communities. Breault's relationship with the communities where he resided or visited provides insights into how we interact with our world today. Unfortunately, this list of communities is limited. Local historians who are excited to know Breault at some point in his career, spent time in their areas of interest can carry this story further by searching for personal artefacts, such as his lost Medal of Honor, which can be identified by the engraving of the details of his heroism on the back.

# Chapter 10

# Uniforms, Cigarettes, Pomade and Other Artefacts of a Material Identity

Part of being American in the twentieth century involved being a participant in consumer culture. Sailors were not immune from cultural motivations, actively striving for opportunities to buy material goods such as cigarettes, alcohol, candy, hair styling pomades and automobiles, as many of their fellow Americans sought to do. As individuals, communities and subcultures began to identify with the goods and services they purchased, the ownership or ability to interact with these brands became symbols of these groups by association. Prospective members sought these goods and services to portray a sense of solidarity or alternatively reject the practice and identify with a competing material.

So how did Breault, likely through unintentional purchases, construct a material identity? Did he seek to portray himself through his purchases in a manner consistent with those of a submariner or sailor subculture? Or did he aim to show himself in a way that was not consistent with the archetype? This research rejects the label of consumer culture, instead seeking to understand the process of construction of a material identity. Material identity is the construction of subcultures surrounding purchasable items, though this label could be extended to technology such as submarines. Through Breault's OMPF, we know there were products he owned and probably identified as being part of his personality.

For most of his contracts, he would have primarily lived aboard the vessel he served on or a submarine tender, though it is possible that due to the unique conditions of the submarine he was allowed a barracks facility.[1] The USS *Holland*, *Canopus* and *Savannah* would be his primary residence throughout his tenure in the submarine force, forcing him to eschew many of the comforts one would associate with a home. Breault lived a relatively spartan existence while underway, as indicated by his reimbursement claim after the *O-5* disaster for lost personal property that consisted only of uniform items, towels, mattress covers and a mattress.[2] No personal items were included, likely because they weren't covered by the USN or Breault stored many of his such things on the *Savannah*.

Breault's lifestyle varied throughout his career. He stated that his profession prior to enlistment was an electric plater, which was either so low-paying or unappealing that he preferred a career in the USN.[3] Considering his likely estrangement from his family and willingness to move for work, Breault had the necessary prerequisites for a career in the service. He had previous experience in naval service and understood the restrictions that it would place on his pursuit of material goods. This did not faze him, and his exuberant adoption of the sailor archetype hints that his motivation was not the accumulation of goods or wealth. Still, Breault had ample opportunities in port to buy goods or services and receive material accolades from his military service.

Breault's initial pay as an apprentice seaman was only $21 per month, but with a reasonable expectation of seeing significant pay raises in his first contract once training was complete. Within a year, Breault had been advanced to GM3/TM3, and by 11 June 1923, at the three-year mark of his naval career, Breault was a TM2 earning $72 a month, with a variable submarine pay.[4] As a TM1 with eight years of service and a Medal of Honor, Breault earned $98.60 in 1928, along with submarine pay.[5] The lack of pay increases into the higher ranks Breault once could have expected ate into his potential buying power, but his essential needs of sustenance and shelter were met so all his pay should be considered his disposable income. By that standard, Breault had ample monetary access, but how he chose to exercise it was dependent upon a variety of factors outside of his control.

## Uniforms

Breault's first list of possessions comes from an insurance claim filed on 8 November 1923 in the aftermath of his rescue from the *O-5*. The list primarily consisted of uniform items, indicating that this was frequently the extent of Breault's possessions aboard the vessel. Alternatively, he may not have been authorized reimbursement for personal items and maybe still had a storage place on the tender, making it likely his loss of personal items outside of what was needed underway would have been minimal.

This is not to discount the importance of uniform items to Breault's self-conception. Sailors were required to wear their uniforms in public, to be seen as walking ambassadors of Uncle Sam. The 'gob' attire was ubiquitous in naval towns, frequently seen and eminently recognizable. The only scenes in *Born to Dance* where the sailors can be seen forgoing their uniforms are after their discharge, while other movies such as *Men Without Women*, *Navy Blues*, *Sweetheart of the Navy* and *Son of the Navy* never show enlisted naval personnel without their uniform. In *Born to Dance*, a frequent joke employed is the misidentification of the sailors, particularly by the CO, who mixes up Tracy and Saks despite their very different physcial appearance. Jenny also initially misidentifies her husband, whom she had not seen in four years, embracing the tall handsome Barker instead of her actual spouse.[6] Both cases of misidentification are galling: Tracy and Saks have served with the CO for four years, but he never bothered to get to know them well enough to tell the two apart; while Jenny forgot what Saks even looked like! Tracy and Saks became the interchangeable Rosencrantz and Guildenstern, the tall, lanky Tracy cutting a different figure to the stocky, short Saks. However, I believe such inattention is more representative of officers in the surface USN than the submarine force, the crews were smaller and more individual responsibility meant that sailors were recalled much more readily.

When Breault walked around a city he visited, he was not known as an individual, but under the collective name of a 'gob' or sailor. His uniform, particularly his undress and dress uniforms, marked him not as Henry Breault, but as a nameless, faceless TM in the USN, frequently seen ashore as a member of a liberty party, carousing ephemerally and disappearing once his ship left in the morning. A sailor simply wasn't a sailor without a uniform; once stripped of it, the sailor is stripped of his identity, such as Thomas Knowlton in Ellsberg's *Pigboats*.[7]

Being identified as a sailor in an American town was not always a desirable experience. Dating potentially to 1906, signs ordering 'Dogs and Sailors keep off the grass' could be seen in numerous American cities, though Norfolk was particularly known for having such signs. A similar one stating 'no solicitors or sailors' hung from the door of the love interest in the film *Navy Blues*.[8] American culture has never been particularly endearing towards transients who have no agency within a community or are seen as lower-class and riotous troublemakers. While sailors had their own communities within these towns, sailors like Breault may not always have been seen as a major constituent part of those who permanently resided there.

Dialogue in film, particularly with women, also indicated sailors were not well respected. In *Born to Dance*, Norma Paige employs terms such as 'not so soon sailor' to Chief Barker's advances, and then denies that she was 'uniform crazy' when Barker accuses her of being unpatriotic.[9] In response to advances by Tracy, a sailor who was not even a chief, the unnamed Lonely Hearts Club server replies that she likes actors 'better than sailors'.[10] When Tracy defends his argument that he is an actor, stating he has an 'inventive mind', the server rebuffs him with, 'yeah, most sailors have', implying that she understood the inventiveness was of a lewd, sexual nature.[11] Similarly, in *Son of the Navy*, the female lead, Stevie Moore, professes she will never marry a sailor, 'even if he were an Admiral', due to her experience waving goodbye to her father, a Navy chief petty officer, on the pier, an argument to which her father has no answer.[12] Sailors lived within American culture and were governed by its rules, but they were also seen as on the periphery due to their frequent time away from American soil.

When it comes to naval servicemen, officers were seen as preferable; as Lucy James put it in *Born to Dance*, 'too bad he's not an officer'.[13] In *Navy Blues*, Gibbs misrepresents himself as a candidate for the Naval Academy at Annapolis to be more attractive to librarian Doris Kimball and her middle-class, academic family, eventually earning a commission as a chief warrant officer.[14] In *Sweetheart of the Navy*, Harris' desire to become an officer is a major plot point, with him grasping with norms he will have to adopt as an officer. The Captain who is writing a letter of recommendation for his acceptance informs him that boxing is acceptable as a form of exercise, but participating in bouts for money is to remain the domain of the common sailors.

As a TM1, Breault never donned the uniform of a chief or an officer, so he was eminently recognizable as a sailor in the traditional crackerjacks. He appeared to wear that moniker proudly, it shaping his perceptions of the world around him, and he actively sought to reinforce his connection in speech, both publicly and privately. Breault's reclamation of his uniform would have been a moment of pride for him. Furthermore, while he possessed the privilege to wear a uniform, the uniforms were expensive. Sailors had to maintain them, keeping them presentable and updated with their current rank and hash stripes representing sea service. Overall, uniforms were, and still are, a significant investment in money and time. We know that Breault at least occasionally spent his own money on his uniform, as the Singer Sewing Company in San Francisco wrote to the Bureau of Navigation for an updated address to forward Breault's bill on 28 April 1939.[15] There are no surviving pictures of Breault in civilian clothing, as the knowledge we have on him is confined to his professional rather than personal life. In essence, the man Breault became was built upon the reputation of the uniform he wore; it defined him and his place in American society.

## Medal of Honor and other Military Accolades

There has been a consistent argument throughout that I believe Breault was a forgotten hero – as much through his own desires and actions as through any socio-cultural impediment to an enlisted sailor rising to prominence. If Breault sabotaged his career and actively kept his name away from public papers, then is it likely he did not actively seek medals and accolades from the USN? His actions in public seem to reflect the desire to remain anonymous – there are no accounts that he ever wore the Medal of Honor publicly. Immediately after receiving the award, the *New York Evening Post* praised his modesty and reported that Breault kept 'the medal and the button in his pocket'.[16] As he remained anonymous in newspaper reporting during his various duty stations, he likely refrained from wearing his Medal of Honor throughout his life, continuing to show the modesty that comes with refraining from public acknowledgment of his award. Despite this behaviour, Breault's attitude toward his other awards reveal an alternative side to his character.

Breault would receive other accolades in time, such as Good ConductMedals, the Yangtze Service Medal and, for service in the RNCVR, the Victory Medal and British War Medal. Breault earned all of these but, the latter two requried extra steps involving an official to write to the Department of National Defence in Ottawa, Canada, for a special exception to receive them due to his status as a Medal of Honor recipient:

> 'Although the time limit has expired I make special request for consideration of the above claim in view of the fact that the man is now the holder of the U.S. Congressional Medal of Honor and to the fact he has been away from the states for a lengthy period and therefor unable to make out the papers.'[17]

While this letter appears to have been written by a Captain F. Kelly, Breault was also willing to invoke his status as a Medal of Honor recipient in a letter to Congressman Benjamin Fairchild to gain a favourable exception.[18] In the conversation Breault had with his superior regarding writing the letter, he likely mentioned his status as a reason the Department of National Defence would grant an exception. Breault's willingness to remind others of his status appears to conflict with his potential motivation to hide the medal in public settings.

Breault wanted to portray that he didn't care about medals, his actions tell a different story. He actively sought accolades when he felt they were deserved, which can be seen in the example above. This behaviour is also displayed when he requested a Good Conduct Medal to be awarded for his enlistment from 1928–32, the only term he would not receive one due to his summary court martial. His request indicates he felt he was deserving of the award and wished to add it to his increasing collection, a potential shift in attitude as he aged.

Breault would write for a replacement Medal of Honor rosette, claiming that he had lost it. Considering Breault professed to carry the medal in his pocket, how did he lose it? Due to the timing of this request, it is possible he had given it to Pearl or Helen, but he may also have lost it in the numerous moves he made. Or perhaps he began wearing it for occasions out in town, and over time it became ragged. Regardless of how Breault lost it in San Diego, his request indicates he genuinely cared about the physical artefact itself, for what it represented in terms of sentiment and status. This desire for material awards potentially detracts from the argument that Breault did not want to advertise his status in a manner that would benefit him and actively sought to prevent his fame from becoming a part of his career.

Breault's loss of the medal was similar to his loss of the physical qualification to serve on a submarine, which would have led to him stripping the submarine warfare device from his sleeve, thereby losing a piece of his identity. Regardless of whether or not he actively sought them, Breault treasured the awards he did receive. It can be difficult to reconcile the modest Breault with the award-seeking Breault, but this could be due to his twin desire to benefit from his status while portraying himself as humble. To seek beyond what one has received could be viewed as vain, but it must be understood that enlisted men did not receive recognition for their actions. However, this does not match his behaviour in actively avoiding the press and other accolades, indicating his relationship to his medals was far more nuanced, as is the case for so many in the military today.

## Automobile

Submarine sailors portrayed in movies did not often interact with automobiles, but there is one example in the film *Navy Blues*. The film begins with four sailors seeking to rent a vehicle so they can enjoy their liberty at a specific spot they have in mind.[19] The owner of the rental agency understands the implications. In Breault's case, he did not seek to rent a car, but to own one. So what did a car, and being able to afford ownership of one, represent at that time?

Young women knew sailors, particularly junior ones, could not own cars without permission from their commands; they further surmised they would be unable to afford one on their salary. Dorothy Reynolds, in *Pigboat 39*, explained that the delicate courtship dance with sailors was in some respects safer because sailors didn't have cars:

> 'Dorothy and Jerry both liked servicemen and knew when the ships were coming in, even the Coast Guard Cutters … they'd haunt the places where the Navy hung out; Louis's Cafe, the Wunderbar, or the Silver Café. They'd dance and flirt, drink Cokes and fruit punch, and in their most sophisticated moments, accept a Camel, Old Gold,

or Lucky and smoke it in short quick puffs ... One of the best things about servicemen was that they didn't have cars. Without a car a girl couldn't be expected to neck, let alone pet, which meant that things progressed a little further anatomically.'[20]

By the end of the period, a car was seen by potential dates as a private spot that implied expected behaviour. In *Navy Blues*, this is commented on by the rental salesman, who asks: 'Four sailors and one car, where are you gonna sit the young ladies?'[21] To which one of the sailors replies: 'We'll take care of that. You just give us one with good strong springs.'[22] The innuendo is unsurprising, considering the perception that the automobile would lead to a private, hopefully intimate, moment with a young woman.

Considering the social status an automobile carried and its appeal for intimate matters, it is no surprise that Breault sought to own one.[23] Breault likely desired the higher social standing, but another possible interpretation is that ownership of a vehicle meant that he sought female companionship. This would be the same year, 1933, that he met his future wife, leading to the possibility that he may have even purchased the vehicle in the hope of attracting Pearl. A sailor owning a vehicle appears to be quite rare in film, which makes sense considering their price. An advertisement for Chevrolet details their cheaper prices as ranging from $445–$475, not unachieveable for a frugal first class petty officer, it would require quite a bit of creative budgeting.[24] Breault earned $96.60 per month from his base salary, an additional $2.00 per month for being a Medal of Honor recipient and a variable income based on the amount of times he dived while underway on the submarine, not exceeding $25.00 per month.[25] Breault's annual income would thus have been $1,183.20 if he didn't go underway, or $1,483.20 if every month he met the maximum submarine pay incentive, but that would also leave him with little time to actually enjoy the vehicle.

Considering maintenance, fuel, insurance and other incidental costs, Breault recognized he needed finance – a recent invention for consumer goods – to afford a new automobile. Breault purchased a vehicle in December 1932, giving Captain Nimitz (the same Chester W. Nimitz of Second World War fame), as a reference.[26] Nimitz and Breault were in contact, and it was likely a known practice for sailors to use their commanding officer as reference as a reputable connection. Before writing to the Bureau of Navigation, the company attempted to mail to Breault's given address, which was that of his sister, Diana, at 4542 Altadena Street, but these letters remained unanswered.[27]

The difficulty of affording a vehicle was magnified by his choice in buying a luxury model. Breault was not content with the more affordable Chevrolet, instead electing to buy a Buick, a vehicle that had achieved the level of status symbol whereby prominent citizens would advertise their ability to purchase a new Buick.[28] Advertisements for Buick would display men with attractive women, extolling the quality of the vehicles and the higher mileage they could achieve for the slightly higher price of $1,045. Breault worked out that he could afford it by being stingy with the rest of the expenses in his life, and made the purchase with automobile dealer Robert D. Maxwell in San Diego.[29]

Unfortunately, Breault learned what so many junior enlisted personnel discover today: an expensive car never stops being expensive, and can be very difficult to maintain on a military salary. It seems likely that Breault's Buick was repossesed, though it is also possible Breault simply missed a payment while underway. Given the exspense, at some point, Breault was likely forced to sell or otherwise get rid of the vehicle. If he owned another vehicle, the Bureau of Navigation did not receive a letter about it. Did Breault feel like a king driving in his Buick? Did he meet Pearl and invite her for a ride? Little did he know, the appeal of sailors was their transience and lack of expectation associated with flirting. It can be safely assumed that his command stepped in and that Breault's first time owning a vehicle ended in sadness. If he owned another in the future, he had learned the difficult financial lesson and bought one he could afford, as there are no more letters for debt collection regarding vehicles. His income was largely disposable, but his time owning a car would show the limits of his salary.

## Possession List upon Death

A list of Breault's possessions is included in the inventory of personal property after his death in 1941. These possessions included a Waltham gold watch, fourteen packages of cigarettes, a litre of alcohol, a can of nutmeg, a bottle of Vitalis hair styling pomade, a month's salary in cash and some other small items.[30] This list was potentially abridged; there may have been smaller things not considered valuable that were not included, such as mementos and letters. By the end of Breault's career, his pay was sufficient to style his hair, smoke cigarettes with regularity, afford vision-correcting eyeglasses and add a bit of flavour to his food. He had paper and a notebook in his quarters, suggesting Breault had picked up writing as a pastime, but this could have been merely for performing his duties.[31]

This list may not be an exhaustive inventory of his possessions at the time of his death, rather it was just what he had in his hospital room. There were surprisingly few uniform items mentioned, indicating that Breault's time in the hospital had stripped him of his immediate identity of being a sailor; sailors do not belong in hospital, there are only patients. While he did have a pair of dungarees for doing manual work such as sweeping hallways, he likely wore a hospital gown during much of his stay, meaning he was symbolically stripped of his material identity as represented by a uniform. It wouldn't surprise me if the dressing of patients was a psychological tool to make them more subservient and much more keen to leave.

The Waltham gold watch is an interesting artefact, one that ties in with his rescue. According to Julius Grigore, Sheppard Shreaves, the diver who rescued Breault and Brown, was presented with a 14-karat gold watch by the sailors of the submarine base, engraved 'To S.J. Shreaves, from Submarine Force, Coco Solo, C.Z., for his heroism in raising the O-5'. It was handed to him by the pair he rescued.[32] We don't know if Shreaves' watch was also a Waltham, but it is a distinct possibility that most submariners had a watch, with the gold watch being a symbol of status. Before the official introduction of the submarine warfare insignia in 1924, a gold watch could have been a common material possession that submariners sought to own as a collective identifier. But submariners did not choose a watch for timekeeping alone: Americans and watches have a long relationship, with them acting as status symbols for the modern man.

Breault's ownership of a watch, even though he probably eschewed wearing one while performing his duties aboard ship, reinforces the idea that he sought to project an image of access to consumer goods through employment. In the 1920s and 1930s, Waltham was a well-known and respected name in the watchmaking world.[33] To many people who recognized the brand, they would have understood that the purchase of a gold wristwatch represented a significant investment. And for an individual sailor, whose essential expenses were accounted for by the Navy and likely had the opportunity to save while out at sea, a gold watch represented a status item that could be flaunted to the general public.

Glasses were not surprising considering the revelation that Breault's eyesight appeared to decline as he aged. Spectacles had already begun to be associated with more intelligent, book-reading types by the 1930s. The three most educated characters in the film *Navy Blues* – Doris, her father and the antagonist Vincent – all wore glasses. Fashion is cyclical, and this was likely an era where wearing glasses was not fashionable for those seeking to portray themselves as masculine and blue-collar. Breault would have attempted to avoid wearing them whenever in public, as he sought to maintain the masculine sailor archetype. No image of a sailor wearing glasses, including officers, can be seen in any of the films I have mentioned that portray sailors.

Breault admitted to his doctor that he smoked around two packs of cigarettes a day, and if his tastes had not changed, he preferred Turkish Trophies or English Ovals when they were available.[34] Breault had fourteen packets of cigarettes and seven boxes of matches, the former likely a week's supply.[35] He also had four cans of 'Smoking Tobacco', indicating it was possible he also had a pipe or rolled his own cigarettes when he had the time or desired a different pleasure. Smoking in the Navy was ubiquitous, being one of the few times a sailor was allowed a break. Even if a sailor did not begin smoking cigarettes upon enlistment, the appeal to start smoking increased the longer one was in the service. The increase in female consumption of tobacco drove growth in the 1920s and 1930s, but it was estimated that 50 per cent of the adult male population in the United States smoked cigarettes.[36] Since cigarettes were so frequently enjoyed, smoking them opened social circles that may have previously been inaccessible to Breault, particularly in military circles.

The final two pictures taken of Breault indicate that he cut his hair regularly and styled it.[37] From his personal property list, we know he used Vitalis hair products.[38] Hair-styling creams, tonics, pomades and gels increased dramatically in popularity in the 1930s. Sailors in particular can be seen with styled hair in numerous pictures and in their portrayal in films. One Vitalis advertisement of the period extolled:

> 'With Vitalis every hair is firmly in place – just the way you want it – without a trace of that very [objectionable] "patent-leather" look. So soak up your summer sun, enjoy your gold – revel in your bath – your boats, your tennis – but [protect] and enhance the good looks of your hair with Vitalis and the "60-Second Workout".'[39]

The '60-Second Workout' consisted of fifty seconds of rubbing Vitalis in the person's hair and then ten seconds of combing and brushing the hair. The advertisements displayed a dapper, handsome young man in the waves on the beach; to the right, there is a headshot of the same man showing his well-groomed hair, implying that the message above was proven. Vitalis products were not expensive, generally under $1.00.[40]

The numerous hygienic and grooming items Breault had in his possession reflect a society that was increasingly focused on hygiene. Nevertheless, while on submarines, concern for hygiene was minimal, which possibly explains the derogatory moniker 'pigboats'. Much of the concern for certain items was likely due to uniform regulations. Breault was required to be clean-shaven, so he had a razor and razor sharpener.[41] He likely didn't particularly enjoy shaving with only water, so he used shaving cream to alleviate the burden slightly and help avoid small cuts and nicks. He then cleaned up the excess water and shaving cream with his face towel.[42] Breault appears to have brushed his teeth regularly, and maintained hygiene when not restricted by operations, reflecting greater cultural emphasis.

Breault also had a bottle of ink, writing materials, loose leaf notebook and one Parker fountain pen.[43] He was literate and likely had duties that required him to write reports. A recommended gift for men and women, the pen itself was a status symbol at over $3.50.[44] Breault would probably have received one or two pens as gifts, rather than buying them. He would have whipped it out to sign important documents whenever necessary, probably keeping it in his undress blue or dungaree jacket chest pocket, similar to how the businessman was portrayed in advertisements, or on his desk.[45] A sailor wielding a pen was no longer an unusual sight, and ballpoint pens were making it much easier for them to always have a pen available for important documentation.

The final consumer good he had that is commonly associated with sailors was the bottle of alcohol. Breault professed multiple times to be a teetotaller, and the lack of distinction means it could have been cleaning alcohol. Sailors are notorious drinkers, but only two films address sailors drinking, likely due to Prohibition-era legal restrictions associated with imbuing alcohol. *Men Without Women*, though released in 1930, manages to have portrayals of sailors drinking while in port in China, where alcoholic beverages were still legal. Once they are recalled, the sailors manage to sober up enough to get the ship underway, something addressed by the CO in a conversation with a newly reported officer. Several sailors are seen attempting to smuggle liquor on board. When on the DISSUB, one of the chief petty officers who was most inebriated and needed assistance getting started, finds the ship's supply of pure alcohol and rejoices. In *Sweetheart of the Navy*, filmed in 1937, the bar and show venue expects the sailors congregating there to drink the business back to solvency.

Most of the other contemporary films simply avoid the topic. *Born to Dance* was an exception, though it attempts to sanitize the sailors by using milkshakes as a stand-in for an alcoholic beverage during one of the songs that pairs several of the characters with a romantic interest. Tracy can be seen setting up a multi-straw tool on six opaque glasses filled with milkshakes. As he sings, he notes he 'hasn't a darned thing to do', then commences to down the arrayed drinks simultaneously, much to the shock and admiration of his shipmates.[46] Tracy's shipmates were expressing the sailors' admiration for the ability to drink rapidly (and hold one's liquor). Drinking was associated with masculinity, and not drinking would have detracted from Breault's insistence of adhering to the sailor archetype.

## Tattoos

Sailors have long been known for having tattoos, but there is no record of Breault having gotten the ink himself. While sailors continue to be known for desiring body art, the fashion appears to have been cyclical. During much of Breault's service, tattoos were out of style. In *Pigboats*, the only known fictional character to have tattoos was Biff Wolters, a torpedoman who had nearly every inch of hairy real estate covered by ink. When Mullaney meets him, he jokes to Knowles/Knowlton, 'I s'pose it took a war to git him away from the sideshow', implying the only place a man with those tattoos belonged was a freakshow or carnival.[47] Wolters ends the discussion by explaining that he's been tattooed since his time on the *Connecticut* in 1907; his tattoos confirm his story when he meets the fictional representation of Admiral Sims, who identifies him as a sailor of the 'old navy'.[48] While a fictional work, Gugliotta confirms that tattoos were still out of style by 1940. Only one of the members of his crew had tattoos, 'Stowaway' Johnson being covered in a similar fashion to Wolters.[49] Gugliotta implies that few young sailors had an interest in receiving tattoos like Wolters or Johnson, indicating that during Breault's tenure, tattoos were simply not in vogue, having fallen out of fashion.

Upon entry to the service, Breault already had several small scars along his arms, on one finger and on his chest.[50] I have offered a possible explanation that these were from industrial accidents or prior naval service, but an alternative answer is that Breault had tattoos in some of the areas. Upon entry into the USN, I had to describe my tattoos, determine the size of them and the location on my body they were imprinted. Was this process also present in Breault's time? Considering that the prevailing attitude of the USN was against tattoos, would they have labelled them as a scar? Wolters was shown as an ideal sailor, a veritable 'man's man' who had no time for women, something Stowaway Johnson also personified as a madman who worked and drank, only stopping to get a new tattoo every once in a while.[51] Only the truest, most devoted sailors had tattoos; as a sailor seeking to adhere to the archetype, Breault may have gotten tattoos during his time in the RNCVR.

However unlikely it is that Breault's scars were actually tattoos, the material culture associated with tattoo artwork remains fashionably cyclical and primarily associated with sailors. It is more likely that Breault did have scars, and looked at tattoos as the sailors of the *S-39* looked at Johnson, as an oddity from a previous era, until they once again became fashionable during the Second World War.

## Other Forms of Access

In a special request for shore leave in 1937, Breault indicated that he considered his home to be in Marysville, Washington. Whether or not that meant he owned property in the town is unknown, but it suggests he had further ties to the community.[52] The level of agency sailors had in deciding their destination, residence or market was comparatively low, but they were compensated well enough to enjoy the ports they frequented. As their storage was limited, sailors like Breault preferred smaller, disposable items. Despite this, Breault still aspired to one day own larger items such as an automobile, so long as it helped him portray an image of higher status.

The negative trade-off to a life as a sailor was the lack of long-term ties to communities. Breault's 'lifer' status prevented him from staying in the areas where he built personal ties, such as Marysville. The only address he gave was PO Box 38, indicating he and Pearl were unable to afford the purchase of a house on the combined income of a sailor and waitress.[53] Breault probably still desired to own property, but was doubtless still waiting for retirement to realize that dream. Breault likely helped his father and stepmother purchase a property in White Plains, NY, and the 1930 census reflects Breault's residence there whenever he returned from the West Coast or Asia. If Joseph died, Breault would have probably been the one who would inherit the house, though he still would have been responsible for housing his sisters and stepmother.

These lists, while exciting are still limited. Breault had access to consumer goods, though we do not know what that level was when stationed in the Philippines and China; it was, however, likely higher than most in the US had access to. Breault would have had access to cheap clubs, cheap goods, handmade clothes and numerous other luxuries a junior enlisted man could not have dreamed of in the States. There are no records of his time in the Philippines, but he would have had access there to all the things a young man wanted, as portrayed by sailors in Gugliotta's *Pigboat 39*. Being a sailor did not prevent him from creating a material identity or participating as a consumer. Breault had access to goods and services and could thereby live a limited version of the 'American Dream', but he could not escape saying goodbye to his loved ones at the pier to earn his living.

# Chapter 11

# Henry Breault Reconstructed

The final chapter will address the titular character by investigating the enigmatic person hidden behind the evidence associated with official correspondence and accounts that have been preserved in newspapers. Due to the scarcity of accounts, examination of the few pieces of research that are available is necessary. All accounts have been examined through a detached, sceptical lens that casts doubt on their authenticity. Despite the valid reasons for scepticism, this chapter will assume all of the personal documents are direct accounts from Breault, his family members or other people who wrote on his behalf. Based on this evidence, who was Breault and, more specifically, what kind of person was he? The evidence is scant, but the attempt is not to assign praise or blame, rather to resurrect the character of Breault through salient details in official documents and newspapers.

**Nonchalant or Oblivious?**

Breault lived in dangerous times, destined for a life of labour that was strenuous at best and downright dangerous in the worst of times. There is an argument to be made that description typifies the existence of humanity, and philosophy frequently revolves around the idea of suffering. For a reader who lives in the present day, surrounded by comforts that many of our ancestors could only dream of, Breault's life was filled with discomfort, pain, poor prospects and an ever-present sense of danger. Before he was rewarded for bravery in the face of this danger, he had likely faced it far more than the three times we are aware of. Breault survived the Halifax Explosion on the *Niobe* and two dangerous events on the *O-5*. After the aftermath of the sinking of the *O-5*, the Breault family forwarded his message home to the *New York Times*:

> 'Just a line to let you know that I am still alive. You have no doubt read about the sinking of the submarine. We were down there for hours and had no food. There was water in the lead tanks, but we did not dare to use it because it had been there for months and we

were afraid of lead poisoning. I sure was a sick boy but am well now. I have been out helping to raise the submarine. She is all right except the central control room where she was struck. The craft will soon be in condition again. But some of the crew will never go down in a submarine again. Fortunately it did not bother me at all.'[1]

This letter, written to a worried family, indicates the character of Breault as being either brave or foolhardy. Was he oblivious to the danger around him, or just nonchalant and accepting of its presence as a fact of life?

To illustrate this point, I wish to focus on Breault's following words: 'But some of the crew will never go down in a submarine again. Fortunately it did not bother me at all.' Such bravery is commendable in the wake of such a close call, but as a young man of 23, did he fully understand that he had come very close to death? As stated, this was not the first time Breault faced his demise; he had been forced to rapidly grow and face his mortality. Breault had been familiar with the dangers of maritime life for seven years at this point, and submarine service in particular was known for the dangers associated with operating the boats. His was not a foolhardy boast, just a recognition that the dangers were always there, and his nonchalant attitude was how he dealt with them.

The message was not intended to be nationally syndicated: Breault wrote thinking only his immediate family would read it. There is an acknowledgement that the letter would be brief, as he likely was ordered to write it in the middle of the day, while he still had duties before liberty was put down. Those who have written while carrying out a dangerous job will understand Breault's intention when writing a letter to inform loved ones he was safe. It would require a comforting tone, one that would conveniently downplay the stress of the event and focus on his current safety and wellbeing. For Breault, the fortunate part is that he did not feel broken by the event. He was probably far from oblivious, but carried a nonchalant air that helped him cope with the stress and danger that accompanied his maritime profession.

## 'I Hope to Tell You'

When Breault was asked whether he planned to stay in the service during a brief leave in New York in 1924, he replied: 'I hope to tell you.'[2] As one of only two known first-hand statements made by Breault, it must be analysed, just as Carlo Ginzburg analysed St Paul's passage, 'so do not become proud, but stand in awe', exploring how the meaning of the phrase changed as the culture that studies it evolved.[3] As Ginzburg notes, 'we can see the extent to which this passage reveals an entire world view', allowing an exploration of how culture affects interpretation and translation.[4] Ginzburg focused on the intellectual history that utilizes that phrase, but this analysis does not always extend to common colloquialisms; but if it did, what would this phrase say about the character of Breault?

The literal definition reflects a desire to have the opportunity to tell someone about a subject, one which they are passionate enough about to entreat the reader to pay close attention. This is a modern definition, but the context of the *New York Evening Post* offers clues that the phrase is imbued with a now defunct meaning signifying positive, enthusiastic affirmation. This is the only instance where we get an unbridled emotion indicated, thus Breault's use of 'I hope to tell you' indicates it is possible the now archaic idiom highlights his outlook on life.

The temptation is great to look into the phrase as deeply as Ginzburg had previously done, but this proves to be difficult. Published intellectual works that embraced the phrase as a reflection of their worldview is one thing; a colloquialism that was uttered as an understandable chic phrase recognizable to those within that period is another. In some respects, Breault's diction reflects the first forays into a hyper-realistic culture, one that was increasingly dissociated from any human group.[5] 'I hope to tell you' has an origin, but it likely was not known to Breault. Americans increasingly invoked simulacra to define themselves and their outlooks, stemming from cultural diffusion. Trends in fashion and language had become intertwined with popular culture. Dictionaries estimate the phrase appeared *circa* 1925, indicating it represented Breault's outlook at that point and potentially a fashionable trend in optimism in the face of danger that permeated 1920s American culture.

Breault's desire and effortless effusiveness for his profession is displayed in each enlistment and his pursuit to rejoin the submarine fleet towards the end of his life. The optimism of Breault, embracing his life and purpose as a sailor, particularly a submariner, would have endeared him to rates young and old. This cheery optimism, embodied by a small phrase, displayed in the harsh and unforgiving world, was embraced by submariners such as the survivors of the *Squalus*, who allegedly laughed and made jokes at the harrowing situation. It was an existential spirit that Jean-Paul Sartre and Albert Camus could only describe.

'I hope to tell you' appears to have been at the end of its usefulness, until one watches the contemporary film *It's Tough to be Famous*. The protagonist, Scotty McClenahan, is a submarine officer who was willing to sacrifice himself to ensure his shipmates would survive a DISSUB circumstance on the fictional *S-89*. Rescued at the last moment by divers, he returns to throngs of crowds praising him for his heroism.[6] While likely an amalgam of contemporary heroes such as Charles

Lindbergh, Edward Ellsberg and others, I forwarded the notion that Breault was possibly one of the heroes that inspired the character. Mary McCall, the author of the book that inspired the film, lived in New York City and was likely a witness to Breault appearing in Brooklyn. McCall, to make the character seem more noble and acceptable, may have changed Breault to be an officer in the mould of Saavy Cooke, CO of the *S-5*. The reception was not as rabid for Breault as it had been for Lindbergh, but it was certainly possible that Breault drew a sizable crowd as well on his return to New York on 13 March 1924.

There is some further potential evidence that Breault at least partially inspired McClenahan. In Breault's OMPF, one can see an inquiry made by telegram on 19 November 1930 by the Campbell-Ewald Company, a marketing firm, requesting the address of 'Henry Breault Medal of Honor Man'.[7] Why was a marketing firm looking for Breault? It is possible that the producer of the film and the marketing company were looking for people the movie could model its protagonist on. Nothing appears to have come out of the request, probably due to Breault's duties keeping him in the Asiatic Fleet at the time. However, there is no better evidence than a line given in the film itself. McClenahan replies to his bride on their honeymoon, 'I hope to tell you', when she mentions a new apartment as she describes their ideal life and marriage.[8] Considering the well-known published response of Breault, either McCall or the screenwriter may well have known that Breault used the colloquialism, and then put it into the mouth of their fictional character.

The assertion that Breault influenced at least one movie in his lifetime could change certain passages of this book, but unfortunately even the inclusion of a well-known phrase is not enough to tease out more evidence from Breault than has already been mined. There are limits to this style of analysis. Unfortunately, without more information, 'I hope to tell you' is more representative of Breault's optimism and connection to American culture, than concrete evidence to support any assertion on his inclusion in popular culture.

## French-Canadian

Breault frequently identified as bilingual, which is not surprising given his heritage. Joseph Breault and Flora Breault were both from Canada, with strong-enough ties that Joseph moved back to Canada with his family to ensure they had work. Still, Joseph Breault did not serve in the Canadian forces at any point, instead enlisting in the Connecticut National Guard before the Spanish-American War. French-Canadians in New England were frequently in both worlds, linguistically and culturally. In Canada, this duality of identity has been a source of friction at times, as cultural values appear to vary. French-Canadians in this era appear to have had a reputation as inefficient farmers (though this has not survived scrutiny in studies today).[9]

French-Canadian communities in Connecticut were well organized. In 1897, the twelfth annual French-Canadian convention was held in Meriden, indicating that an organized, sizeable French-Canadian presence had been in New England since at least 1885.[10] Their agenda was well communicated and indicates what they valued as a community around the time of Breault's birth:

1. The clergy and the intervention of the laity in religious matters; practical plan for continuing the demand for French Canadian priests in Canadian centers and at the same time preserve the faith of our ancestors.
2. The French and English languages in our schools and families; means to be taken for increasing the number of [Canadian] and French books in our public libraries.
3. Nationality and Americanism; are they compatible? The welfare of the French Canadians in Connecticut and the blessing of naturalization.
4. Our national association and the future of the French Canadians of the states; the reciprocal advantage of a closer union with our convention.
5. The convention; the importance of printing the minutes of our annual [reunion] in order that we may have the current history of our race in Connecticut.
6. The press. How to recompense the papers for their sympathetic regard for the French Canadians of Connecticut and pay the debt of gratitude due them.
7. Somplete reports of the French [Canadian] societies and centers.[11]

From this, the highest priority was on religious matters, language and resolving the difficulty of integration into American society as a community. Other concerns were primarily communication to the community, and those outside of it, of the goals of the convention. Breault was part of a community that had existed in the English worlds of the Dominion of Canada and the United States, and had survived with their ancestors' religion, language and customs intact, and he likely shared these values throughout his life.

Two remarks stand out as unexpected, the 'blessing of naturalization' and their desire to repay a 'debt of gratitude' to members of the Connecticut press.[12] French-Canadians in New England and other northern states were increasingly common between 1860 and 1920 due to the same pull factors that enticed other immigrants to America, namely employment.[13] By 1914, Norwich, Connecticut, recorded that there were over 400 French-Canadian voters residing in the city, a total that a reporter estimated was a third of the total voting population.[14] The press of Connecticut generally seemed to embrace French-Canadians, something that was recognized and appreciated by the community. This ties in with espousing naturalization and integration while maintaining a cohesive identity. While serving in the RNCVR, Breault managed to enlist and stated his birthplace was in Quebec. However, in his enlistment paperwork, Breault always referred to Putnam, CT, as his birthplace, reflecting how industrialization created a challenge for traditional identification based on birthplace. Coming from a French-Canadian family, Breault likely had dual British Dominion and United States citizenship, so which did he identify as? Would he have said he was French-Canadian or American? The answer is that he identified as both French-Canadian and American, but utilized whichever matched the cultural expectation of the audience he was attempting to be a part of.

Breault's bilingual status likely influenced his worldview in ways that even he was unaware of. Contemporary philosopher Ludwig Wittgenstein, continuing a line of thought extending from Wilhelm Humboldt and Immanuel Kant, believed that language shapes our *Weltanschauung* (world view). As described in the previous section, Breault openly embraced American military service and the common American colloquialisms. His French-Canadian identity may have even been commented upon by shipmates, but he was certainly no more unusual than the former German Imperial Navy sailor Stanley Mandekic, who served in the USN after the war and rose to the rank of chief petty officer. Mandekic was well respected, to the point he was the frontrunner to replace the COB who was departing, losing only due to his impending transfer date.[15] The sailors aboard any submarine were of varying backgrounds, reflecting the status of the United States as a magnet for immigration. A French-Canadian sailor in the heterogonous USN environment would not have merited much attention, at least any more than the usual taunting that sailors of all ethnicities would receive.

Breault was increasingly detached from his French-Canadian heritage, choosing to live on the West Coast and in the Philippines whenever he had a chance to. Even after his numerous cardiac episodes, his last request for duty was in Anchorage, Alaska, a far cry from the sunny and warm years he had spent in Asiatic ports and far from any bastion of French-Canadian communities. One of the few places he had indicated he considered home was Marysville, Washington, but even this was in official documentation requesting shore duty in the area. This may have been a stable place for his family, more so than for Breault, but it is possible that he had built community ties as a member of the small town. As he was disconnected from his parents, did he also feel his ties to his French-Canadian family diminish and his identity in connection with the US increase? As researchers have previously observed, French-Canadians maintained a cohesive identity in both Canada and New England, frequently characterized by linguistic and religious ties. Throughout his career, Breault professed to maintain a competency for French and maintained he was Roman Catholic. It is assessed as likely that Breault still considered French an important language in his life, even if English was increasingly his common language. Breault was probably influenced by his French language in service, perhaps even providing the root of his apparently endless drive and optimism.

## Catholic

The relationship of American culture with its Catholic contributors has a history that would politely be described as turbulent. Immigrants in the nineteenth and twentieth centuries were increasingly Catholic, sparking waves of resentment from the Protestant establishment. The 1920s was one of these periods of resentment. A major part of the Ku Klux Klan's bandwagon was Anti-Catholic resentment and the supposed incompatibility of Catholicism and democracy.[16] Even H.P. Lovecraft's work was permeated with Catholic immigrant characters, who were portrayed in a rather unflattering fashion.[17] As Dumenil writes, it is important to note that Catholics were far from a homogenous grouping; they had their own conflicts and this reactionary pressure stimulated unity among the factions and she offers the example of the tension between Polish and Irish groups as a specific example.[18]

Breault professed to be Roman Catholic throughout his career and received a Catholic burial. In the spartan room on a submarine, a chaplain was not always a commodity one could expect. Lay leaders could have been assigned among the crew, so attending Sunday services in the crew's mess or the torpedo room did occur and were likely included in the Plan of the Day. Unfortunately, we have no other evidence that Breault was one of these lay leaders, attended services of any kind or even if he participated in the greater customs that defined Catholicism. The latter option has become increasingly common in the present day, but it is evaluated that if Breault did eschew his obligations, he would have felt justified should his duties have prevented it.

One instance that was surprising was that the funeral service for Pearl Breault in 1939 was a cremation. The *San Diego Union* obituary for Pearl indicated the service would be at Benbough Funeral Parlors at two in the afternoon, specifically at the Benbough crematory.[19] Catholics who believe in the resurrection of the body would have insisted a full burial be performed. As St Paul stated in *Corinthians*:

> 'For whether I, or they, so we preach, and so you have believed. Now if Christ be preached, that he arose again from the dead, how do some among you say, that there is no resurrection of the dead? But if there be no resurrection of the dead, then Christ is not risen again. And if Christ be not risen again, then is our preaching vain, and your faith is also vain. Yea, and we are found false witness of God: because we have given testimony against God, that he hath raised up Christ; whom he hath not raised up, if the dead rise not again. And if Christ be not risen again, your faith is vain, for you are yet in your sins. Then they also that are fallen asleep in Christ, are perished. If in this life only we have hope in Christ, we are of all men most miserable. But now Christ is risen from the dead, the firstfruits of them that sleep: For by a man came death, and by a man the resurrection of the dead. And as in Adam all die, so also in Christ all shall be made alive.'[20]

This passage, taken from the contemporary standard Catholic Bible, was referenced by the most famous priest of the period, Father Charles E. Coughlin, a radio personality who gained a large audience over the airwaves:

> 'In one sense the Resurrection of Christ from the dead becomes almost equally important as the passing of Christ from the living to the dead. "If Christ be not risen again, then is our preaching vain, and your faith is also vain," says St Paul.'[21]

Father Coughlin's quotation is close to the verbatim passage from the Bible and his sermon consists of the resurrection of the body of Christ on Easter Sunday. This passage cannot be underestimated in understanding Catholic practices surrounding burial. The belief of resurrecting the body was a strong influence in Catholic burials, so Pearl's cremation would be odd for a man who would identify as a devout Catholic.

    A few possibilities can be gained from this insight. It is assessed as highly likely that the funeral service was carried out in accordance with the wishes of Pearl. If she had a will or had mentioned precisely how she wished to be buried, this may have been reason enough. A more cynical interpretation is that Breault was a devout Catholic and the cremation was both economically motivated and a spiritual punishment for Pearl's infidelity. This does not fit within the Catholic concept of forgiveness, another tenant of the faith, nor does it seem to be in line with any other interpretation of Breault's personality. I think it probable that Breault was simply not a perfect or devout Catholic, and followed his own interpretation of his faith, without the focus on the resurrection of the body. This is an attitude that could have been shared with many of his sailor compatriots, combined with seeking to fulfil the last wishes of his wife.

Breault's service does serve as evidence that there was a focus on manpower and competence, rather than religion, in creating American heroes. In the dynamic demography of the United States in the 1920s and 1930s, this was likely a pragmatic decision. While sailors who were in coastal regions were still an important part of the naval manpower pool, they were no longer the defining factor of it. The USN was a force that constructed Bluejackets, rather than recruiting them, utilizing institutions such as Recruit Training Commands, further socialization in rating schools and the ever-present *Bluejacket's Manual*, first written in 1902. Religious diversity would have been the norm, rather than the exception. Considering the names of his shipmates, Breault was far from the only Catholic aboard the ships he served on, and likely saw little or no bias against his religious beliefs while aboard naval vessels, as indicated by his receipt of the nation's highest honour.

## Sailor/Submariner

Breault appeared to be positively inclined to a life at sea, even before his time in the RNCVR. Fred St Onge noted that Breault mentioned one of his ancestors had spent a life at sea, using it as an ancestral reason for a predicted maritime career.[22] Joseph J. Breault, while not a sailor, had likely been transported via ship to assignments during the Spanish-American War and this may have caused Breault to dream of a maritime life. Life at sea has an appealing romantic quality, one that continues to attract men and women of diverse backgrounds. I have some experience in this regard. My boyhood room was filled with model ships of all sorts from different eras. I was an introverted boy, one who preferred reading and writing over companionship. From many descriptions of Breault – a potential interpretation of his willing descent to anonymity, eschewing mentions of his service and requests for service in the Asiatic theatre – he may be seen as an introverted, quiet soul who simply desired a life out to sea.

Many introverts lived aboard ships, but their special conditions created an insular group, one that many had never had the privilege to be a part of. It is described as a coming out of one's shell process, but must not be mistaken as a departure from an introverted life. The group is moulded by shared conditions, danger, competence and of course trust. As a sailor who was discharged, I can tell you there is no other place in the civilian world that I have been a part of with that bond. This is something that remains a common complaint for those who leave the service. One can imagine Breault in what are commonly described as 'dead-end' civilian jobs and feeling the need for the connection he had in the RNCVR, to recapture the romantic feelings of a life at sea that he described to St Onge.

From Breault's OMPF, there are indications that identity factors were primary motivators ranking as highly as monetary considerations. His desire for service in the submarine fleet, one already notorious in the 1920s for close bonds and no-frills decorum, in all likelihood reflected this initial desire for camaraderie, and his attempts to return to submarines after his initial disqualification despite serving on a platform that had a similar, though more formal, reputation. Submariners going to other communities are not an unusual occurrence, as the rigours of duty on pigboats were known for injuring sailors. Even on today's much more habitable submarines, injuries can and will occur; if they are debilitating, a sailor may be sent for shore duty for the remainder of their contract, get a medical discharge or, once they convalesce, join a different community that needs their skillset.

Breault's tenure had shore-duty-like stops, such as time in the Torpedo Shop on board the submarine tender USS *Holland* in 1929. These stops were few and still entailed duty aboard seagoing vessels, as the USN did not have the manpower to perform all the duties that had to be carried out. Every sailor was overworked and underpaid in the peacetime interwar USN. Breault likely appreciated the break for a spell, but in 1929 he found the change so unappealing that he swapped duties with a sailor on board the *V-2* instead of staying on the cosier *Holland*.[23] This move, characteristic of many submariners on shore duty remembering their time out at sea, is typical of the submariner seeking out the submarine culture, often to the detriment of their health.

## Modest/Unassuming

Fred St Onge remembered Breault as average, good-natured, sociable and open minded.[24] The reporter who interviewed him for the *New York Evening Post* similarly identified Breault as 'modest', due to his practice of not wearing the Medal of Honor, but rather keeping it in his pocket.[25] This modesty extended to a belief in his lack of intellectual capacity, which he expressed personally to his commanding officer when approached about the Gunner examination. Through Breault's portrayal of himself, we can discern that he wanted to live life as an enlisted sailor.

It is possible that Breault purposefully conducted himself in this manner to continue living life as he wished. Though speculative at best, perhaps Breault acted in this manner to fit in with the enlisted ratings, purposefully sabotaging his results in the Gunner examination, refusing to ask to be advanced to chief and consistently making himself unassuming through modesty. Both instances were similar to how two-time Medal of Honor recipient Dan Daly allegedly refused advancement to an officer rank, stating that he would rather be a good sergeant than just another officer.[26] While officers enjoyed higher social status and pay, there were disadvantages that an introvert who had finally found a home among the enlisted men would have struggled with, such as representing the USN and surrendering even more agency.

This is even more likely when one considers that Breault potentially did not believe he was a hero. Author Mary McCall offers a possible insight – though the exact situation is not the same – as to how Breault may have felt in the immediate aftermath of being trapped with Brown on the *O-5* in her depiction of Scotty McClenahan's experience:

> 'The first few hours in that torpedo room had been bad. There was the being scared first, when he realized the sub was crippled and couldn't rise ... Then a kind of frenzy of resentment at being trapped there, penned in so you couldn't help yourself. Then everything coming clear, and a thin voice he didn't know giving orders. Then terrible loneliness and fear again as he saw the last pair of feet going into the tube. He'd cried. That's what he'd done. Blubbered. They didn't know that, these people who were slobbering about his being a hero. He'd cried like a kid because he was afraid, and so dammed mad at having to die like a poisoned pup all alone there. Then the agony of the eight hours, feeling the sweat pouring into his eyes, listening to himself breathe, louder, louder with the pain growing worse every time until his tongue was thick and his throat raw meat.'[27]

Breault would have had the company of Brown, but that was little solace when it was still highly likely they would die without being rescued. They also probably had the conversation of who, if it was possible, would escape from the submarine via the torpedo tubes in a last-ditch effort, and who would stay. Escaping from a DISSUB was a common trope employed in film. The scene in *The Goldfish Bowl* could have been inspired by Breault, but films such as *Men Without Women* have scenes where the protagonist (in this case Burke/Quartermain) melodramatically sacrifices himself to ensure the rescue of the remaining crew.[28] He is then left alone, as McClenahan also found himself.

Ultimately, Breault's reluctance to wear the medal was likely a display of true modesty, a selfless belief that he did not deserve praise. Breault and Brown may have felt that the divers and canal workers who rescued them were more deserving of praise. Perhaps Breault assumed that any sailor, had they the information he had, would have conducted themselves in the same manner, conveniently forgetting that most of the sailors in the *O-5* collision had abandoned ship despite knowing several of their shipmates were likely below decks. This is not a condemnation, but the product of rational self-preservation. Breault was the irrational one, running below to rescue someone, even if he thought he had enough time to escape after finding Brown. Breault's modesty reflects his likely desire to remain anonymous whenever possible.

**Father/Husband**

Breault married Pearl around 10 April 1935 and adopted her daughter, Helen, as his own. While Helen was aged 10 or 11 at the time, Breault indicated in numerous clues in his official documentation that he treated her like his daughter, and considered himself her father. The first document is a travel claim for reimbursement of his dependents, Pearl and Helen Breault, moving from Bremerton, Washington State, to San Diego between 1 and 4 September 1938.[29] In it, Breault attested that he was the girl's father:

> 'I, Henry Breault, certify that Helen Breault is my legitimate child, will be 15 years of age at next birthday, and is a member of my household; that said child is not possessed of property or income adequate for its support and education; is not the beneficiary, or beneficiaries, either directly or through others, of any trust or estate entitling them it to income adequate for its support and education; that said child is in fact now and at all times solely dependent on me; that in all respects I maintain the child at my own expense and from my own resources and am not reimbursed therefore directly or indirectly in any manner or form whatsoever.'[30]

In this case, it was essential for Breault to identify as her father for legal purposes, as it would be the only way that he would be reimbursed for her travel. But there are hints that Breault potentially saw Helen as his daughter without regard to blood.

Even after Pearl's death in Los Angeles on 10 February 1940, Breault maintained Helen as his next of kin, as indicated on his medical history sheet on 29 April 1941.[31] A more cynical person would say this was due to the benefits provided by marriage in the military, such as medical insurance for the dependent and extra pay for the service member, but there is no record in Breault's OMPF that he received extra money other than the travel claim for having a dependent in his care. The only extra incentive for which Breault received any money at the end of his career was his Medal of Honor pay, which equated to an additional $2 per month. It does not appear that Breault kept in contact with Helen, as he indicated her last known address was in Marysville, with no full postal address, but the 1940 census stated that she was living with her father in Los Angeles.[32] Helen could have made the move to be closer to her father, return to California or seek employment in the area, as so many others did.

There are numerous explanations for the relationship, but the only one that is backed up by surviving evidence is that Breault adopted Helen as his own child. Another explanation may be that Pearl and Henry had much met earlier, and Helen was his biological child, but there is absolutely no evidence to support this assertion, and nor is it unlikely to surface. William Slaughter stated in his letter that he had been married for twelve years before 24 December 1932, meaning he and Pearl had been together since 1920.[33] Helen's birthdate of 24 January 1924 is also problematic, as Breault was then in the Panama Canal Zone aboard the *O-5* and his movements were monitored and recorded. Unless Pearl happened to be vacationing in the area roughly nine months prior to this, around 24 March 1923 – which is assessed to be unlikely as it invokes too many unknown variables – it is impossible for Breault to have fathered Helen. Finally, Helen returned to San Diego to live with her biological father after the death of her mother, indicating that regardless of her feelings for Breault, she felt William Slaughter was her father.

The most likely explanation is the adoption theory, but documents from William, Pearl or Helen Slaughter that would offer clarity on the subject are currently unavailable. What is likely is that Breault wanted to be a father to Helen and thought of himself as responsible for her care. The building of a relationship came into being during the Great Depression, which has been noted to have had a profound effect on the perception of fatherhood in America due to the cultural and economic realities of the period.[34] Breault was a provider, but he was one whose job necessitated a high degree of independence for the woman he married. Pearl exercised her independence by working and raising her child as she saw fit. The ability to rear children was important to conceptions of masculinity, even if Helen was not biologically his child. This could even explain why Breault informed others that she was his own child, as it would justify to himself that he was able to rear a child that was his own. Being a father and a husband were thus pillars of Breault's identity during and after his marriage.

## An Optimistic, Nonchalant, French-Canadian, Catholic, Sailor/Submariner and Husband/Father: a Man of His Times

Breault's identity can be teased out through clues, as Carlo Ginzburg intimated was possible. Unfortunately, these clues only offer so much. They require an understanding of the period as an American from 1900–41 would have, a cultural context I am limited in understanding through representations that survive from popular culture. Further, the limitations of the source material are self-evident. Describing a person through military records can only offer so much, the records themselves frequently being on the periphery of events on the outside looking in.

The major example of this is the character of Breault's service and his corresponding descent into relative anonymity. The evidence is that Breault, despite being offered the ability to take an officer examination, remained an enlisted sailor throughout his career, never even rising to the rank of chief petty officer. This is a complicated question to answer, as we have no argument from Breault or anyone who knew him as to why he should remain a torpedoman's mate first class. The alternatives I have presented, in order of magnitude of the leap of faith required to believe them, are as follows:

> **Luck of the draw**: Breault is not the only sailor to be deserving of advancement, even with recommendations from his Commanding Officer. The recommendation was made when the manpower in the Navy was reduced to an incredibly low number, likely due to budgetary and billet issues. Breault's advancement to TM1 had already been a favour; it is possible that was the extent of the favour allowed. Oftentimes, advancement comes down to timing as much as it does to skill and despite his numerous recommendation, the USN simply wasn't looking for more TMCs while Breault served.
>
> **Brave but clueless**: Breault struggled with academic ventures, likely due to cultural pressures and a lack of intellectual curiosity promoted as part of the sailor archetype. He was clearly a gifted sailor, but that required a practical knowledge that could be taught. His limits were in intellectual capability, and he showed he could be clueless when a bit of situational awareness would be wise.

**The Dan Daly approach**: Breault never had a desire to be anything but a sailor, so he actively strove to sabotage any chance he had to be advanced to chief or officer. This explains his lack of urgency in taking the test, his failing in the gunner examination and lack of follow-up to becoming a chief. Breault simply wanted to be a good TM1, rather than just another officer.

Again, these are possibilities, and the truth was likely some variation incorporating elements of all three. There can be no further insight on my part without artefacts of a personal nature. This chapter must end without a grand conclusion, but rather a request to visit family artefacts and see if your ancestor served with Breault or was an old friend or romantic partner of the still unknown submariner.

To oversimplify, sailors were complex creatures, subject to a variety of individual, social and economic factors. Breault was no exception.

# Conclusion

# History Seen Through the Eyes of a Submariner

A sailor exists both within and outside the culture they serve, granting them a privileged view of their society should they desire to reframe their existence. Many choose not to, but examining their life in context allows for original historical analysis that contradicts the popular myths surrounding their contemporary context. By looking at the world from how Breault sought to construct his own life, rather than imposition from an external myth's context, a surprising view emerges of American history that does not conform to the myths.

By analysing Breault's life, I offer some insights, give fewer answers but ask more questions that other scholars who may be in a more privileged position than myself can access sources for. I seek to break the feedback loop of structuralist tendencies, viewing each era with a frame so wide that no individual picture can fit within it. As Baudrillard described the map that completely covered the world, so too have misconceptions suffocated the actual historical analysis, preventing it from disseminating through cultural diffusion to popular audiences. Breault is a hero, but he is also a person, who experienced life and had influences that shaped how he experienced them.

I have attempted to survey some of these avenues of research, particularly medical history, to the best of my ability. I lack the prerequisite knowledge to properly analyse this topic, and I invite a researcher with the background to conduct such analysis. The same request goes to local historians who seek to understand Breault's experience in their particular town or city, or researchers who study the movement of military personnel. There are numerous fields I have neglected to mention or may not have thought about, and to them I apologize. I believe the documentation surrounding Breault could be impactful in numerous studies that have not considered close examination of an enlisted sailor. The survival of career-oriented documentation such as Breault's OMPF is always a treasure, fortuitous for numerous disciplines.

Seeing history through the eyes of Breault has been insightful and helped me make peace with my own naval career. I believe the work could also help others in a similar vein. I ask the dear readers who also swell with pride at the sight of the dolphins that sit in their sea chest: did your career contain some of the excitement and hurdles that Breault had? While some may focus on the positives of a career, Breault had numerous roadblocks as well. Did you ever buy a car you couldn't afford? Were you ever party at an NJP proceeding? Did you ever deal with marital infidelity? Did going out to sea take a toll on your personal and familial relations? Did you ever get passed over for an award you felt you had earned? Did you ever get physically disqualified from submarine duty and sent to the surface fleet? Did you ever fail an examination for advancement to officer? If the answer to any of those questions is 'yes', don't worry. You are in good company, as Breault did all of these, and likely more shenanigans we are unaware of. Reading about a Medal of Honor recipient as a person, rather than a personage, is far more insightful and interesting to the person reading than just another 'Great Man' or 'Military Hero' story.

While military history always seems to be a vogue topic, studying military men and women outside of conflict is fruitful too. They are not war machines, who exist only in war to serve a singular purpose and then are deactivated. The ones who stood ready for war are members of our society; understanding their motivations in peacetime could also prove to be insightful, just as this study into Breault's life has been.

Unfortunately, many do not understand this link. There is a collective tendency to refer to ships as a singular unit and ascribe all human achievement to the ship alone. When this is not done, the CO is often raised to an exulted status to illustrate the efforts of the crew. This latter tendency can be seen in awards in the submarine fleet, as COs are given the highest award for actions performed by the ship. Of the eight submarine Medal of Honor recipients, Breault was the only one who was an enlisted man, and the only one who was not commanding officer. There are arguments to be made that I should include Master Chief Hospital Corpsman William R. Charette and Vice-Admiral Paul F. Foster in the tally, but I do not; even though they became submariners, they were awarded the Medal of Honor for combat-related actions before their time as submariners. To illustrate a point, if they are included, 80 per cent of Medals of Honor awarded to submariners went to officers; this figure compares to the aggregate recipients comprising 77 per cent enlisted personnel and only 23 per cent officers.[1]

This imbalance in Navy awards is a result of the anthropomorphization of the ship to equal its CO, and the CO alone, which is harmful to understanding naval service in general. Historians should be above such measly concerns of assigning blame or praise, but the very act of getting a ship, let alone a fleet, underway speaks volumes for the range of societies devoted to maintaining such complex beasts in war and peace. Breault's Medal of Honor, though it guaranteed the survival and accessibility of these documents, was a drop of water from the top of a wave. For those seeking authentic insight into the lives of service members, not just sailors, I offer a template as to how to explore an OMPF for the purpose of original insight. The topics may vary depending on the nature of the inquiry, but analysis can come organically, then be linked into other realms of research when applicable.

Microhistory is an insight into the unknown and what had previously been the unknowable. Breault's life, and that of sailors and submariners like him, is equally worthy of investigation as any admiral, president, general, business head or other prominent personas from any generation. I admit that exploring Breault's conduct, identity and character requires further investigation into realms I may not have thought of. I invite other researchers who may be interested to add to the mosaic, with the hope that more personal documentation can forward the conversation in a manner that adds new insight into the life and times of Henry Breault.

# Bibliography

## Archives

Congressional Medal of Honor Society, Medal of Honor Recipients, Henry Breault Collection. Shared with author by Archivist & Historical Collections Manager Laura Jowdy.

Submarine Force Library and Museum, *Submarine Archives, Biography Collection, Medal of Honor, Henry Breault Collection.*

## Books

Appleton, Victor, *Tom Swift and His Submarine Boat* (New York: Grosset & Dunlap, 1910).

Baudrillard, Jean, *Simulacra and Simulation*, trans. Sheila F. Glaser (Ann Arbor: University of Michigan Press, 1994).

Beach, Edward L., *Salt and Steel: Reflections of a Submariner* (Annapolis: Naval Institute Press, 1999).

Bishop, David J., *Images of America: Naval Submarine Base New London* (Portsmouth: Arcadia, 2006).

Bureau of the Census Department of Commerce and Labor, *Thirteenth Census of the United States Taken in 1913: Statistics for New York* (Washington D.C.: Government Printing Office, 1913).

Bureau of Navigation, *U.S. Navy Ports of the World: San Francisco* (Washington D.C.: Ditty Box Guide Book Series, 1920).

Connecticut Adjutant General, *Roster of Connecticut Volunteers Who Served in the War Between the United States and Spain: 1898–1899* (Hartford: The Case, Lockwood and Brainard Company, 1899).

Conner, Claude C., *Nothing Friendly in the Vicinity: My Patrols on the submarine USS Guardfish during WWII* (Annapolis: Naval Institute Press, 1999).

Dubay, Ted E., *Three Knots to Nowhere* (Jefferson: McFarland & Company, 2014).

Durham, Victor G., *The Submarine Boys on Duty: Life on a Diving Torpedo Boat* (Akron: The Saalfield Publishing Co, 1909).

Ellsberg, Edward, *Pigboats* (Rahway: Quinn and Boden, 1931).
Federal Writer's Project of the Works Progress Administration, *San Diego in the 1930s: The WPA Guide to America's Finest City* (Los Angeles: University of California Press, 2013).
Galantin, Ignatius J., *Take Her Deep!: A Submarine Against Japan in World War II* (Chapel Hill: Algonquin Books, 1987).
Gimblett, Richard H., and Michael L. Hadley (eds), *Citizen Sailors: Chronicles of Canada's Naval Reserve, 1910–2010* (Toronto: Dundurn, 2010).
Ginzburg, Carlo, *Clues, Myths, and the Historical Method*, trans. John Tedeschi and Anne C. Tedeschi (Baltimore: Johns Hopkins University Press, 1989).
Gugliotta, Bobette, *Pigboat 39* (Lexington: University of Kentucky, 1984).
Heaslip, Matthew, *Gunboats, Empire and the China Station: The Royal Navy in 1920s East Asia* (London: Bloomsbury Publishing, 2020).
Herodotus, *The History*, trans. David Greene (Chicago: University of Chicago Press, 1987).
Howard, Alice S., *Seaman's Handbook for Shore Leave* (Boston: Custom House, 1920).
Holwitt, Joel I., *'Execute Against Japan': The US Decision to Conduct Unrestricted Submarine Warfare*, Vol. 121 of Williams-Ford Texas A&M University military history series (College Station: Texas A&M University Press, 2009).
Jackson, Stephen L., *The Men: American Enlisted Submariners in World War II; Why They Joined, Why They Fought, and Why They Won* (Indianapolis: Dog Ear Publishing, 2010).
Kammen, Carol, *On Doing Local History: Third Edition* (New York: Rowman & Littlefield, 2014).
LaRossa, Ralph, *The Modernization of Fatherhood: A Social and Political History* (Chicago: University of Chicago Press, 1997).
Marshall, Benjamin T. (ed.), *A Modern History of New London County, Connecticut: Vol. 1* (New York: Lewis Historical Publishing Company, 1922).
Mears, Dwight S., *The Medal of Honor: The Evolution of America's Highest Military Decoration* (Lawrence: University Press of Kansas, 2018).
Nasser, Alan, *Overripe Economy: American Capitalism and the Crisis of Democracy* (Chicago: Pluto Press, 2018).
Nietzsche, Friedrich W., *The Gay Science*, trans. Walter Kaufmann (New York: Vintage Books, 1974).
O'Kane, Richard H., *Clear the Bridge!: The War Patrols of the U.S.S. Tang* (Novato: Presidio Press, 1977).

# BIBLIOGRAPHY

Partridge, Eric, *A Dictionary of Catch Phrases, American and British, from the Sixteenth Century to the Present Day*, ed. Paul Beagle (Lanham: Scarborough House, 1992).

Paul, Heike, *The Myths That Made America* (Bielefeld: Transcript Verlag, 2014).

Roberts, Mark K., *Sub: An Oral History of US Navy Submarines* (New York: Berkley Caliber, 2007).

Schultz, Robert, and James Shell, *We Were Pirates: A Torpedoman's Pacific War* (Annapolis: Naval Institute Press, 2009).

Serans, Luis P., 'From Pole to Pole; Or, Frank Reade, Jr.'s Strange Submarine Voyage', *Frank Reade Weekly Magazine: Containing Stories of Adventures on Land, Sea, and in the Air*, 4 (2 November 1902).

Steinbeck, John, *The Grapes of Wrath* (New York: Modern Library, 1939).

Stillwell, Paul, *Submarine Stories: Recollections from the Diesel Boats* (Annapolis: Naval Institute Press, 2013).

The Day, *First & Finest: The 100-Year Anniversary of Naval Submarine Base New London* (Battle Ground: Pediment, 2015).

*United States Navy Regulations, 1920* (United States: U.S. Government Printing Office, 1941), 551–556.

*United States Navy Uniform Regulations* (United States: U.S. Government Printing Office, 1922), 20–20A.

Uruburu, Paula M., *American Eve: Evelyn Nesbit, Stanford White, the Birth of the 'It' Girl, and the Crime of the Century* (New York: Riverhead Books, 2008).

Verne, Jules, *Twenty Thousand Leagues Under the Sea* (New York: Grosset & Dunlap, 1917).

Verrill, A. Hyatt, *Panama Past and Present* (New York: Dodd, Mead, and Co, 1921).

Wright, Ernest V., *Thoughts and Reveries of an American Bluejacket* (self-published, 1918).

## Court Case

*The Abangarez*, 60 F.2d 543 (E.D. La. 1932). U.S. District Court for the Eastern District of Louisiana – 60 F.2d 543 (E.D. La. 1932) 3 August 1932.

## Films

Ashby, Hal, dir., *The Last Detail*, 1973 (Columbia Pictures, Amazon.com Collection).

Bacon, Lloyd, dir., *Submarine D-1*, 1937 (Cosmopolitan Productions, Campbell Films Collection).

Capra, Frank, dir., *Submarine*, 1928 (Columbia Pictures, Campbell Films Collection).
Conway, Jack, dir., *Hell Below*, 1933 (Metro-Goldwyn-Mayer, Presumed Lost).
Del Ruth, Roy, dir., *Born to Dance*, 1936 (Metro-Goldwyn-Mayer, Amazon.com Collection).
Ford, John, dir., *Men Without Women*, 1930 (Fox Film Corporation, Campbell Films Collection).
Green, Alfred, dir., *It's Tough to be Famous*, 1932 (Warner Bros Pictures Inc, Amazon.com Collection).
Mansfield, W. Duncan, dir., *Sweetheart of the Navy*, 1937 (Grand National Films Inc, https://www.youtube.com/watch?v=y9N1U0U19bU&t=2s).
Sewell, Vernon and Gustav Ucicky, dirs, *Morgenrot* (Dawn), 1933 (Universum Film AG, Amazon.com Collection).
Staub, Ralph, dir., *Navy Blues*, 1937 (Republic Pictures, https://www.youtube.com/watch?v=Y_m7P7BLOMM).

## Journal Articles

Anderson, William L., and Derek W. Little, 'All's Fair: War and Other Causes of Divorce from a Beckerian Perspective', *The American Journal of Economics and Sociology* 58, no. 4 (October 1999), 901–22, http://www.jstor.org/stable/3488013.
Antoine, Eric H., 'Chief of the Boat!', *The Submarine Review* (January 2014), 88–93, Archive Reprint, accessed 31 December 2022, https://archive.navalsubleague.org/2014/articles-chief-of-the-boat.
Armstrong, John G., 'Letters from Halifax: reliving the Halifax explosion through the eyes of my grandfather, a sailor in the Royal Canadian Navy', *The Northern Mariner/Le marin du nord* 8, no. 4 (1998), 55–74.
Arnould, Eric J., and Craig J. Thompson, 'Consumer Culture Theory (CCT): Twenty Years of Research', *Journal of Consumer Research* 31, no 4 (March 2005), 868–82, https://doi.org/10.1086/426626.
Barounis, Cynthia, '"Not the Usual Pattern": James Baldwin, Homosexuality, and the *DSM*', *Criticism* 59, no. 3 (Summer 2017), 395–415, https://doi.org/10.13110/criticism.59.3.0395.
Bélanger, Claude, 'French Canadian Emigration to the United States 1840–1930', *The Levasseur Newsletter* 14, no 2 (July 2002).
Blair, Leon B., 'Dogs and Sailors Keep Off!', *Proceedings*, Vol. 76/10/572 (October 1950), accessed 26 November 2022, https://www.usni.org/magazines/proceedings/1950/october/dogs-and-sailors-keep.

# BIBLIOGRAPHY

Blake, Joseph A., and Suellen Butler, 'The Medal of Honor, Combat Orientations and Latent Role Structure in the United States Military', *The Sociological Quarterly* 17, no. 4 (Autumn 1976), 561–67, http://www.jstor.org/stable/4105556.

Brault, Gerard J., 'New England French Culture', *The French Review* 45, no. 4 (March 1972), 831–37, http://www.jstor.org/stable/388382.

Brewer, John, 'Microhistory and the histories of everyday life', *Cultural and Social History* 7, no. 1 (2010), 87–109, https://www.tandfonline.com/doi/abs/10.2752/147800410X477359.

Brown, Eric, 'A Boy Seaman in the King's Service William Miles, RNCVR', *Canadian Military History* 23, no. 1 (Winter 2014), 111–20.

Byers, J. Andrew, 'The Sailors of 1898: Identity, Motivations, and Experiences of Naval Enlisted Personnel at the Dawn of an Age of American Empire', *International Journal of Naval History* 7, no. 2 (August 2008), https://www.ijnhonline.org/wp-content/uploads/2012/01/Byers.pdf.

Carosso, Vincent P., 'The Waltham Watch Company: A Case History', *Bulletin of the Business Historical Society* 23, no. 4 (December 1949), 165–87, https://doi.org/10.2307/3110545.

Chapman, John E., 'How to Fail at the NTC', *Army Logistician: Professional Bulletin of United States Army Logistics* (January–February 1998).

Chauncey, George, 'Christian Brotherhood or Sexual Perversion? Homosexual Identities and the Construction of Sexual Boundaries in the World War One Era', *Journal of Social History* 19, no. 2 (Winter 1985), 189–211, http://www.jstor.org/stable/3787467.

Cooke, Laquana, and Gaines S. Hubbell, 'Working out Memory with a Medal of Honor Complex', *Game Studies* 15, no. 2 (December 2015), https://gamestudies.org/1502/articles/cookehubbell.

Doyle, Michael K., 'The U.S. Navy and War Plan Orange, 1933–1940: Making Necessity a Virtue', *Naval War College Review* 33, no. 3 (May–June 1980), 49–63, http://www.jstor.org/stable/44642633.

Drennan, Jimmy, 'Self, Shipmate, and Ship: Bringing Balance to Naval Leadership', *Center for International Maritime Security* (25 July 2018), https://cimsec.org/self-shipmate-and-ship-bringing-balance-to-naval-leadership/.

Dumenil, Lynn, 'The Tribal Twenties: "Assimilated" Catholics' Response to Anti-Catholicism in the 1920s', *Journal of American Ethnic History* 11, no. 1 (Fall 1991), 21–49, http://www.jstor.org/stable/27500903.

Ewart, Gavin, 'All The Nice Girls Love A Sailor', *Ambit*, no. 138 (1994), 24–25, http://www.jstor.org/stable/44341213.

Fawcett, Waldon, 'The Submarine Boat Protector', *Scientific American* 87, no. 21 (1902), 346–47, http://www.jstor.org/stable/24985633.

Ginzburg, Carlo, John Tedeschi and Anne C. Tedeschi, 'Microhistory: Two or Three Things That I Know about It', *Critical Inquiry* 20, no. 1 (Autumn 1993), 10–35, https://www.journals.uchicago.edu/doi/abs/10.1086/448699.

Grigore, Julius, 'The Luck of the Submarine O-5', *The Military Engineer* 61 (July–August 1969), 267–69, http://www.jstor.org/stable/44565478.

Grigire, Julius, 'The O-5 Is Down!', *Proceedings*, 98 (February 1972), 54–60, https://www.usni.org/magazines/proceedings/1972/february/o-5-down.

Hamilton, C.I., 'Naval Hagiography and the Victorian Hero', *The Historical Journal* 23, no. 2 (June 1980), 381–98, http://www.jstor.org/stable/2638674.

Hennessey, Gregg R., 'San Diego, the U.S. Navy, and Urban Development: West Coast City Building, 1912–1929', *California History* 72, no. 2 (1993), 128–49, https://doi.org/10.2307/25177342.

Herr, Cheryl, '"One Good Turn Deserves Another": Theatrical Cross-Dressing in Joyce's "Circe" Episode', *Journal of Modern Literature* 11, no. 2 (July 1984), 265, http://www.jstor.org/stable/3831247.

Hess, Aaron, '"You Don't Play, You Volunteer": Narrative Public Memory Construction in Medal of Honor: Rising Sun', *Critical Studies in Media Communication* 24, no. 4 (2007), 339–56.

Holland, John P., 'The Submarine Boat and Its Future', *The North American Review* 171, no. 529 (1900), 894–903, http://www.jstor.org/stable/25105099.

Hone, Trent, 'U.S. Navy Surface Battle Doctrine and Victory in the Pacific', *Naval War College Review* 62, no. 1 (Winter 2009), 67–106, http://www.jstor.org/stable/26396991.

Howenstine, E. Jay, 'Demobilization After the First World War', *The Quarterly Journal of Economics* 58, no. 1 (1943), 91–105, https://doi.org/10.2307/1885757.

Hoswenstine, E. Jay, 'Lessons of World War I', *The Annals of the American Academy of Political and Social Science* 238 (March 1945), 180–87, http://www.jstor.org/stable/1025298.

Hurl-Eamon, Jeanine, 'Insights into Plebeian Marriage: Soldiers, Sailors, and their Wives in the Old Bailey Proceedings', *The London Journal* 30, no. 1 (2005), 22–38, https://doi.org/10.1179/ldn.2005.30.1.22.

Imbert, Michel, 'The Handsome Sailor, the Cult of Beauty, Moral Dilemmas and Political Imperatives in "Billy Budd, Sailor"', *Revue TIES* 3 (2019), 59–78.

Jackson, Elmo L., 'Trends in the Consumption of Tobacco Products, United States, 1900–1950', *Journal of Farm Economics* 32, no. 4 (November 1950), 881–93, https://doi.org/10.2307/1233840.

Keene, Jennifer, 'A "Brutalizing" War? The USA after the First World War', *Journal of Contemporary History* 50, no. 1 (January 2015), 78–99, http://www.jstor.org/stable/43697364.

Lachmann, Richard, and Abby Stivers, 'The Culture of Sacrifice in Conscript and Volunteer Militaries: The US Medal of Honor from the Civil War to Iraq, 1861–2014', *American Journal of Cultural Sociology* 4 (2016), 323–58.

Lake, Simon, 'Submarines That Are Strictly Invisible', *Scientific American* 112, no. 3 (1915), 68–75, http://www.jstor.org/stable/26015512.

Lepore, Jill, 'Historians Who Love Too Much: Reflections on Microhistory and Biography', *The Journal of American History* 88 (June 2001), 129–44, https://doi.org/10.2307/2674921.

Lewis, Frank, and Marvin McInnis, 'The Efficiency of the French-Canadian Farmer in the Nineteenth Century', *The Journal of Economic History* 40, no. 3 (1980), 497–514, doi:10.1017/S002205070008520X.

MacDonald, William, 'The French Canadians in New England', *The Quarterly Journal of Economics* 12, no. 3 (April 1898), 245–79, https://doi.org/10.2307/1881895.

MacKinnon, Mary, 'Canadian Railway Workers and World War I Military Service', *Labour/Le Travail* 40 (1997), 213–34, https://doi.org/10.2307/25144169.

Magnússon, Sigurður Gylfi, 'Tales of the Unexpected: The "Textual Environment", Ego-Documents and a Nineteenth-Century Icelandic Love Story – An Approach in Microhistory', *Cultural and Social History* 12 (2015), 77–94.

Magnússon, Sigurður Gylfi, 'Far-reaching microhistory: the use of microhistorical perspective in a globalized world', *Rethinking History* 21 (2017), 312–41.

McBride, William M., 'The Unstable Dynamics of a Strategic Technology: Disarmament, Unemployment, and the Interwar Battleship', *Technology and Culture* 38, no. 2 (April 1997), 386–423, https://doi.org/10.2307/3107127.

Meyer, Scott, 'Diabolists and Decadents: H.P. Lovecraft as Purveyor, Indulger, and Appraiser of Puritan Horror Fiction Psychohistory', *Lovecraft Annual*, no. 13 (2019), 175–88, https://www.jstor.org/stable/26868584.

Mobbs, Meaghan C., and George A. Bonanno, 'Beyond War and PTSD: The Crucial Role of Transition Stress in the Lives of Military Veterans', *Clinical Psychology Review* 59 (2018), 137–44, https://doi.org/10.1016/j.cpr.2017.11.007.

Newton, Jason L., '"These French Canadian of the Woods Are Half-Wild Folk": Wilderness, Whiteness, and Work in North America, 1840–1955', *Labour/Le Travail* 77 (2016), 121–50, http://www.jstor.org/stable/44122945

Nicolosi, Anthony S., The Navy, Newport and Stephen B. Luce', *Naval War College Review* 37, no. 5 (September–October 1984), 117–31, http://www.jstor.org/stable/44642363.

Nye, B.H., 'A Canadian Port in War Time', *History Teacher's Magazine* (1 June 1916), 189–90.

Nye, Robert A., 'Western Masculinities in War and Peace', *The American Historical Review* 112, no. 2 (April 2007), 417–38, http://www.jstor.org/stable/4136608.

Peters, Jason, '"Speak White": Language Policy, Immigration Discourse, and Tactical Authenticity in a French Enclave in New England', *College English* 75, no. 6 (July 2013), 563–81, http://www.jstor.org/stable/24238126.

Price, Joseph E., 'The French Language in New England: Past, Present, and Future', *The French Review* 88, no. 4 (May 2015), 59–71, http://www.jstor.org/stable/24549631.

Restad, Penne, 'The Third Sex: Historians, Consumer Society, and the Idea of the American Consumer', *Journal of Social History* 47, no. 3 (Spring 2014), 769–86, http://www.jstor.org/stable/43305959.

Savage, Stephanie, 'Evelyn Nesbit and the Film(ed) Histories of the Thaw-White Scandal', *Film History* 8, no. 2 (1996), 159–75, http://www.jstor.org/stable/3815332.

Smith, Mark A., 'Religion, Divorce, and the Missing Culture War in America', *Political Science Quarterly* 125, no. 1 (Spring 2010), 57–80, http://www.jstor.org/stable/25698955.

Stephenson, Andrew, '"Our jolly marin wear": The Queer Fashionability of the Sailor Uniform in Interwar France and Britain', *Fashion, Style & Popular Culture* 3, no. 2 (March 2016), 157–72, https://doi.org/10.1386/fspc.3.2.157_1.

Talbott, J.E., "Weapons Development, War Planning and Policy: The US Navy and the Submarine, 1917–1941', *Naval War College Review* 37, no. 3 (May–June 1984), 53–71, http://www.jstor.org/stable/44636561.

Unknown author, 'How to Escape From a Sunken Submarine', *Scientific American* 102, no. 23 (1910), 460, http://www.jstor.org/stable/26038682.

Unknown author, 'Submarine Torpedo Boats', *Scientific American* 85, no. 24 (1901), 387–88, http://www.jstor.org/stable/24983887.

Warren, Jean-Philippe, 'The French Canadian Press in the United States', *The Journal of Modern Periodical Studies* 7, nos 1–2 (2016), 74–95, https://doi.org/10.5325/jmodeperistud.7.1-2.0074

Wingate, Jennifer, 'Over the Top: The Doughboy in World War I Memorials and Visual Culture', *American Art* 19, no. 2 (2005), 26–47, https://doi.org/10.1086/444480.

Wirsching, Andreas, 'From Work to Consumption: Transatlantic Visions of Individuality in Modern Mass Society', *Contemporary European History* 20, no. 1 (2011), 9, http://www.jstor.org/stable/41238339.

Zane, Sherry, 'I did it for the uplift of humanity and the Navy: Same-Sex Acts and the Origins of the National Security State 1919–1921', *The New England Quarterly* 91, no. 2 (June 2018), 279–306, https://www.jstor.org/stable/26497565.

# BIBLIOGRAPHY

## Library of Congress Online

Bain News Service, Publisher, 'Evelyn Thaw dodging a camera, White Plains, July 14, 1909', photograph, https://www.loc.gov/item/2014684043/.

Bain News Service, Publisher, 'Mrs. Wm. Thaw, veiled, on street, White Plains, July 14, 1909', photograph, https://www.loc.gov/item/2014684045/.

Clark, Luther A., and L. La Rose, 'Submarine Johnny', Library of Congress, LCN, 2013564388, Notated Music, 1911, https://www.loc.gov/item/2013564388/.

'Here is Opportunity, See the World, Serve Your Country, Save Your Money', USN Recruiting Poster, Photograph, POS – WWI – US, no. 104 (C size), LCN 00651875, https://www.loc.gov/item/00651875/.

Historic American Buildings Survey, 'Israel Putnam School, Putnam, Windham County, Connecticut, Windham County, Putnam, 1933', photograph, https://www.loc.gov/item/ct0390/.

Historic American Buildings Survey, 'Israel Putnam School (View from the Southeast), Putnam, Windham County, Connecticut, Windham County, Putnam, 1933', photograph, https://www.loc.gov/item/ct0390.

Historic American Buildings Survey, 'Israel Putnam School (View from the South), Putnam, Windham County, Connecticut, Windham County, Putnam, 1933', photograph, https://www.loc.gov/item/ct0390/.

Monaco, James V., and Roger Lewis, 'Torpedo Jim', Image and Sheet Music, 1917, Notated Music, LCN: 2013567908, https://www.loc.gov/item/2013567908/.

Royale, Edwin Milton, Silvio Hein and George V. Hobart, Marie Cahill, 'In My Submarine', Library of Congress, LCN, 201676218. Notated Music, 1905, https://www.loc.gov/item/2016762181/.

'Sanborn Fire Insurance Map from Putnam, Windham County, Connecticut', Sanborn Map Company, August 1903, Map, https://www.loc.gov/item/sanborn01167_004/.

'Sanborn Fire Insurance Map from Putnam, Windham County, Connecticut', Sanborn Map Company, September 1910, Map, https://www.loc.gov/item/sanborn01167_005/.

United States Navy Department, 'Information on living conditions in the Canal Zone', (Washington D.C.: Government Printing Office, 1920), https://www.loc.gov/item/24014341/.

Unknown Artist, 'Here is Opportunity, See the World, Serve Your Country, Save Your Money', USN Recruiting Poster, Photograph, POS – WWI – US, no. 104 (C size), LCN 00651875, https://www.loc.gov/item/00651875/.

Unknown Photographer, 'Henry Breault, 3/8/24', Photograph, Library of Congress Prints and Photographs Division Washington, D.C., LCN, 2016836978.

Unknown Photographer, 'Coolidge & Henry Breault, 3/8/24', Photograph, Library of Congress Prints and Photographs Division Washington, D.C., LCN, 2016836982, https://www.loc.gov/item/2016836978/.

Unknown Photographer, 'Denby, Coolidge, & Henry Breault, [3/8/24]', Photograph, Library of Congress Prints and Photographs Division Washington, D.C., LCN, 2016836979, https://www.loc.gov/item/2016836979/.

Unknown Photographer, 'Naval Training Station, Newport: Sailors in Formation for Calisthenics', Library of Congress, LCN 2016821325, LC-DIG-npcc-19745 (digital file from original), 1900–1920, https://www.loc.gov/resource/npcc.19745/.

Unknown Photographer, 'Naval Training Station, Newport: Sailors Performing Boat Drill', Library of Congress, LCN 2016821326, LC-USZ62-16082 LC-DIG-npcc-19746 (digital file from original), ca. 1908–1919, https://www.loc.gov/resource/npcc.19746/.

Unknown Photographer, 'Naval Training Station, Newport: Sailors Preparing to Swim', Library of Congress, LCN 2022634782, LC-USZ62-16082 (b&w film copy neg.), ca. 1900–1920, https://lccn.loc.gov/2022634782.

Unknown Photographer, '[President Coolidge] decorating Henry Breault of the submarine O-5 with Congressional Medal of Honor', Photograph, Library of Congress Prints and Photographs Division Washington, D.C., LCN, 2002712385, https://www.loc.gov/item/2016836981/.

## Mike France Genealogy Report

*Burlington Daily News*, 'Former Grand Isle Boy Tells Of Submarine Tomb', newspaper clipping, Burlington, VT, 2 November 1923, Page 6.

*Burlington Suburban List*, 30 March 1940, newspaper clipping.

*Dominion Bureau of Statistics: Population*, Sixth Census of Canada, 1921, Brault, Joseph.

Drennan, Everett Dewey, 'Ohio, Roster of Soldiers, Sailors, and Marines in World War I, 1917–1918'.

*Los Angeles Times*, 'Bodies of Pair Found in Cabin', newspaper clipping, Los Angeles, CA, 10 February 1939, Part 1, Page 1.

*Los Angeles Times*, 'Pair Found Dead in Auto Court', newspaper clipping, Los Angeles, CA, 10 February 1939, Part 1, Page 10.

*Order of Publication (Divorce) – Underhill Enterprise, Essex Junction, Chittenden, VT*, 8 February 1923, Page 7, newspaper clipping.

State of Rhode Island, 'Death Certificate, Henry Breault', *Rhode Island, Vital records, 1846–1898, 1901–1953*.

# BIBLIOGRAPHY

## Naval History and Heritage Command (NHHC) Online Sources

Mario DeMarco, 'NH 86982 Torpedoman Second Class Henry Breault, US', originally published in *Navy Times*, 27 October 1956, https://www.history.navy.mil/our-collections/photography/numerical-list-of-images/nhhc-series/nh-series/NH-86000/NH-86982.html.

Unknown Photographer, 'NH 43954 Rear Admiral Montgomery M. Taylor, USN', ca. 1927, Naval History and Heritage Command (NHHC), accessed 26 February 2023, https://www.history.navy.mil/our-collections/photography/numerical-list-of-images/nhhc-series/nh-series/NH-43000/NH-43954.html.

## Official Military Personnel File (OMPF)

The National Archives (US), St Louis, Persons of Exceptional Prominence, 'Series: Record Group 24 Records of the Bureau of Naval Personnel 1798–2007 Official Military Personnel Files, 1885–1998, Official Military Personnel File for Henry Breault 145766579'. Accessed 16 October 2021, https://catalog.archives.gov/id/145766579.[2]

## Online Census & Newspaper Databases

Ancestry, 'Newspapers.com by Ancestry', accessed 12 March 2023, https://www.newspapers.com.

Center for Bibliographical Studies and Research, 'California Digital Newspaper Collection', accessed 12 March 2023, https://cdnc.ucr.edu/.genealogy.

Genealogy Bank, 'Newspaper Archives – 1690–2016', accessed 12 March 2023, https://www.genealogybank.com/explore/newspapers/all.

Genealogy Bank, 'Obituaries – 1690–Present', accessed 12 March 2023, https://www.genealogybank.com/explore/all-obits.

Genealogy Bank, 'U.S. Census Records – 1790–1940', accessed 12 March 2023, https://www.genealogybank.com/explore/census/all.

Library of Congress, 'Chronicling America: Historic American Newspapers', accessed 12 March 2023, https://chroniclingamerica.loc.gov/.

## Social Media

Dubay, Ted, 'Response to LinkedIn Inquiry By Ryan Walker', 20 October 2021.

Neville, Kenny, 'Facebook Post Replying to Poll Created By Ryan Walker, (Do you know who Henry Breault is?)', 19 October 2021, https://www.facebook.com/groups/usnsubmariners/?multi_permalinks=10158032892331927&comment_

id=10158033005096927&notif_id=1634702557490226&notif_t=feedback_reaction_generic&ref=notif.

## Theses/Dissertations

Collins, Jeanette Maria, 'Style in the New Story', MA Thesis, University of Wisconsin, 1924.

Richardson, E. Mark J., 'Manpower and the Orphan Service: Recruiting, Training and Personnel Retention in the Royal Canadian Navy, 1910–1940', MA Thesis, University of Calgary, 2002.

Van Meter, Larry A., 'The Officer Fetish', Ph.D Dissertation, Texas A&M University, 2004.

## United States Navy Sources

COMSUBLANT/COMSUBPACINST 1650.6D. *AWARDS SPONSORED BY THE NAVAL SUBMARINE LEAGUE. Department of the Navy*, 2017. Accessed 17 October 2021. https://www.navalsubleague.org/wp-content/uploads/2017/11/CSLCSPINST_1650.6D.pdf.

## Websites and Online Personal Collections

Anderson, James W. (photographer), 'American Submarines in Bermuda, Just Returned From the War Front', *Naval Source Organization*, accessed 26 December 2022, http://navsource.org/archives/08/O-boats/0806609.jpg.

Canadian War Museum, 'The Halifax Explosion', accessed 23 December 2022, https://www.warmuseum.ca/firstworldwar/history/life-at-home-during-the-war/wartime-tragedies/the-halifax-explosion/.

Christley, Jim, 'Submarine Hero: TM2 Henry Breault', *Undersea Warfare Spring 1999* 1, no. 3, accessed 12 March 2023, https://web.archive.org/web/20110629063832/http://www.navy.mil/navydata/cno/n87/usw/issue_3/sub_hero.htm.

Congressional Medal of Honor Society (CMOHS), 'Statistics & FAQs', accessed 30 April 2022, https://www.cmohs.org/medal/faqs.

CMOHS, 'Henry Breault', accessed 26 February 2023, https://www.cmohs.org/recipients/henry-breault.

CMOHS, 'William Adger Moffett', accessed 26 February 2023, https://www.cmohs.org/recipients/william-a-moffett.

Dougherty, Phil. 'Marysville – Thumbnail History', accessed 20 January 2023, https://www.historylink.org/file/8227.

# BIBLIOGRAPHY

Eternal Patrol, 'Fred C. Smith', accessed 14 February 2023, https://www.oneternalpatrol.com/smith-f-c.htm.

Freeman, David J., 'Substantive and Non-Substantive Rates in the RCN', accessed 21 December 2022, https://navalandmilitarymuseum.org/article/substantive-and-non-substantive-rates-the-rcn/.

Fretz, Robert E., 'Qualification Notebook Week 1', private collection of Ric Hedman, accessed 26 December 2022, http://www.pigboats.com/subs/qualsweek1.pdf.

Government of Canada, 'Heroes of the Halifax Explosion', accessed 18 February 2023, https://www.canada.ca/en/navy/services/history/heroes-halifax-explosion.html.

Gow, Bonar A. (Sandy), 'Canada's Boy Seamen', accessed 21 December 2022, https://navalandmilitarymuseum.org/article/canadas-boy-seamen/.

Mrazek, Courtney, 'Frank Baker's Diary', Dartmouth Heritage Museum, accessed 23 December 2022, https://www.dartmouthheritagemuseum.ns.ca/2017/08/06/frank-bakers-diary/.

Naval History and Heritage Command (NHHC), 'O-5', accessed 26 December 2022, https://www.history.navy.mil/research/histories/ship-histories/danfs/o/o-5.html.

NHHC, 'U.S. Navy Personnel Strength, 1775 to Present', accessed 24 January 2023, https://www.history.navy.mil/research/library/online-reading-room/title-list-alphabetically/u/usn-personnel-strength.html.

NHHC, 'Yangtze River Patrol and Other US Navy Asiatic Fleet Activities in China, 1920–1942, as Described in the Annual Reports of the Navy Department', accessed 18 February 2023, https://www.history.navy.mil/content/history/nhhc/research/library/online-reading-room/title-list-alphabetically/y/yangtze-river-patrol-and-other-us-navy-asiatic-fleet-activities-in-china.html.

Population.us, 'Population of Marysville, WA', accessed 20 January 2023, https://population.us/wa/marysville/.

Ray, Ricky (original contributor), '1920s – Newport, Rhode Island in 1920', Shutterstock ID: 4117099, accessed 11 March 2023, https://www.shutterstock.com/video/clip-4117099-1920s---newport-rhode-island-1920. (The sailor can be seen around the 30-second mark, and reappears in the video.)

Retford, Ella, 'Ship Ahoy (All the Nice Girls Love a Sailor)', accessed 5 March 2023, https://www.youtube.com/watch?v=YMP1hQT7EnY.

State of Connecticut, 'Population of Connecticut Towns 1900–1960', accessed 15 January 2023, https://portal.ct.gov/SOTS/Register-Manual/Section-VII/Population-1900-1960.

Unknown photographer, 'O-Class Submarines of Submarine Division Eight at Boston 16 Aug 1921', *Naval Source Organization*, accessed 26 December 2022, http://navsource.org/archives/08/O-boats/0806705.jpg.

Unknown photographer, 'US Submarine base at Coco Solo, Panama 1923', *Naval Source Organization*, accessed 26 December 2022, http://navsource.org/archives/08/r-boats/0810304.jpg.

# Endnotes

## Chapter 1: Enlisted Submarine Folk Hero

1. *The Abangarez*, 60 F.2d 543 (E.D. La. 1932), U.S. District Court for the Eastern District of Louisiana – 60 F.2d 543 (E.D. La. 1932) August 3, 1932.
2. Julius Grigore, 'The Luck of the Submarine O-5', *The Military Engineer* 61, no. 402 (July–August 1969), 267–69, http://www.jstor.org/stable/44565478; Edwin Denby, 'General Order No. 125: Award of Medal of Honor, Washington D.C. February 20, 1924', in *Official Military Personnel File for Henry Breault. Series: Official Military Personnel Files, 1885–1998* (OMPF), accessed October 16, 2021, https://catalog.archives.gov/id/145766579, 43.
3. Denby, 'No. 125', OMPF, 43.
4. Grigore, 'The Luck of the Submarine O-5', 268.
5. Grigore, 'The Luck of the Submarine O-5', 268.
6. Julius Grigore, 'The O-5 Is Down!', *Proceedings*, 98 (February 1972), 54–60, Proceedings Website Reprint, https://www.usni.org/magazines/proceedings/1972/february/o-5-down; verified in several newspapers.
7. 'How to Escape from a Sunken Submarine', *Scientific American* 102, no. 23 (June 1910), 460, http://www.jstor.org/stable/26038682.
8. Grigore, 'The Luck of the Submarine O-5', 268.
9. Grigore, 'The Luck of the Submarine O-5', 267–69; 267; Grigore, 'The O-5 Is Down!', website reprint.
10. Grigore, 'The O-5 Is Down!', website reprint. Breault knew how to swim; it is verified in his OMPF that he was qualified to swim.
11. 'They Stared at the Clock for 15 Hours', *United Press Associations*, October 31, 1923, newspaper clipping, *Submarine Archives, Biography Collection, Medal of Honor, Breault Collection*, SFLM.
12. Bureau of Navigation, 'Medical History', OMPF, 478–85.
13. 'Submarine Hero Writes: Breault Tells His Mother About Panama Disaster', *New York Times*, November 20, 1923, page 23, newspaper clipping, SFLM.
14. Jeanette Maria Collins, 'Style in the New Story' (MA Thesis, University of Wisconsin, 1924), 48–53.

15. Collins, 'Style', 58.
16. *The Sunday Bee* (Omaha), November 4, 1923, page 8.
17. Lachmann & Stivers, 'The Culture of Sacrifice', 323.
18. Ship, shipmate, self is a useful euphemism that enlisted leader use to teach the priorities of a 'good' sailor. See also: Jimmy Drennan, 'Self, Shipmate, and Ship: Bringing Balance to Naval Leadership', *Center for International Maritime Security*, originally published July 25, 2018, https://cimsec.org/self-shipmate-and-ship-bringing-balance-to-naval-leadership/.
19. Kenny Neville, 'Facebook Post Replying to Poll Created by Ryan Walker: (Do you know who Henry Breault is?)'. I asked Mr Neville if I could use his quotation and he graciously agreed. Of note, the USS *Virginia* was laid down in 1999 and delivered in 2004, closely mirroring the development of Breault as an icon. M-Div is a contraction of Machinery Division, a part of engineering.
20. Grigore, 'The Luck of the Submarine O-5', website reprint.
21. Ryan C. Walker, 'Henry Breault: Construction of a Naval Hero', *International Journal of Maritime History* 35, no. 1 (December 2022), 46–70, https://doi.org/10.1177/08438714221145491.
22. Mario DeMarco, 'NH 86982 Torpedoman Second Class Henry Breault, US', *Navy Times*, accessed October 17, 2021, https://www.history.navy.mil/our-collections/photography/numerical-list-of-images/nhhc-series/nh-series/NH-86000/NH-86982.html.
23. DeMarco, 'Henry Breault', 40. Most accounts agree that Breault and Brown were trapped for over 30 hours; the general consensus was 31–38 hours and the Medal of Honor citation states 31.
24. DeMarco, 'Henry Breault', 40.
25. Mark K. Roberts, *SUB: An Oral History of US Navy Submarines* (New York: Berkley Caliber, 2007); Paul Stillwell, *Submarine Stories: Recollections from the Diesel Boats* (Annapolis: Naval Institute Press, 2013); Ted E. Dubay, *Three Knots to Nowhere* (Jefferson: McFarland & Company, 2014); Claude C. Conner, *Nothing Friendly in the Vicinity: My Patrols on the Submarine USS Guardfish During WWII* (Annapolis: Naval Institute Press, 1999).
26. Ted Dubay, 'Response to LinkedIn Inquiry By Ryan Walker', October 20, 2021. Mr Dubay wrote *Three Knots to Nowhere*, a book on his experiences in the submarine fleet on Boomers (Fleet Ballistic Submarines). While he is humble and states he is not an expert, his first-hand account tells the story of many men whose stories will not be told. I do believe his account displays expertise in the culture of the submarine fleet in the period he served.

## ENDNOTES

27. Dwight S. Mears, *The Medal of Honor: The Evolution of America's Highest Military Decoration* (Lawrence: University Press of Kansas, 2018), 92.
28. Mears, *The Medal of Honor*, 2.
29. Grigore, 'The Luck of the Submarine O-5', 267; Grigore, 'The O-5 Is Down!', website reprint.
30. I have worked closely with the staff of the Submarine Force Library and Museum throughout this project. Finnegan and Gully were unable to narrow this timeline further but insist this occurred in the late 1990s. Both Finnegan and Christley deserve a level of acknowledgement for introducing this to the larger submarine community.
31. Shewman McClain, 'Pier Dedicated to Enlisted Medal of Honor Recipient', COMSUBPAC News Release, June 18, 1999, newspaper clipping, SFLM.
32. McClain, 'Pier Dedicated', SFLM.
33. McClain, 'Pier Dedicated', SFLM.
34. Robert A. Hamilton, 'Memorial Honors Enlisted Hero', *The Day*, May 19, 2001, newspaper clipping, SFLM. This is the same one I also saw.
35. Hamilton, 'Memorial Honors', SFLM.
36. Hamilton, 'Memorial Honors', SFLM.
37. Hamilton, 'Memorial Honors', SFLM. See also Appendix 1; those who served prior to 2000 were much less likely to hear about Breault than those who served later.
38. James E. Ratte Jr., 'Speech Given During TM1 Henry Breault Bridge Dedication, November 11, 2003', speech transcript, SFLM.
39. Larry A. Van Meter, 'The Officer Fetish' (Ph.D Dissertation, Texas A&M University, 2004), 37.
40. COMSUBLANT/COMSUBPACINST 1650.6D, *AWARDS SPONSORED BY THE NAVAL SUBMARINE LEAGUE, Department of the Navy*, 2017, accessed October 17, 2021, https://www.navalsubleague.org/wp-content/uploads/2017/11/CSLCSPINST_1650.6D.pdf.
41. Jimmy Drennan, 'Ship, Shipmate, Self', CIMSEC Online.
42. Mears, *The Medal of Honor*, 94; see also Appendices 2, 3 & 4.
43. See Appendix 1.
44. Ross T. McIntire, 'CA JEJ: Enclosure 1, March 5, 1942', OMPF, 403; Basil Filardi Jr., 'In Re: March 12, 1942', OMPF, 404; Basil Filardi Jr., 'In Re: March 14, 1942', OMPF, 406; Bureau of Medicine and Surgery, 'Subject: Statement of Funeral Expenses, March 19, 1942', OMPF, 202.
45. *Observer Extra* (Putnam), November 19, 1988, SFLM.
46. 1910 US Census, MFGR.
47. Bureau of Navigation, 'Medical History', OMPF, 478.

## Chapter 2: Historiography & Methodology

1. Statistics gathered from Congressional MOH Society, 'Statistics & FAQs', accessed April 30, 2022, https://www.cmohs.org/medal/faqs.
2. Aaron Hess, '"You Don't Play, You Volunteer": Narrative Public Memory Construction in Medal of Honor: Rising Sun', *Critical Studies in Media Communication* 24, no. 4 (2007), 339–56; Laquana Cooke and Gaines S. Hubbell, 'Memory and Complex capitalize', *Game Studies* 15, no. 2 (December 2015), https://gamestudies.org/1502/articles/cookehubbell.
3. Joseph A. Blake and Suellen Butler, 'The Medal of Honor, Combat Orientations and Latent Role Structure in the United States Military', *The Sociological Quarterly* 17, no. 4 (Autumn 1976), 561, http://www.jstor.org/stable/4105556.
4. Blake & Butler, 'Medal of Honor', 561.
5. Richard Lachmann & Abby Stivers, 'The Culture of Sacrifice in Conscript and Volunteer Militaries: The U.S. Medal of Honor From the Civil War to Iraq, 1861–2014', *American Journal of Cultural Sociology* Vol. 4 (2016), 333, https://doi.org/10.1057/s41290-016-0002-x.
6. Mears, *The Medal of Honor*, 82–83, 94; see also Appendices 2, 3 & 4.
7. An honorable mention belongs to William R. Charette, a Corpsman who became a submariner later in his career. He was awarded the Medal of Honor during the Korean War for actions performed as a Corpsman.
8. Blake & Butler, 'Medal of Honor', 566–67.
9. Joel I. Howlitt, *'Execute Against Japan': The US Decision to Conduct Unrestricted Submarine Warfare* (College Station: Texas A&M University Press, 2009); J.E. Talbott, 'Weapons Development, War Planning and Policy: The US Navy and the Submarine, 1917–1941', *Naval War College Review* 37, no. 3 (May–June 1984), 53–71, http://www.jstor.org/stable/44636561.
10. William M. McBride, 'The Unstable Dynamics of a Strategic Technology: Disarmament, Unemployment, and the Interwar Battleship', *Technology and Culture* 38, no. 2 (April 1997), 386–423, https://doi.org/10.2307/3107127; Trent Hone, 'U.S. Navy Surface Battle Doctrine and Victory in the Pacific', *Naval War College Review* 62, no. 1 (Winter 2009), 70–72, 95, http://www.jstor.org/stable/26396991; Michael K. Doyle, 'The U.S. Navy and War Plan Orange, 1933–1940: Making Necessity a Virtue', *Naval War College Review* 33, no. 3 (May–June 1980), 50, http://www.jstor.org/stable/44642633.
11. National Archives (USA), 'Persons of Exceptional Prominence (PEP)', accessed March 14, 2023, https://www.archives.gov/st-louis/pep. William Badders and Floyd Bennett appear, but their records have not been digitized yet.

12. Matthew Heaslip, *Gunboats, Empire and the China Station: The Royal Navy in 1920s East Asia* (London: Bloomsbury Publishing, 2020).
13. Heaslip, *Gunboats*, 107.
14. Heaslip, *Gunboats*, 18–19, 21–22, 210, 215.
15. Jill LePore, 'Historians Who Love Too Much: Reflections on Microhistory and Biography', *The Journal of American History* 88, no. 1 (June 2001), 130, https://doi.org/10.2307/2674921.
16. LePore, 'Historians Who Love Too Much', 129.
17. LePore, 'Historians Who Love Too Much', 141.
18. Lepore, 'Historians Who Love Too Much', 141.
19. Lepore, 'Historians Who Love Too Much', 141. It is from this proposition that I utilize first-person, as both a subject and investigator into a military hero.
20. Carlo Ginzburg, John Tedeschi and Anne C. Tedeschi, 'Microhistory: Two or Three Things That I Know about It', *Critical Inquiry* 20, no. 1 (Autumn 1993), 10–35, https://www.journals.uchicago.edu/doi/abs/10.1086/448699.
21. Ginzburg, Tedeschi and Tedeschi, 'Microhistory' 34, http://www.jstor.org/stable/1343946.
22. Sigurður Gylfi Magnússon, 'Tales of the Unexpected: The "Textual Environment", Ego-Documents and a Nineteenth-Century Icelandic Love Story – An Approach in Microhistory', *Cultural and Social History* 12 (2015), 84, https://doi.org/10.2752/147800415X14135484867180.
23. Magnússon, 'Tales of the Unexpected', 84–85.
24. Magnússon, 'Tales of the Unexpected', 86.
25. Magnússon, 'Tales of the Unexpected', 86.
26. Carol Kammen, *On Doing Local History: Third Edition* (New York: Rowman & Littlefield, 2014), 1.
27. Kammen, *On Doing Local History*, 1.
28. Kammen, *On Doing Local History*, 29.
29. Joseph E. Price, 'The French Language in New England: Past, Present, and Future', *The French Review* 88, no. 4 (May 2015), 59, http://www.jstor.org/stable/24549631.
30. William MacDonald, 'The French Canadians in New England', *The Quarterly Journal of Economics* 12, no. 3 (September 1898), 260, https://doi.org/10.2307/1881895.
31. *Norwich Bulletin*, July 28, 1914, Tuesday.
32. Claude Bélanger, 'French Canadian Emigration to the United States 1840–1930', *The Levasseur Newsletter* 14, no. 2 (July 2002), 27.
33. Gerard J. Brault, 'New England French Culture', *The French Review* 45, no. 4 (March 1972), 831–37, http://www.jstor.org/stable/388382; Jason

L. Newton, '"These French Canadian of the Woods Are Half-Wild Folk": Wilderness, Whiteness, and Work in North America, 1840–1955', *Labour/Le Travail* 77 (2016), 121–50, http://www.jstor.org/stable/44122945; Jean-Philippe Warren, 'The French Canadian Press in the United States', *The Journal of Modern Periodical Studies* 7, nos 1–2 (2016), 74–95, https://doi.org/10.5325/jmodeperistud.7.1-2.0074.
34. Newton, 'These French Canadian of the Woods',122–24; Warren, 'The French Canadian Press', 88.
35. *Norwich Bulletin*, July 28, 1914, Tuesday.
36. Jason Peters, '"Speak White": Language Policy, Immigration Discourse, and Tactical Authenticity in a French Enclave in New England', *College English* 75, no. 6 (July 2013), 563, http://www.jstor.org/stable/24238126.
37. Gavin Ewart, 'All The Nice Girls Love A Sailor', *Ambit*, no. 138 (1994), 24–25, http://www.jstor.org/stable/44341213. Alternative lyrics include 'Falls in love with Kate and Jane/Then he's out to sea again'.
38. Cheryl Herr, '"One Good Turn Deserves Another": Theatrical Cross-Dressing in Joyce's "Circe" Episode', *Journal of Modern Literature* 11, no. 2 (July 1984), 265, http://www.jstor.org/stable/3831247.
39. Ella Retford, 'Ship Ahoy (All the Nice Girls Love a Sailor)', accessed March 5, 2023, https://www.youtube.com/watch?v=YMP1hQT7EnY.
40. Sherry Zane, 'I did it for the uplift of humanity and the Navy: Same-Sex Acts and the Origins of the National Security State 1919–1921', *The New England Quarterly* 91, no. 2 (June 2018), 279–306, https://www.jstor.org/stable/26497565; George Chauncey, 'Christian Brotherhood or Sexual Perversion? Homosexual Identities and the Construction of Sexual Boundaries in the World War One Era', *Journal of Social History* 19, no. 2 (Winter 1985), 189–211, http://www.jstor.org/stable/3787467; Cynthia Barounis, '"Not the Usual Pattern": James Baldwin, Homosexuality, and the *DSM*', *Criticism* 59, no. 3 (Summer 2017), 405–06, https://doi.org/10.13110/criticism.59.3.0395; Michel Imbert, 'The Handsome Sailor, the Cult of Beauty, Moral Dilemmas and Political Imperatives in "Billy Budd, Sailor"', *Revue TIES* 3 (2019), 59–78.
41. Imbert, 'The Handsome Sailor', 69.
42. Andrew Stephenson, '"Our jolly marin wear": The Queer Fashionability of the Sailor Uniform in Interwar France and Britain', *Fashion, Style & Popular Culture* 3, no. 2 (2016), 157–72, https://doi.org/10.1386/fspc.3.2.157_1.
43. Ralph LaRossa, *The Modernization of Fatherhood: A Social and Political History*. (Chicago: University of Chicago Press, 1997).
44. Ellsberg, *Pigboats*, 157–58.

45. Friedrich W. Nietzsche, *The Gay Science*, trans. Walter Kaufmann (New York: Vintage Books, 1974), 115. While some may object to this section, I have interdisciplinary interests that have profoundly impacted my interpretation of the subject. In this respect, philosophy and semiotics are employed to illustrate a historical trend that is muddied by marketers who seek to sell to us the idea they can predict consumer behaviour through historical analysis.
46. Eric J. Arnould and Craig J. Thompson, 'Consumer Culture Theory (CCT): Twenty Years of Research', *Journal of Consumer Research* 31, no 4 (March 2005), 871, https://doi.org/10.1086/426626.
47. Arnould & Thompson, 'Consumer Culture Theory (CCT)', 871.
48. Arnould & Thompson, 'Consumer Culture Theory (CCT)', 872–73.
49. Arnould & Thompson, 'Consumer Culture Theory (CCT)', 875.
50. Penne Restad, 'The Third Sex: Historians, Consumer Society, and the Idea of the American Consumer', *Journal of Social History* 47, no. 3 (2014), 770, http://www.jstor.org/stable/43305959.
51. Restad, 'The Third Sex', 780–81.
52. Heike Paul, *The Myths That Made America* (Bielefeld: Transcript Verlag, 2014), 379.
53. Paul, *The Myths That Made America*, 379.
54. Jean Baudrillard, *Simulacra and Simulation*, trans. Sheila F. Glaser (Ann Arbor: University of Michigan Press, 1994).
55. Baudrillard, *Simulacra and Simulation*, 24.
56. Andreas Wirsching, 'From Work to Consumption: Transatlantic Visions of Individuality in Modern Mass Society', *Contemporary European History* 20, no. 1 (2011), 9, http://www.jstor.org/stable/41238339.
57. Wirsching, 'From Work to Consumption', 23.

## Chapter 3: Pre-Award Life and Career (1900–23)

1. C.I. Hamilton, 'Naval Hagiography and the Victorian Hero', *The Historical Journal* 23, no. 2 (June 1980), 382, http://www.jstor.org/stable/2638674.
2. Henry Breault, 'U.S. Navy Enlistment, July 20, 1920', OMPF, 1.
3. 1900 US Census, Windham County, CT, Putnam Town, 3rd Ward, ED 523, Sheet 33, MFGR.
4. 1910 US Census, Westchester County, NY, White Plains Village, 5th Ward, ED 130, Sheet 5A, MFGR.
5. Breault Family Headstone, St Mary Cemetery, Putnam, CT, 1988.
6. Bureau of Navigation, U.S. Navy Enlistment, July 20, 1920', OMPF, 1; Bureau of Navigation, 'Enlistment Service Book, December 26, 1936', OMPF,

295; Bureau of Navigation, 'Enlistment Service Book, February 23, 1937', OMPF, 311.
7. D.B. Peters, 'Medical History Sheet Page 3, March 24, 1930', OMPF, 462.
8. Henry Breault, 'Application for Enlistment, January 5, 1929', OMPF, 120; Henry Breault, 'Service Record, November 22, 1924', OMPF, 257; Henry Breault, 'Service Record, February 23, 1937', OMPF, 311.
9. Henry Breault, 'Application to be Enrolled in the Royal Naval Canadian Volunteer Reserve', SFLM.
10. Eric Brown, 'A Boy Seaman in the King's Service William Miles, RNCVR', *Canadian Military History* 23, no. 1 (Winter 2014), 111–20.
11. Henry Breault, 'Application to be Enrolled', SFLM.
12. Henry Breault, 'Application to be Enrolled', SFLM.
13. Breault, 'U.S. Navy Enlistment, July 20, 1920', OMPF, 1.
14. Bonar A. (Sandy) Gow, 'Canada's Boy Seamen', accessed December 21, 2022, https://navalandmilitarymuseum.org/article/canadas-boy-seamen/.
15. Henry Breault, 'Application to be Enrolled', SFLM.
16. Louis Christ, 'My Dear Hose ... It Can't be Done: Splicing Traditions in the Early Years', in *Citizen Sailors: Chronicles of Canada's Naval Reserve, 1910–2010*, eds Richard H. Gimblett and Michael L. Hadley (Toronto: Dundurn, 2010), 9.
17. W. David Parsons, 'Codfish, Cruisers and Courage: The Newfoundland Division of the Royal Naval Reserve, 1900–1922', in *Citizen Sailors*, 23, 30.
18. The largest ships that Breault served on were likely the submarine tenders that acted like motherships, which ranged from the smaller *Canopus* at 6,000 tons to the *Savannah* at 10,000 tons.
19. Henry Breault, 'Service Record, R.N.C.V.R.', SFLM.
20. Henry Breault, 'Service Record, R.N.C.V.R.', SFLM.
21. Henry Breault, 'Service Record, R.N.C.V.R.', SFLM.
22. David J. Freeman, 'Substantive and Non-Substantive Rates in the RCN', accessed December 21, 2022, https://navalandmilitarymuseum.org/article/substantive-and-non-substantive-rates-the-rcn/.
23. Mark J.E. Richardson, 'Manpower and the Orphan Service: Recruiting, Training and Personnel Retention in the Royal Canadian Navy, 1910–1940', (MA Thesis, University of Calgary, 2002), 47–48.
24. Mary MacKinnon, 'Canadian Railway Workers and World War I Military Service', *Labour/Le Travail* 40 (Fall 1997), 225, https://doi.org/10.2307/25144169.
25. MacKinnon, 'Canadian Railway Workers', 225.

## ENDNOTES

26. Connecticut Adjutant General, *Roster of Connecticut Volunteers Who Served in the War Between the United States and Spain: 1898–1899* (Hartford: The Case, Lockwood and Brainard Company, 1899), 31.
27. Connecticut Adjutant General, *Roster of Connecticut Volunteers*, 31.
28. *Observer Extra* (Putnam), November 19, 1988, SFLM.
29. B.H. Nye, 'A Canadian Port in War Time', *History Teacher's Magazine* (June 1, 1916), 189–90.
30. Canadian War Museum, 'The Halifax Explosion', accessed December 23, 2022, https://www.warmuseum.ca/firstworldwar/history/life-at-home-during-the-war/wartime-tragedies/the-halifax-explosion/.
31. John G. Armstrong, 'Letters from Halifax: Reliving the Halifax Explosion Through the Eyes of my Grandfather, a Sailor in the Royal Canadian Navy', *The Northern Mariner/Le Marin du Nord* 8, no. 4 (1998), 55–74.
32. Armstrong, 'Letters from Halifax', 60.
33. Armstrong, 'Letters from Halifax', 60.
34. Armstrong, 'Letters from Halifax', 61.
35. Armstrong, 'Letters from Halifax', 61.
36. Armstrong, 'Letters from Halifax', 61.
37. Armstrong, 'Letters from Halifax', 61–66.
38. *Observer Extra* (Putnam), November 19, 1988, SFLM.
39. Courtney Mrazek, 'Frank Baker's Diary: December 6, 1941', *Dartmouth Heritage Museum* (online exhibit), accessed December 23, 2022, https://www.dartmouthheritagemuseum.ns.ca/2017/08/06/frank-bakers-diary/.
40. Mrazek, 'Frank Baker's Diary', *Dartmouth Heritage Museum*.
41. Armstrong, 'Letters from Halifax', 66.
42. Armstrong, 'Letters from Halifax', 68.
43. Richardson, 'Manpower and the Orphan Service', 21.
44. Henry Breault, 'Service Record, R.N.C.V.R.', SFLM.
45. Henry Breault, 'Service Record, R.N.C.V.R.', SFLM.
46. Henry Breault, 'Final Discharge Form', SFLM.
47. *Observer Extra* (Putnam), November 19, 1988, SFLM.
48. *Observer Extra* (Putnam), November 19, 1988, SFLM.
49. Hal Ashby, *The Last Detail* (1973), Columbia Pictures, 01:07:13–01:08:40.
50. *The Last Detail*, 01:07:56.
51. *Observer Extra* (Putnam), November 19, 1988, SFLM.
52. Jennifer Keene, 'A "Brutalizing" War? The USA after the First World War', *Journal of Contemporary History* 50, no. 1 (January 2015), 88, 94, http://www.jstor.org/stable/43697364; William M. McBride, 'The Unstable Dynamics of a Strategic Technology: Disarmament, Unemployment, and the Interwar

Battleship', *Technology and Culture* 38, no. 2 (April 1997), 386–423, https://doi.org/10.2307/3107127. The problem of demobilization was recognized as the discussion gained steam from 1943–45. See E. Jay Howenstine, 'Demobilization After the First World War', *The Quarterly Journal of Economics* 58, no. 1 (1943), 91–105, https://doi.org/10.2307/1885757; E. Jay Howenstine, 'Lessons of World War I', *The Annals of the American Academy of Political and Social Science* 238 (1945), 180–87, http://www.jstor.org/stable/1025298.

53. At an unknown date between 1921 and 1923, the Breault's immediate family moved back to White Plains, NY. The Canadian Census and the letters to Breault indicate the family had moved before the *O-5* collision in 1923.
54. Breault, 'U.S. Navy Enlistment, July 20, 1920', OMPF, 1.
55. Breault, 'U.S. Navy Enlistment, July 20, 1920', OMPF, 1.
56. Meaghan C. Mobbs and George A. Bonanno, 'Beyond War and PTSD: The Crucial Role of Transition Stress in the Lives of Military Veterans', *Clinical Psychology Review* 59 (2018), 139.
57. Richardson, 'Manpower and the Orphan Service', 24.
58. Breault, 'U.S. Navy Enlistment, July 20, 1920', OMPF, 1.
59. Breault, 'U.S. Navy Enlistment, July 20, 1920', OMPF, 1.
60. Unknown photographer, 'Naval Training Station, Newport: Sailors Preparing to Swim', LCN 2022634782, LC-USZ62-16082 (b&w film copy neg.), *ca.* 1900–20, https://lccn.loc.gov/2022634782; unknown photographer, 'Naval Training Station, Newport: Sailors Performing Boat Drill', LCN 2016821326, LC-USZ62-16082 LC-DIG-npcc-19746 (digital file from original), *ca.* 1908–19, https://www.loc.gov/resource/npcc.19746/.
61. C.B. Hatch, 'Memorandum for Navy Press Room, February 20, 1924', OMPF, 30.
62. *The Sun* (New York), March 8, 1914, *Chronicling America: Historic American Newspapers, Lib. of Congress*, https://chroniclingamerica.loc.gov/lccn/sn83030272/1914-03-08/ed-1/seq-36/.
63. J. Andrew Byers, 'The Sailors of 1898: Identity, Motivations, and Experiences of Naval Enlisted Personnel at the Dawn of an Age of American Empire', *International Journal of Naval History* 7, no. 2 (August 2008), 12.
64. Hatch, 'Memorandum', OMPF, 30.
65. Naval Submarine School, 'Henry Breault Submarine School Attendance Card', SFLM.
66. Hatch, 'Memorandum', OMPF, 30.
67. Hatch, 'Memorandum', OMPF, 30.
68. Henry Breault, 'Agreement to Extend Enlistment, July 13, 2022', OMPF, 7.
69. James W. Anderson (photographer), 'American Submarines in Bermuda, Just Returned From the War Front', Naval Source Organization, accessed

December 26, 2022, http://navsource.org/archives/08/O-boats/0806609.jpg; NHHC, 'O-5', accessed December 26, 2022, https://www.history.navy.mil/research/histories/ship-histories/danfs/o/o-5.html.
70. *New York Tribune*, October 8, 1918; *The Boston Globe*, August 13, 1919; *News Pilot* (San Pedro), Monday, July 21, 1919.
71. *The Pittsburgh Press*, August 7, 1921.
72. Unknown photographer, 'O-Class Submarines of Submarine Division Eight at Boston 16 Aug 1921', Naval Source Organization, accessed December 26, 2022, http://navsource.org/archives/08/O-boats/0806705.jpg.
73. *News Pilot* (San Pedro), January 18, 1923; unknown photographer, 'US Submarine base at Coco Solo, Panama 1923', Naval Source Organization, accessed December 26, 2022, http://navsource.org/archives/08/r-boats/0810304.jpg.
74. Robert E. Fretz, 'Qualification Notebook Week 1', private collection of Ric Hedman, accessed December 26, 2022, http://www.pigboats.com/subs/qualsweek1.pdf.
75. Gugliotta, *Pigboat 39*, 113, 125.
76. Bureau of Navigation, 'Transcript of Record', OMPF, 82.
77. Benjamin Fairchild, 'Letter on Behalf of Henry Breault, October 13, 1924', OMPF, 353.
78. Bureau of Navigation, 'Small Arms Qualification Record', OMPF, 251.
79. Henry Breault, 'Agreement to Extend Enlistment, July 13, 2022', OMPF, 30.
80. Bureau of Navigation, 'Breault, Henry, 2108003, TM3c. to TM2c. June 18, 1923', OMPF, 14.
81. Fairchild, 'Letter', OMPF, 353.

## Chapter 4: Heroism and Recognition (1923–24)

1. 'Submarine Hero Writes Home', *New York Times*, November 20, 1923, newspaper clipping, SFLM.
2. *The Daily Argus* (White Plains), November 2, 1923, Friday, page 29. Curiously, the title of the passage is 'I am alive and well'. More of a reason to distrust the *Argus*.
3. 'They Stared at the Clock', newspaper clipping, SFLM.
4. 'They Stared at the Clock', newspaper clipping, SFLM.
5. Robert F. Jones, 'Medical History Sheet', OMPF, 452.
6. *Sunday Star* (Washington D.C.) December 9, 1923; *Omaha Morning Bee*, March 10, 1924; *Evening Star* (Washington D.C.) March 9, 1924.
7. Collins, 'Style in the New Story', 48–53.

8. Collins, 'Style in the News Story', 58.
9. 'Submarine Hero Writes', newspaper clipping, SFLM.
10. *Dominion Bureau of Statistics: Population*, Sixth Census of Canada, 1921, Breault, Joseph, MFGR.
11. Henry Breault, 'Enlistment, 1920', OMPF, 1.
12. Henry Breault, 'U.S. Navy Enlistment/Enrollment of Henry Breault, November 22, 1924', OMPF, 60; Henry Breault, 'U.S. Navy Enlistment/Enrollment of Henry Breault, January 5, 1929', OMPF, 122; Henry Breault, 'U.S. Navy Enlistment/Enrollment of Henry Breault, December 29, 1932', OMPF, 129; Henry Breault, 'U.S. Navy Enlistment/Enrollment of Henry Breault, February 23, 1937', OMPF, 143.
13. J.J. Breault, 'Western Union Telegram', OMPF, 344.
14. Unknown photographer, 'Picture of the Cofferdam on the O-5', from the collection of Ric Hedman, http://pigboats.com/subs/o-boats.html; unknown photographer, 'Picture of the Damage Done to the O-5', from the collection of Ric Hedman, accessed March 16, 2023, http://pigboats.com/subs/o-boats.html.
15. *The Portsmouth Herald*, April 22, 1924, Tuesday, page 5.
16. Bureau of Navigation, 'U.S. Naval Message, November 12, 1923', OMPF, 24; Hatch, 'Memorandum', OMPF, 30.
17. 'They Stared at the Clock', newspaper clipping, SFLM; *Sunday Star* (Washington D.C.), December 9, 1923; *Omaha Morning Bee*, March 10, 1924; *Evening Star* (Washington D.C.), March 9, 1924; *Indianapolis Times*, October 31, 1923. See also Collins, 'Style', 58, for more examples.
18. Grigore, 'The O-5 Is Down!', website reprint.
19. *Indianapolis Times*, October 31, 1923.
20. *The Abangarez*, court case.
21. 'They Stared at the Clock', newspaper clipping, SFLM.
22. 'They Stared at the Clock', newspaper clipping, SFLM.
23. 'They Stared at the Clock', newspaper clipping, SFLM.
24. 'They Stared at the Clock', newspaper clipping, SFLM.
25. 'They Stared at the Clock', newspaper clipping, SFLM; Robert F. Jones, 'Medical History Sheet', OMPF, 452.
26. Jones, 'Medical History Sheet', OMPF, 452.
27. 'They Stared at the Clock', newspaper clipping, SFLM.
28. 'They Stared at the Clock', newspaper clipping, SFLM.
29. H. Avery, 'BREAULT, Henry, TM2c, (#210-83-03) Recommendation for Navy Cross, Coco Solo, November 19, 1923', OMPF, 415.
30. Avery, 'Navy Cross', OMPF, 415.
31. Avery, 'Navy Cross', OMPF, 415.

# ENDNOTES

32. A. Bronson & R.H. English, 'BREAULT, Henry, TM2c, (210-83-03) Recommendation for Navy Cross (U.S.S. *O-5*), Coco Solo, November 23, 1923', OMPF, 416; M.M. Taylor, 'BREAULT, Henry, TM2c, (210-83-03) Recommendation for Congressional Medal of Honor, New London, December 5, 1923', OMPF, 417.
33. M.M. Taylor, 'BREAULT, Henry, TM2c', OMPF, 417.
34. There is no source that outright states this, but the smiling moustached man pictured to the left of Breault in his portrait shot was Taylor, verified by viewing his other pictures. See unknown photographer, 'Henry Breault, 3/8/24', photograph, *Library of Congress Prints and Photographs Division Washington, D.C., LCN, 2016836978*.
35. The Chief of the Bureau of Navigation, 'BREAULT, Henry, TM2c, (210-83-03) Recommendation for Congressional Medal of Honor, February 12, 1924', OMPF, 421.
36. *United States Navy Regulations, 1920* (Washington D.C.: U.S. Govt. Press, 1920), 551–53.
37. Unknown photographer, 'Henry Breault, 3/8/24', photograph, *Library of Congress Prints and Photographs Division Washington, D.C., LCN, 2016836978*; unknown photographer, 'Coolidge & Henry Breault, 3/8/24', photograph, *Library of Congress Prints and Photographs Division Washington, D.C., LCN, 2016836982*; unknown photographer, 'Coolidge & Henry Breault, 3/8/24', photograph, *Library of Congress Prints and Photographs Division Washington, D.C., LCN, 2016836981*; unknown photographer, 'Denby, Coolidge, & Henry Breault, [3/8/24]', photograph, *Library of Congress Prints and Photographs Division Washington, D.C., LCN, 2016836979*.
38. *The Baltimore Sun*, February 20, 1924, Thursday, page 11.
39. *The Commercial Appeal* (Memphis), March 7, 1924, Friday, page 1.
40. *Buffalo Morning Express*, March 9, 1924, Sunday, page 39, Henry Breault, 'Claim for Reimbursement for Personal Property Lost in a Marine Disaster, November 8, 1923', OMPF, 22.
41. *New York Evening Post*, March 15, 1924, newspaper clipping, Congressional Medal of Honor Society.
42. *Buffalo Morning Express*, March 9, 1924, Sunday, page 39, Breault's home state did not appear to play a role in his award, but it likely pleased Coolidge to bring another Medal of Honor to Vermont.
43. *Oakland Tribune*, March 9, 1924, Sunday, page 69.
44. *Oakland Tribune*, March 9, 1924, Sunday, page 69.
45. CMOHS, 'William Adger Moffett', accessed February 26, 2023, https://www.cmohs.org/recipients/william-a-moffett.

46. Unknown photographer, 'NH 43954 Rear Admiral Montgomery M. Taylor, USN', *ca.* 1927, (NHHC), accessed February 26, 2023, https://www.history.navy.mil/our-collections/photography/numerical-list-of-images/nhhc-series/nh-series/NH-43000/NH-43954.html; unknown photographer, 'NH 43955 Will Rogers and Rear Admiral Montgomery M. Taylor', *ca.* 1927, NHHC, accessed February 26, 2023, https://www.history.navy.mil/our-collections/photography/numerical-list-of-images/nhhc-series/nh-series/NH-43000/NH-43955.html.
47. CMOHS, 'Henry Breault', accessed February 26, 2023, https://www.cmohs.org/recipients/henry-breault.
48. *Daily Pilot* (San Pedro), March 26, 1924, Wednesday evening, page 9; *New York Times*, March 9, 1924; *The San Bernardino County Sun*, April 13, 1924, Sunday, page 11.
49. *The Brooklyn Daily Eagle*, March 10, 1924, Monday, page 22.
50. *The Commercial Appeal* (Memphis), Friday, March 7, 1924.
51. *The Buffalo Evening News*, March 11, 1924, Tuesday, page 17.
52. Bureau of Navigation, 'BREAULT, Henry, TM2c, 210-80-03, USN re: Leave and transfer of. March 8, 1924', OMPF, 41.
53. *The Daily Argus* (White Plains), November 2, 1923, Friday, page 29.
54. J.J. Breault, 'Western Union Telegram', OMPF, 344.
55. Bureau of Navigation, 'Transfer Card, March 12, 1924', OMPF, 213.
56. Alfred Green (dir.), *It's Tough to be Famous* (1932), Warner Bros Pictures Inc, Amazon.com Collection, 18:00–22:55.
57. Bureau of Navigation, 'Transfer Card, March 15, 1924', OMPF, 215.
58. *New York Evening Post*, March 15, 1924, newspaper clipping, Congressional Medal of Honor Society Archives (CMOHS).
59. *New York Evening Post*, March 15, 1924, newspaper clipping, CMOHS.
60. *The Daily Argus* (White Plains), November 2, 1923, Friday, page 29.
61. *New York Evening Post*, March 15, 1924, newspaper clipping, CMOHS.
62. Alfred Green, *It's Tough to be Famous*, 18:00–22:55.
63. *Pittsburgh Post-Gazette*, May 19, 1932, Thursday, page 17.
64. Murphy, photograph of - request for', OMPF, 64.
65. W.R. Shoemaker, 'Reply: BREAULT, Henry, TM2c, USN, 210-83-03 photograph of- request for, Brooklyn, December 8, 1924', OMPF, 65.

## Chapter 5: Post-award Career (1924–41)

1. Benjamin Fairchild, 'Letter on Behalf of Henry Breault, October 13, 1924', OMPF, 353.

# ENDNOTES

2. Bureau of Navigation, 'Transfer Card, March 24, 1924', OMPF, 216.
3. *The Portsmouth Herald*, April 22, 1924, Tuesday.
4. Bureau of Navigation, 'Record of BREAULT, Henry', OMPF, 245.
5. Bureau of Navigation, 'Record of BREAULT, Henry', OMPF, 247.
6. J.B. Hoover, 'Breault, Henry, T.M.2cl, U.S.N. (210-80-03) – recommendation for examination for Gunner, July 8, 1924', OMPF, 46.
7. W.R. Shoemaker, 'Breault, Henry, T.M.2cl, U.S.N. (210-80-03) – recommendation for examination for Gunner. August 27, 1924', OMPF, 50.
8. *New York Evening Post*, March 15, 1924, newspaper clipping, CMOHS; Eric Partridge, *A Dictionary of Catch Phrases, American and British, from the Sixteenth Century to the Present Day*, ed. Paul Beagle (Lanham: Scarborough House, 1992), 143; Bureau of Navigation, 'Application for Enlistment, November 22, 1924', OMPF, 58.
9. Bureau of Navigation, 'Application for Enlistment, November 22, 1924', OMPF, 58.
10. *New York Evening Post*, March 15, 1924, newspaper clipping, CMOHS; Bureau of Navigation, 'Application for Enlistment, November 22, 1924', OMPF, 58.
11. *Observer Extra* (Putnam), November 19, 1988, SFLM.
12. Catherine O'Rourke, 'Letter to the Bureau of Navigation Requesting Henry Breault's Address, January 24, 1928', OMPF, 359–60.
13. *Born to Dance*, Roy Del Ruth (1936), Metro-Goldwyn-Mayer, 1:24:08–1:24:40.
14. Fairchild, 'Letter on Behalf of Henry Breault', OMPF, 353.
15. Shoemaker, 'BREAULT, Henry, #2108003, Ex-TM2c', OMPF, 56.
16. J.M. Smeallie, 'SUBJECT: Breault, Henry; course of instruction for, October 22, 1924', OMPF, 57.
17. E.J.A. Murphy, 'BREAULT, Henry, TM2c, USN, 210-83-03 photograph of-request for, November 26, 1924', OMPF, 64.
18. Bureau of Navigation, 'Professional Qualifications, Conduct, and Marks, January 26, 1925', OMPF, 262.
19. Bureau of Navigation, 'Professional Qualifications, Conduct, and Marks, February 8, 1925', OMPF, 263.
20. Gugliotta, *Pigboat 39*, 3, 8, 34, 54, 58. The entire book should be considered an ode to the S-boat sailor, but the first several chapters of the book detail how close they were.
21. Gugliotta, *Pigboat 39*, 54.
22. Edward L. Beach, *Salt and Steel: Reflections of a Submariner* (Annapolis: Naval Institute Press, 1999), 70.

23. Gugliotta, *Pigboat 39*, 11, 54.
24. Bureau of Navigation, 'Medical History', OMPF, 473.
25. Hoover, 'Breault, Henry', OMPF, 46.
26. Breault, Henry, 'TM 2c1, 210-80-03; Medal of Honor Man; Course of Instruction for, January 26, 1925', OMPF, 69; Bureau of Navigation, 'Syllabus of Study for Gunner (Ordnance)', OMPF, 70–75.
27. Edward Ellsberg, *Pigboats* (Rahway: Quinn and Boden, 1931), 215–17.
28. Ellsberg, *Pigboats*, 218.
29. Ellsberg, *Pigboats*, 219.
30. Ralph Staub, dir., *Navy Blues* (1937), Republic Pictures, https://www.youtube.com/watch?v=Y_m7P7BLOMM.
31. Ralph Staub, *Navy Blues* (1937), film.
32. W. Duncan Mansfield, *Sweetheart of the Navy* (1937), Grand National Films Inc, https://www.youtube.com/watch?v=y9N1U0U19bU&t=2s.
33. R.A. Koch, 'Memorandum for Chief of Bureau: --, February 17, 1928', OMPF, 106.
34. Unknown author, 'Handwritten Note on Enlisted Personnel Division Mailing Slip', OMPF, 104.
35. Bureau of Navigation, 'Permanent Appointment', OMPF, 114. This is similar to the 'MAP' or 'CAP' programme in the present-day military. Considering there was a procedure to meritoriously promote people in the timeframe, it can seen as rewarding those for service, rather than professional knowledge.
36. Government of Canada, 'Heroes of the Halifax Explosion', accessed February 18, 2023, https://www.canada.ca/en/navy/services/history/heroes-halifax-explosion.html.
37. This is an observation having studied both British and American history. The enlisted sailor, Jack Tar, is a major cultural influence on British society, but American Bluejackets did not have the same cultural pull. They were subject to influences as frequently as they commanded them.
38. John E. Chapman, 'How to Fail at the NTC', *Army Logistician: Professional Bulletin of United States Army Logistics* (January–February 1998), 29. This quote has taken a life of its own, but it likely was similar to Daly's actual opinion.
39. (NHHC), 'U.S. Navy Personnel Strength, 1775 to Present', accessed January 24, 2023, https://www.history.navy.mil/research/library/online-reading-room/title-list-alphabetically/u/usn-personnel-strength.html.
40. Bureau of Navigation, 'Award of Campaign Medal, July 21, 1936', OMPF, 445.

## ENDNOTES

41. Bureau of Navigation, 'Professional Qualifications, Conduct, and Marks, February 18, 1930', OMPF, 281.
42. Bureau of Navigation, 'Professional Qualifications, Conduct, and Marks, July 13, 1928', OMPF, 268.
43. Bureau of Navigation, *U.S. Navy Ports of the World: San Francisco* (Washington D.C.: Ditty Box Guide Book Series, 1920), 20.
44. Bureau of Navigation, 'Professional Qualifications, Conduct, and Marks, January 5, 1929', OMPF, 271.
45. Bureau of Navigation, 'Professional Qualifications, Conduct, and Marks, February 21, 1929', OMPF, 279.
46. L.D. McCormick, 'Professional Qualifications, Conduct and Marks', OMPF, 279.
47. *The Bluejackets' Manual: 1927, Seventh Edition Revised May, 1927* (Washington D.C: United States Government Printing Office, 1928), 241.
48. *Bluejackets' Manual 1927*, 247.
49. Ellsberg, *Pigboats*, 1–6.
50. Bureau of Navigation, 'Professional Qualifications, Conduct, and Marks, April 30, 1930', OMPF, 282; Bureau of Navigation, 'Professional Qualifications, Conduct, and Marks, June 4, 1930', OMPF, 283.
51. Bureau of Navigation, 'Medical History Sheet', OMPF, 461.
52. Bureau of Navigation, 'Professional Qualifications, Conduct, and Marks, April 30, 1930', OMPF, 282; Bureau of Navigation, 'Professional Qualifications, Conduct, and Marks, June 4, 1930', OMPF, 283; Bureau of Navigation, 'Medical History Sheet', OMPF, 462.
53. NHHC 'Yangtze River Patrol and Other US Navy Asiatic Fleet Activities in China, 1920–1942, as Described in the Annual Reports of the Navy Department', accessed February 18, 2023, https://www.history.navy.mil/content/history/nhhc/research/library/online-reading-room/title-list-alphabetically/y/yangtze-river-patrol-and-other-us-navy-asiatic-fleet-activities-in-china.html.
54. S.W. DuBois, 'Letter of Commendation, in the case of, -- BREAULT, Henry 210-80-03, TM1c. USN', OMPF, 442.
55. *Honolulu Star-Bulletin*, Thursday, December 10, 1931.
56. Eric H. Antoine, 'Chief of the Boat!', *The Submarine Review* (January 2014), 88–93, archive reprint, accessed December 31, 2022, https://archive.navalsubleague.org/2014/articles-chief-of-the-boat.
57. Schultz & Snell, *We Were Pirates*, 175.
58. O'Kane, *Clear the Bridge*, 137; Galantin, *Take Her Deep*, 57.
59. Gugliotta, *Pigboat 39*, xii.

60. Gugliotta, *Pigboat 39*, 3, 13.
61. Gugliotta, *Pigboat 39*, 3, 8, 13, 47.
62. Gugliotta, *Pigboat 39*, 58–60.
63. Gugliotta, *Pigboat 39*, 59.
64. Gugliotta, *Pigboat 39*, 59.
65. Bureau of Navigation, 'Professional Qualifications, Conduct, and Marks, October 28, 1932', OMPF, 289. The same Nimitz who would lead the Pacific Fleet in the Second World War. This is not the only document that contains Nimitz's name and illustrates how many Second World War sailors were present in the fleet during the interwar period.
66. Bureau of Navigation, 'Professional Qualifications, Conduct, and Marks, December 29, 1932', OMPF, 294; Bureau of Navigation, 'Enlistment of Henry Breault, December 29, 1932', OMPF, 129.
67. William L. Slaughter, 'Letter concerning Henry Breault to the Bureau of Navigation, December 24, 1933', OMPF, 377–78. This connection will be explored in much greater detail in Chapter 7.
68. Bureau of Navigation, 'Professional Qualifications, Conduct, and Marks, December 29, 1932', OMPF, 300.
69. Bureau of Navigation, 'Professional Qualifications, Conduct, and Marks, December 29, 1932', OMPF, 302.
70. *The Los Angeles Times*, December 16, 1933, Saturday, page 13; *Honolulu Star-Bulletin*, September 22, 1934, Saturday, page 10, 43; *Oakland Tribune*, May 4, 1935, Saturday, page 3; *Oakland Tribune*, March 19, 1935, Tuesday, page 18; *Rutland Daily Herald*, March 19, 1935, Tuesday, page 1.
71. *Honolulu Star-Bulletin*, September 22, 1934, Saturday, page 43.
72. *The Los Angeles Times*, December 16, 1933, Saturday, page 13.
73. *Honolulu Star-Bulletin*, September 22, 1934, Saturday, page 10.
74. Bureau of Navigation, 'Medical History', OMPF, 473.
75. Bureau of Navigation, 'Enlistment', OMPF, 129.
76. Bureau of Navigation, 'Enlistment', OMPF, 129.
77. Bureau of Navigation, 'Enlistment', OMPF, 129.
78. Bureau of Navigation, 'Medical History', OMPF, 475.
79. Bureau of Navigation, 'Medical History', OMPF, 477.
80. Bureau of Navigation, 'Medical History', OMPF, 477.
81. Bureau of Navigation, 'Medical History', OMPF, 478.
82. Bureau of Navigation, 'Medical History', OMPF, 478.
83. Bureau of Navigation, 'Medical History', OMPF, 481.
84. Bureau of Navigation, 'Medical History', OMPF, 482.

# ENDNOTES

85. Bureau of Navigation, 'Medical History', OMPF, 483.
86. Bureau of Navigation, 'Medical History', OMPF, 483–84.
87. Frank Capra, *Submarine* (1928), Columbia Pictures, Campbell Films; John Ford, *Men Without Women* (1930), Fox Film Corporation, Campbell Films; Alfred E. Green, *It's Tough to be Famous* (1932), Warner Bros Pictures Inc, Amazon.com; Jack Conway, *Hell Below* (1933), Metro-Goldwyn-Mayer, Presumed Lost; Vernon Sewell and Gustav Ucicky, *Morgenrot* (Dawn) (1933), Universum Film AG, Amazon.com; Lloyd Bacon, *Submarine D-1* (1937), Cosmopolitan Productions, Campbell Films.
88. Koch, 'Memorandum for Chief of Bureau', OMPF, 106; Henry Breault, 'Duty on Asiatic Station – request for', OMPF, 134–35; Henry Breault, 'Duty-Request for, July 30, 1941', OMPF, 189.
89. *Honolulu Star-Bulletin*, September 22, 1934, Saturday, page 10.

## Chapter 6: 'A Pigboat Sailor's Lament': Danger and Discomfort

1. Nye, 'A Canadian Port in War Time', 190.
2. *Bluejackets' Manual 1927*, 250.
3. Schultz & Shell, *We Were Pirates*, 20.
4. Roberts, *Sub*, 6.
5. Gugliotta, *Pigboat 39*, 129.
6. Jules Verne, *Twenty Thousand Leagues the Sea* (New York: Grosset & Dunlap, 1917).
7. Victor Appleton, *Tom Swift and His Submarine Boat* (New York: Grosset & Dunlap, 1910); Luis P. Serans, 'From Pole to Pole; Or, Frank Reade, Jr.'s Strange Submarine Voyage', *Frank Reade Weekly Magazine: Containing Stories of Adventures on Land, Sea, and in the Air*, 4 (November 2, 1902); G. Harvey Ralphson, *Boy Scouts in a Submarine or, Searching the Ocean Floor* (New York: M.A. Donohue & Company, 1912); Victor G. Durham, *The Submarine Boys on Duty: Life on a Diving Torpedo Boat* (Akron: The Saalfield Publishing Co, 1909). There are many more examples, but these give the possible breadth of influence.
8. Edwin Milton Royale, Silvio Hein and George V. Hobart, *In My Submarine*, Image and Sheet Music (1905), notated music, accessed November 2, 2022, https://www.loc.gov/item/2016762181/; Luther A. Clark and L. La Rose, *Submarine Johnny*, notated music (1911), accessed November 2, 2022, https://www.loc.gov/item/2013564388/.
9. This will be explored in greater detail in Chapter 9 but is worthy of introduction as part of this section.

10. 'Pray for Son, He Returns', *Los Angeles Examiner*, May 26, 1939, SFLM, newspaper clipping.
11. 'Her Fiancée Among Those Missing', *Los Angeles Examiner*, May 26, 1939, SFLM, newspaper clipping.
12. 'L.A. Man Among Dead', *Los Angeles Examiner*, May 26, 1939, SFLM, newspaper clipping.
13. 'Submarine Hero Writes', newspaper clipping, SFLM.
14. *New York Evening Post*, March 15, 1924, newspaper clipping, CMOHS.
15. 'Survivor Tells How He Opened Door to Save 5 as Water Rose', *Associated Press*, May 25, 1939, SFLM, newspaper clipping.
16. 'The Cold Was Worst Say Squalus Men', *International News Service*, May 25, 1939, SFLM, newspaper clipping.
17. Mary F. Romig, *Fatal Submarine Accidents; A Bibliography, 1900–1965* (Santa Moncia: Rand Corporation, 1966), report.
18. Gugliotta, *Pigboat 39*, 12.
19. Lloyd Bacon (dir.), *Submarine D-1* (1937), Warner Bros. Pictures, Campbell Films remastered and edited; Frank Capra (dir.), *Submarine: A Mighty Drama of the Sea* (1928), Columbia Pictures, Campbell Films remastered and edited; Jack Conway (dir.), *Hell Below* (1933), Metro-Goldwyn-Mayer (presumed lost, no known copies, but based on Edward Ellsberg's *Pigboats*). John Ford (dir.), *Men Without Women* (1930), Fox Film Corporation, Fox Cinema Archives, remastered; Gustav Ucicky (dir.), *Dawn* (*Morgenrot*) (1933), Protex Picture Corporation (USA), https://rarefilmm.com/2018/10/morgenrot-1933/.
20. Gugliotta, *Pigboat 39*, 23.
21. James R. Reckner, *A Sailor's Log: Water-Tender Frederick T. Wilson, USN, on Asiatic Station, 1899–1901* (London: Kent University Press, 2004).
22. Reckner, *A Sailor's Log*, 46.
23. Jackson, *The Men*; Gugliotta, *Pigboat 39*.
24. Jackson, *The Men*, 10–11.
25. Jackson, *The Men*, 33; Gugliotta, *Pigboat 39*, 8, 10.
26. Gugliotta, *Pigboat 39*, 66–67.
27. Gugliotta, *Pigboat 39*, 129.
28. Gugliotta, *Pigboat 39*, 128–30. These examples are all from the passages contained within the page range.
29. Submarine Research Center, *Submarine Cuisine* (Bangor, Washington: Submarine Research Center, 2004), 21.
30. Submarine Research Center, *Submarine Cuisine*, 41.
31. Submarine Research Center, *Submarine Cuisine*, 41.

# ENDNOTES

32. Gugliotta, *Pigboat 39*, 24.
33. Gugliotta, *Pigboat 39*, 82–84, 120.
34. Jackson, *The Men*, 33–34.
35. 1929 Deck Log, Submarine V-2, The National Archives (US), RG 24, 2599/2766, January 1, 1929–December 31, 1929, 817.
36. 1929 Deck Log, Submarine V-2, The National Archives (US), RG 24, 2599/2766, January 1, 1929–December 31, 1929, 857.
37. Gugliotta, *Pigboat 39*, 3–5, 57, 75.
38. Gugliotta, *Pigboat 39*, 54.
39. Gugliotta, *Pigboat 39*, 8.
40. Gugliotta, *Pigboat 39*, 104–05.
41. Gugliotta, *Pigboat 39*, 137.
42. *The Los Angeles Times*, June 23, 1931, Tuesday, page 11.
43. *The Los Angeles Times*, June 23, 1931, Tuesday, page 11.
44. Jackson, *The Men*, 23.

## Chapter 7: Family, Friends and Forced Alienation

1. *The Virginian-Pilot* (Norfolk), November 2, 1923, Friday, page 9.
2. DuBois, 'Letter of Commendation', OMPF, 442.
3. Gugliotta, *Pigboat 39*, 126, 130, 174.
4. Breault, 'RNCVR Final Discharge Form', SFLM.
5. Bureau of Navigation, 'Enlistment', OMPF, 1.
6. Bureau of Navigation, 'Letters to Mrs. L.R.B. Hale Regarding Status of Friend Henry Breault, October 28–30, 1923', OMPF, 15–20
7. Josephine Breault, 'Telegram to Bureau of Navigation, November 6, 1923', OMPF, 338.
8. A.M. Brady, 'Telegram to Bureau of Navigation, November 6, 1923', OMPF, 341.
9. A.A. Brault, 'Letter to Bureau of Navigation, November 6, 1923', OMPF, 347–48.
10. Bureau of Navigation, 'Reply to A.A. Brault', OMPF, 349; Bureau of Navigation, 'Reply to Louis A. Breault', OMPF, 350; Bureau of Navigation, 'Reply to Josephine A. Breault', OMPF, 340; Bureau of Navigation, 'Reply to A.M. Brady', OMPF, 343; Bureau of Navigation, 'Reply to J.J. Breault', OMPF, 346.
11. Joseph J. Breault, 'Telegram to Bureau of Navigation, November 1, 1923', OMPF, 346.
12. Bureau of Navigation, 'Reply to J.J. Breault', OMPF, 346.

13. *New York Evening Post*, March 15, 1924, newspaper clipping, CMOHS.
14. *The Daily Argus* (White Plains), November 2, 1923, Friday, page 29.
15. Bureau of Navigation, 'Subject: BREAULT, Henry, EX T.M.2c USN – Address of, September 25, 1924', OMPF, 352.
16. Breault, 'Enlistment November 22, 1924', 60.
17. Diana Breault, 'Letter to U.S. Navy Dept – July 8, 1926', OMPF, 357; Diana B. Drennan, 'Letter to Bureau of Navigation, September 14, 1933', OMPF, 374; Diana B. Drennan, 'Letter to Bureau of Navigation, January 1, 1940', OMPF, 383; Diana B. Drennan, 'Letter to Bureau of Navigation, ca. February 14, 1941', OMPF, 392; Diana B. Drennan, 'Letter to Bureau of Navigation, ca. July 7, 1941', OMPF, 394–95.
18. Beatrice C. Breault, 'Letter to Bureau of Navigation, March 8, 1940', OMPF, 385–86.
19. *Observer Extra*, newspaper, SFLM.
20. *Men Without Women*, 00:01:30–00:18:30.
21. *The Last Detail*, 01:40:34–01:41:40.
22. *The Boston Globe* (Boston, Massachusetts), October 29, 1923, Monday, page 1.
23. *Times* (Picayune), August 9, 1936.
24. Grigore, 'The O-5 Is Down!', website reprint.
25. *The Buffalo News*, October 31, 1923, Wednesday, page 2.
26. *The Buffalo News*, October 31, 1923, Wednesday, page 2.
27. Slang for someone from the state of Connecticut.
28. *The Philadelphia Inquirer*, October 29, 1923, Monday, page 9.
29. *The Philadelphia Inquirer*, October 29, 1923, Monday, page 9; Navsource.org, 'From the Collection of Ric Headman, photo id. By John Hart', accessed February 14, 2023, http://navsource.org/archives/08/O-boats/0806608.jpg.
30. Jackson, *The Men*, 31, Gugliotta, *Pigboat 39*, 61.
31. Eternal Patrol, 'Fred C. Smith', accessed February 14, 2023, https://www.oneternalpatrol.com/smith-f-c.htm.
32. H. Avery, 'Breault, Henry, T.M.2cl, U.S.N. (210-80-03) – recommendation for examination for Gunner, July 8, 1924', OMPF, 46.
33. *Sweetheart of the Navy*, 18:50–19:40.
34. Ellsberg, *Pigboat*, 115.
35. Drennan, Everett Dewey, 'Ohio, Roster of Soldiers, Sailors, and Marines in World War I, 1917–1918', MFGR.
36. *The Portsmouth Times*, Portsmouth, Scioto, OH, October 27, 1932, page 9, MFGR; *Honolulu Star-Bulletin*, Honolulu, Hawaii, October 24, 1932, pages 1 & 2, MFGR.

37. *The Portsmouth Times*, October 27, 1932, page 9, MFGR; *Honolulu Star-Bulletin*, October 24, 1932, pages 1 & 2, MFGR.
38. *1930 US Census, San Diego Co, CA, San Diego Town, San Diego City*, ED 37-76, Sheet 8A, MFGR.
39. *The Honolulu Advertiser*, October 29, 1932, Saturday, page 7.
40. Gugliotta, *Pigboat 39*, 14–15.
41. *Navy Blues*, 00:02:00–00:02:35.
42. Herodotus, *The History*, trans. David Greene (Chicago: University of Chicago Press, 1987), 46–48. The story of Cleobis and Biton (alt.spelling Kleobis and Bito) is often used to illustrate legacy and happiness.

## Chapter 8: 'Falls in love with Kate and Jane, then he's out to sea again'

1. *Born to Dance*, 1:24:08–1:24:40.
2. Robert A. Nye, 'Western Masculinities in War and Peace', *The American Historical Review* 112, no. 2 (2007), 423, 431–32, http://www.jstor.org/stable/4136608; Jennifer Wingate, 'Over the Top: The Doughboy in World War I Memorials and Visual Culture', *American Art* 19, no. 2 (2005), 26–47, https://doi.org/10.1086/444480.
3. Ernest V. Wright, *Thoughts and Reveries of an American Bluejacket* (self-published, 1918), 5.
4. *Observer Extra*, newspaper, SFLM.
5. Chauncey, 'Christian Brotherhood or Sexual Perversion?', 190.
6. Cynthia Barounis, '"Not the Usual Pattern": James Baldwin, Homosexuality, and the *DSM*', *Criticism* 59, no. 3 (Summer 2017), 405–06, https://doi.org/10.13110/criticism.59.3.0395.
7. Sherry Zane, 'I did it for the uplift of humanity and the Navy: Same-Sex Acts and the Origins of the National Security State 1919–1921', *The New England Quarterly* 91, no. 2 (June 2018), 279–306, https://www.jstor.org/stable/26497565; Chauncey, 'Christian Brotherhood', *Journal of Social History* 19, no. 2 (Winter 1985), 189–211, http://www.jstor.org/stable/3787467.
8. *Born to Dance*, film, 00:03:00.
9. *Born to Dance*, film, 01:05:20.
10. Barounis, 'Not the Usual Pattern', 405–06; Chauncey, 'Christian Brotherhood', 190.
11. *Born to Dance*, film, 01:20:00.
12. Gugliotta, *Pigboat 39*, 14–15.

13. *Times* (Picayune), August 9, 1936.
14. Barounis, 'Not the Usual Pattern', 405–06.
15. *Daily Times* (Seattle), November 25, 1936.
16. *Daily Times* (Seattle), November 25, 1936.
17. *Imperial Valley Press* (El Centro, California), August 12, 1936.
18. *Born to Dance*, film, 00:41:43.
19. *Born to Dance*, film, 00:41:43.
20. *Born to Dance*, film, 00:01:32.
21. *Born to Dance*, film, 00:02:43.
22. *Born to Dance*, film, 00:03:54.
23. *Born to Dance*, film, 00:03:40.
24. *Born to Dance*, film, 00:02:43.
25. *Born to Dance*, film, 00:03:57.
26. *Born to Dance*, film, 00:16:00.
27. *Born to Dance*, film, 00:17:22.
28. *Born to Dance*, film, 00:17:37.
29. *Born to Dance*, film, 00:21:18.
30. *Born to Dance*, film, 00:22:00.
31. *Born to Dance*, film, 00:22:38.
32. *Born to Dance*, film, 00:23:34.
33. *Born to Dance*, film, 00:23:45.
34. *Observer Extra* (Putnam), SFLM.
35. *Burlington Daily News*, November 2, 1923, newspaper clipping, MFGR.
36. *Boston Globe*, October 29, 1923, Monday, page 9.
37. *Burlington Suburban List*, March 30, 1940, newspaper clipping, MFGR.
38. *Order of Publication (Divorce) - Underhill Enterprise, Essex Junction, Chittenden, VT*, February 8, 1923, page 7, MFGR.
39. *Burlington Suburban List*, March 30, 1940, newspaper clipping, MFGR.
40. *Burlington Suburban List*, March 30, 1940, newspaper clipping, MFGR.
41. Mark A. Smith, 'Religion, Divorce, and the Missing Culture War in America', *Political Science Quarterly* 125, no. 1 (Spring 2010), 68–70, http://www.jstor.org/stable/25698955; William L. Anderson and Derek W. Little, 'All's Fair: War and Other Causes of Divorce from a Beckerian Perspective', *The American Journal of Economics and Sociology* 58, no. 4 (October 1999), 904, http://www.jstor.org/stable/3488013.
42. *Born to Dance*, film, 01:24:20.
43. Catherine O'Rourke, 'Letter Requesting Mailing Address for Henry Breault, January 24, 1928', OMPF, 359–60; Catherine O'Rourke, 'Thank You Letter, January 31, 1928', OMPF, 363.

# ENDNOTES

44. Bureau of Navigation, 'Reply to Miss Catherine O'Rourke', OMPF, 362; O'Rourke, 'Thank You Letter', 363.
45. O'Rourke, 'Letter Requesting Mailing Address', OMPF, 359–60.
46. 'United States Census, 1930', database with images, GenealogyBank (https://genealogybank.com/#), Catherine O'Rourke, White Plains, Westchester, New York, United States (Original index: United States Census, 1930, FamilySearch, 2014).
47. William L. Slaughter, 'Letter concerning Henry Breault to the Bureau of Navigation, December 24, 1933', OMPF, 377–78.
48. Slaughter, 'Letter', OMPF, 377–78.
49. William D. Leahy & J.F. Donelson, 'Reply – January 3, 1934', OMPF, 379.
50. Slaughter, 'Letter', 377.
51. 'United States Census, 1930', database with images, FamilySearch, William L. Slaughter, San Diego, San Diego, California, United States; citing enumeration district (ED) 148, sheet 13A, line 16, family 347, NARA microfilm publication T626, roll 193; FHL microfilm 2,339,928 (Washington D.C.: National Archives and Records Administration, 2002), accessed May 17, 2022, https://www.familysearch.org/ark:/61903/1:1:XC6L-28D.
52. 'United States Census, 1930', FamilySearch Database.
53. *Submarine*, 00:01:00–00:30:00. The introductory sequences illustrate the friendship, marriage, infidelity and surprise on discovering the love triangle.
54. Bureau of Navigation, 'U.S. Navy Enlistment/Enrollment(s) of Henry Breault', OMPF, 129; 130 143–44, 171.
55. Henry Breault, 'Public Voucher for Reimbursement of Travel and Other Expenses Including Per Diem', OMPF, 171.
56. *Los Angeles Times*, 'Pair Found Dead in Auto Court', Los Angeles, CA, February 11, 1939, Part 1, page 10, MFGR.
57. *Los Angeles Times*, 'Pair Found Dead in Auto Court', MFGR.
58. Bureau of Navigation, 'Documents relating to Death, Funeral and Funeral Reimbursement', OMPF, 194–202, 401–09.
59. *Submarine*, 00:01:00–00:30:00.
60. Gugliotta, *Pigboat 39*, 11.
61. James V. Monaco and Roger Lewis, *Torpedo Jim*, Image and Sheet Music (1917), notated music, https://www.loc.gov/item/2013567908/.
62. Jeanine Hurl-Eamon, 'Insights into Plebeian Marriage: Soldiers, Sailors, and their Wives in the Old Bailey Proceedings', *The London Journal* 30, no. 1 (2005), 27–33, https://doi.org/10.1179/ldn.2005.30.1.22.
63. Bureau of Navigation, 'Medical History', OMPF, 483.

## Chapter 9: Permanent Change of Home Station

1. 1910 US Census, MFGR.
2. State of Connecticut, 'Population of Connecticut Towns 1900–1960', accessed January 15, 2023, https://portal.ct.gov/SOTS/Register-Manual/Section-VII/Population-1900-1960.
3. *Sanborn Fire Insurance Map from Putnam, Windham County, Connecticut*, Sanborn Map Company, August 1903, map, https://www.loc.gov/item/sanborn01167_004/. *Sanborn Fire Insurance Map from Putnam, Windham County, Connecticut*, Sanborn Map Company, September 1910, map, https://www.loc.gov/item/sanborn01167_005/.
4. *Sanborn Fire Insurance Map from Putnam*, August 1903; *Sanborn Fire Insurance Map from Putnam, Windham County*, September 1910.
5. Historic American Buildings Survey, *Israel Putnam School, Putnam, Windham County, Connecticut, Windham County, Putnam, 1933*, photograph, https://www.loc.gov/item/ct0390/; Historic American Buildings Survey, *Israel Putnam School (View from the Southeast), Putnam, Windham County, Connecticut, Windham County, Putnam, 1933*, photograph, https://www.loc.gov/item/ct0390/; Historic American Buildings Survey, *Israel Putnam School (View from the South), Putnam, Windham County, Connecticut, Windham County, Putnam, 1933*, photograph, https://www.loc.gov/item/ct0390/.
6. 'Local Man Dies at Naval Hospital', newspaper clipping, SFLM.
7. Bureau of the Census Department of Commerce and Labor, *Thirteenth Census of the United States Taken in 1913: Statistics for New York* (Washington D.C.: Government Printing Office, 1913), 588.
8. 'Submarine Torpedo Boats', *Scientific American* 85, no. 24 (1901), 387–88, http://www.jstor.org/stable/24983887; John P. Holland, 'The Submarine Boat and Its Future', *The North American Review* 171, no. 529 (1900), 894–903, http://www.jstor.org/stable/25105099; Simon Lake, 'Submarines That Are Strictly Invisible', *Scientific American* 112, no. 3 (1915), 68–75, http://www.jstor.org/stable/26015512; Waldon Fawcett, 'The Submarine Boat "Protector"', *Scientific American* 87, no. 21 (1902), 346–47, http://www.jstor.org/stable/24985633.
9. Paula M. Uruburu, *American Eve: Evelyn Nesbit, Stanford White, the Birth of the 'It' Girl, and the Crime of the Century* (New York: Riverhead Books, 2008), 361.
10. Stephanie Savage, 'Evelyn Nesbit and the Film(ed) Histories of the Thaw-White Scandal', *Film History* 8, no. 2 (1996), 159–75, http://www.jstor.org/stable/3815332.

# ENDNOTES

11. Bain News Service, publisher, 'Evelyn Thaw dodging a camera, White Plains, July 14, 1909', photograph, https://www.loc.gov/item/2014684043/; Bain News Service, publisher, 'Mrs. Wm. Thaw, veiled, on street, White Plains, July 14, 1909', photograph, https://www.loc.gov/item/2014684045/.
12. Bain News Service, 'Evelyn Thaw dodging a camera', LOC.
13. *The Sun* (New York), April 14, 1907, *New York Tribune*, May 13, 1906, *New York Tribune*, April 18, 1909.
14. *The Sun* (New York), April 14, 1907.
15. *New York Tribune*, May 13, 1906.
16. *New York Evening Post*, March 15, 1924, newspaper clipping, CMOHS.
17. Bureau of Navigation, 'Application for Enlistment, November 22, 1924', OMPF, 60.
18. Bureau of Navigation, 'Application for Enlistment, November 22, 1924', OMPF, 60; 1925 New York State Census, Westchester County, White Plains, 1st Ward, page 7, MFGR; 1940 US Census, Westchester County, New York, White Plains, 1st Ward, ED 60-353, Sheet 16A, MFGR.
19. Alice S. Howard, *Seaman's Handbook For Shore Leave* (Boston: Custom House, 1920), 50–51.
20. Nye, 'A Canadian Port in War Time', 190.
21. *The Evening Mail* (Halifax, Nova Scotia), January 4, 1917, Thursday, page 8.
22. *The Evening Mail* (Halifax), October 13, 1917, Saturday, page 5.
23. *The Evening Mail* (Halifax), October 28, 1918, Monday, page 4.
24. Anthony S. Nicolosi, 'The Navy, Newport and Stephen B. Luce', *Naval War College Review* 37, no. 5 (September–October 1984), 117–18, http://www.jstor.org/stable/44642363.
25. Ricky Ray (original contributor), '1920s – Newport, Rhode Island in 1920', Shutterstock ID: 4117099, access March 11, 2023, https://www.shutterstock.com/video/clip-4117099-1920s---newport-rhode-island-1920. The sailor can be seen around the 30-second mark, and reappears in the video.
26. *Newport Mercury*, May 28, 1921, Saturday, page 4.
27. *Newport Mercury*, May 21, 1921, Saturday, page 8; *Newport Mercury*, May 28, 1921, Saturday, page 8.
28. *Newport Mercury*, May 21, 1921, Saturday, page 8; *Newport Mercury*, May 28, 1921, Saturday, page 8.
29. Benjamin T. Marshall (ed.), *A Modern History of New London County, Connecticut: Vol. 1* (New York: Lewis Historical Publishing Company, 1922), 585–86.
30. The Day, *First & Finest: The 100-Year Anniversary of Naval Submarine Base New London* (Battle Ground: Pediment, 2015), 9.

31. David J. Bishop, *Images of America: Naval Submarine Base New London*, (Portsmouth: Arcadia, 2006), 46–47, 52; The Day, *First & Finest*, 18–22.
32. Bishop, *Naval Submarine Base*, 43.
33. *Norwich Bulletin*, Monday, January 27, 1919; *Norwich Bulletin*, Friday, March 12, 1920; *Norwich Bulletin*, Friday, January 16, 1920; *Norwich Bulletin*, Wednesday, September 1, 1920.
34. This is the subject of my future history.
35. *The Bridgeport Times and Evening Farmer*, August 16, 1920, Monday, page 4; *Rutland Daily Herald*, August 30, 1922, Wednesday, page 11.
36. *The Charlotte News*, May 4, 1921, Wednesday, page 2.
37. *The Lakeland Evening Telegram*, May 15, 1920, Saturday, page 2.
38. Fairchild, 'Letter on Behalf of Henry Breault', OMPF, 353.
39. A. Hyatt Verrill, *Panama Past and Present* (New York: Dodd, Mead, and Co, 1921), vii–viii.
40. Verrill, *Panama*, 76–84.
41. Verrill, *Panama*, 85–89.
42. United States Navy Department, *Information on living conditions in the Canal Zone* (Washington D.C.: Government Printing Office, 1920), https://www.loc.gov/item/24014341/.
43. Grigore, 'The O-5 is Down', *Proceedings*, online.
44. Fairchild, 'Letter', OMPF, 353.
45. Beach, *Salt and Steel:* 70.
46. Gugliotta, *Pigboat 39*, 11.
47. Henry Breault, 'Subject: Duty on Asiatic Station – Request for, June 29, 1933', OMPF, 134.
48. V.L. Kirkman and William D. Leahy, 'BREAULT, Henry TM1c., USN, Subject: Duty on Asiatic Station – Request for, June 29, 1933', OMPF, 137.
49. *Rochester Democrat and Chronicle*, February 2, 1932, Tuesday, page 8.
50. Gugliotta, *Pigboat 39*, 36.
51. *Los Angeles Evening Citizen News*, August 23, 1929, Friday, page 12.
52. Gugliotta, *Pigboat 39*, 35–36.
53. *Spokesman-Review* (Spokane), March 27, 1932, Sunday morning, page 50.
54. Gugliotta, *Pigboat 39*, 37.
55. Gugliotta, *Pigboat 39*, 38.
56. *Reading Times*, May 21, 1928, Monday, page 1.
57. *Lancaster New Era*, May 8, 1928, Tuesday, page 22.
58. Gugliotta, *Pigboat 39*, 38. See also picture 4.
59. Alan Nasser, *Overripe Economy: American Capitalism and the Crisis of Democracy* (Chicago: Pluto Press, 2018), 100.

# ENDNOTES

60. John Steinbeck, *The Grapes of Wrath*, 73, 86, 89, 97, 109, 112.
61. Steinbeck, *The Grapes of Wrath*, 122–24.
62. Gregg R. Hennessey, 'San Diego, the U.S. Navy, and Urban Development: West Coast City Building, 1912–1929', *California History* 72, no. 2 (1993), 143–44, https://doi.org/10.2307/25177342.
63. Federal Writer's Project of the Works Progress Administration (WPA), *San Diego in the 1930s: The WPA Guide to America's Finest City* (Los Angeles: University of California Press, 2013), 4.
64. WPA, *San Diego in the 1930s*, 4.
65. Keystone View Company, 'Balboa Park, San Diego, California – the Botanical Gardens, San Diego California, ca. 1931', photograph, https://www.loc.gov/item/2018646158/.
66. WPA, *San Diego in the 1930s*, 2–8.
67. *The Chula Vista Star* (San Diego), October 20, 1933, Friday, page 5.
68. *The Chula Vista Star*, October 20, 1933, Friday, page 5. The same *Indianapolis* that was sunk by a Japanese submarine on 30 July 1945, the surviving crew having to fend off numerous sharks.
69. WPA, *San Diego in the 1930s*, 63.
70. Breault, 'Shore duty, January 6, 1938', OMPF, 168.
71. Population.us, 'Population of Marysville, WA', accessed January 20, 2023, https://population.us/wa/marysville/.
72. Phil Dougherty, 'Marysville – Thumbnail History', accessed January 20, 2023, https://www.historylink.org/file/8227.
73. Henry Breault, 'Itemized Schedule of Travel and Other Expenses', OMPF, 173.
74. 'Here is opportunity, See the world, serve your country, save your money', USN Recruiting Poster, Photograph, POS – WWI – US, no. 104 (C size), LCN 00651875, https://www.loc.gov/item/00651875/.

## Chapter 10: Uniforms, Cigarettes, Pomade and Other Artefacts of a Material Identity

1. This is the situation in the present day: sailors aboard surface vessels live on board in port and out to sea; submariners are afforded a barracks due to the lack of racks for personnel. This is the more likely scenario, especially considering the lack of room on the O-class subs, but it was not unusual for sailors to live on board the vessel during fleet manoeuvres.
2. Henry Breault, 'Claim for Reimbursement for Personal Property Lost in a Marine Disaster, November 8, 1923', OMPF, 22.

3. Breault, 'U.S. Navy Service Record, July 20, 1920', OMPF, 1.
4. Breault, 'U.S. Navy Service Record, July 20, 1920', OMPF, 1; Bureau of Navigation, 'Placing on eligibility list for advancement in rate: Breault, Henry, 2108003, TM3c to TM2c', OMPF, 9; Bureau of Navigation, 'Transcript Record', OMPF, 80; Rutherford Platt, *The Manual of Occupations* (New York: G.P. Putnam's Sons, 1929), 405–06.
5. Bureau of Navigation, 'Professional Qualifications, Conduct, and Marks', OMPF, 266.
6. *Born to Dance*, 6:50–7:05, 16:45–17:15, 29:00–29:20, 01:20:15–1:20:30.
7. Ellsberg, *Pigboats*, 1–3.
8. Leon B. Blair, 'Dogs and Sailors Keep Off!', *Proceedings*, Vol. 76/10/572 (October 1950), accessed November 26, 2022, https://www.usni.org/magazines/proceedings/1950/october/dogs-and-sailors-keep.
9. *Born to Dance*, 18:30–18:45.
10. *Born to Dance*, 18:30–18:45.
11. *Born to Dance*, 19:45–20:00.
12. *Son of the Navy*, 07:00–07:30.
13. *Born to Dance*, 42:10–42:15.
14. *Navy Blues*, 07:00–07:15, 12:00–12:30, 01:06:35–01:06:45.
15. A.A. Fagerberg, 'Singer Sewing Company Letter to Bureau of Navigation, April 28, 1939', OMPF, 381.
16. *New York Evening Post*, March 15, 1924, newspaper clipping, CMOHS.
17. Harold H. Levy, 're Henry Breault: "H.M.C.S Niobe", December 1, 1925', SFLM.
18. Fairchild, 'Letter on Behalf of Henry Breault', OMPF, 353.
19. *Navy Blues*, 2:25–2:35.
20. Gugliotta, *Pigboat 39*, 14–15.
21. *Navy Blues*, 2:25–2:35.
22. *Navy Blues*, 2:35–2:40.
23. T.D. Trumbo, 'Robert D. Maxwell Co. Letter Regarding Breault's Whereabouts, March 29, 1933', OMPF, 367.
24. *Daily Times-Advocate* (Escondido), March 11, 1933, Saturday, page 3.
25. Bureau of Navigation, 'Professional Qualifications, Conduct, and Marks, November 29, 1933', OMPF, 291.
26. Trumbo, 'Robert D. Maxwell Co. March 29, 1933', OMPF, 367.
27. Bureau of Navigation, 'Henry Breault Enlistment, December 29, 1929', OMPF, 129.
28. *Daily Times-Advocate* (Escondido), August 2, 1933, Wednesday, page 4, *National City Star-News*, January 13, 1933, Friday, page 4.

# ENDNOTES

29. *The Los Angeles Times*, May 17, 1933, Wednesday, page 4; *The Los Angeles Times*, April 18, 1933, Tuesday, page 4, Newspaper.com archive; *The Los Angeles Times*, December 27, 1933, Wednesday, page 5.
30. T.L. Ryan, 'Inventory of Henry Breault's Possessions at Time of Death', OMPF, 194.
31. Bryan, 'Inventory', OMPF, 194.
32. Grigore Jr., 'The O-5 is Down', website reprint.
33. Vincent P. Carosso, 'The Waltham Watch Company: A Case History', *Bulletin of the Business Historical Society* 23, no. 4 (December 1949), 175–76, https://doi.org/10.2307/3110545.
34. *Observer Extra* (Putnam), November 19, 1988, SFLM; Bureau of Navigation, 'Medical History', OMPF, 478.
35. Bryan, 'Inventory', OMPF, 194.
36. Elmo L. Jackson, 'Trends in the Consumption of Tobacco Products, United States, 1900–1950', *Journal of Farm Economics* 32, no. 4 (November 1950), 886, https://doi.org/10.2307/1233840.
37. Unknown photographer, 'I.D. Picture of Henry Breault', OMPF, 495; unknown photographer, 'I.D. Picture of Henry Breault', OMPF, 497; unknown photographer, 'United States Navy Identification Card, Breault, H.', OMPF, 495.
38. Bryan, 'Inventory', OMPF, 194.
39. *The San Francisco Examiner*, August 26, 1937, Thursday, page 27.
40. *The San Francisco Examiner*, August 26, 1937, Thursday, page 27; *The San Francisco Examiner*, June 17, 1934, Sunday, page 8; *The Modesto Bee*, April 10, 1936, Friday, page 3.
41. Bryan, 'Inventory', OMPF, 194.
42. Bryan, 'Inventory', OMPF, 194.
43. Bryan, 'Inventory', OMPF, 194.
44. *The Brainerd Daily Dispatch*, December 21, 1931, Monday, page 7; *The Oklahoma County Register*, December 15, 1932, Thursday, page 1; *Oakland Tribune*, August 13, 1931, Thursday, page 25.
45. *Los Angeles Evening Citizen News*, March 6, 1930, Thursday, page 11; *Oakland Tribune*, October 8, 1931, Thursday, page 14.
46. *Born to Dance*, film, 00:23:45.
47. Ellsberg, *Pigboats*, 53.
48. Ellsberg, *Pigboats*, 200.
49. Gugliotta, *Pigboat 39*, 67.
50. Bureau of Navigation, 'Medical History', OMPF, 455.
51. Gugliotta, *Pigboat 39*, 67.
52. Breault, 'Shore duty, January 6, 1938', OMPF, 168.

53. Bureau of Navigation, 'Professional Qualifications, Conduct, and Marks', OMPF, 38.

## Chapter 11: Breault Reconstructed

1. 'Submarine Hero Writes Home', newspaper clipping, SFLM.
2. *New York Evening Post*, March 15, 1924, newspaper clipping, CMOHS.
3. Ginzburg, *Clues, Myths and the Historical Method*, 54–69.
4. Ginzburg, *Clues, Myths and the Historical Method*, 57.
5. For more on hyperrealism theory, see Jean Baudrillard and Umberto Eco.
6. *It's Tough to be Famous*, 02:11–24:00.
7. M.A. Holinshead, 'Copy of Telegram, November 19, 1930', OMPF, 364.
8. *It's Tough to be Famous*, 40:20–40:40.
9. Frank Lewis and Marvin McInnis, 'The Efficiency of the French-Canadian Farmer in the Nineteenth Century', *The Journal of Economic History* 40, no. 3 (1980), 497–514. doi:10.1017/S002205070008520X.
10. *The Daily Morning Journal and Courier* (New Haven), August 3, 1897.
11. *The Daily Morning Journal and Courier*, August 3, 1897. It is evaluated that 'Somplete' is likely an error and the intended word is 'Complete'.
12. *The Daily Morning Journal and Courier*, August 3, 1897.
13. *Norwich Bulletin*, July 28, 1914.
14. *Norwich Bulletin*, July 28, 1914.
15. Gugliotta, *Pigboat 39*, 59.
16. Lynn Dumenil, 'The Tribal Twenties: "Assimilated" Catholics' Response to Anti-Catholicism in the 1920s', *Journal of American Ethnic History* 11, no. 1 (Fall 1991), 21–49, http://www.jstor.org/stable/27500903.
17. Scott Meyer, 'Diabolists and Decadents: H.P. Lovecraft as Purveyor, Indulger, and Appraiser of Puritan Horror Fiction Psychohistory', *Lovecraft Annual*, no. 13 (2019), 178, https://www.jstor.org/stable/26868584. Meyer's work is an excellent primer into the Puritan mindset. In reference to a specific example, see the characters Paul Choynski and Landlord Dombrowski from *Dreams in the Witch House*, who cowardly avoid responsibility to tell the protagonist of the strange lights emanating from his room.
18. Dumenil, 'The Tribal Twenties', 24.
19. *San Diego Union*, February 14, 1939.
20. 1 Cor. 15:11–23. From the Douay-Rheims Bible, considered the standard for contemporary Catholic mass in the period.
21. Chas. E. Coughlin and M.J. Gallagher, *Father Coughlins Radio Sermons Complete: October 1930–April, 1931 Complete* (Austin: Knox and O'Leary, 1931), 248.

22. *Observer Extra* (Putnam), SFLM.
23. Henry Breault, 'Subject: Transfer in Exchange – request for, February 13, 1929', OMPF, 125.
24. *Observer Extra* (Putnam), November 19, 1988, SFLM.
25. *New York Evening Post*, March 15, 1924, newspaper clipping, CMOHS.
26. Chapman, 'How to Fail at the NTC', 29.
27. McCall, *The Goldfish Bowl*, 13–14.
28. *Men Without Women*, 01:10:00–01:17:00.
29. Henry Breault, 'Itemized Schedule of Travel and Other Expenses', OMPF, 171.
30. Breault, 'Itemized Schedule', OMPF, 171.
31. Henry Breault, 'Physical Examination', OMPF, 466.
32. US Census, 1940.
33. Slaughter, 'Letter', 377.
34. La Rossa, *The Modernization of Fatherhood*, 3.

## Conclusion: History Seen Through the Eyes of a Submariner

1. CMOHS, 'Statistics & FAQs', accessed March 12, 2023, https://www.cmohs.org/medal/faqs: 'For the military service members for whom we have ranks, 77% of Medals of Honor have gone to enlisted personnel; 23% to officers.'
2. Important note on the PDF document numbers: to actually see them in the compiled order, one must download the entire file, which is then put into a consistent viewing format. The web page appears to randomize the images.